A Rose For Jonathan

By
Beth Green

Copyright April 2015
All rights reserved

ISBN-13: 978-1511770804
ISBN-10: 1511770805

First Edition

This is a work of fiction. Names, characters, businesses, places, events and incidents are either the products of the author's imagination or used in a fictitious manner. Any resemblance to actual persons, living or dead, or actual events is purely coincidental.

Preface

As I began the journey to write this book, I felt strongly that I wanted to write about the love and sacrifice between the families who donated the organs of a loved one and those families that received them. The story began with that idea; but it became too emotional for me, as I have worked with these families through my job as a pediatric physical therapist. After prayer and reflection, the story evolved into a representation of the spiritual war that rages around us but with the underlying theme of organ donation as the driving force for a unique spiritual gift. The Bible says in Ephesians 6:12 in the King James Version (KJV)

12 For we wrestle not against flesh and blood, but against principalities, against powers, against the rulers of the darkness of this world, against spiritual wickedness in high places.

I quote several scriptures throughout this book and reference several Bible versions. This was done because I simply don't favor any of the Bible types and find that a combination of several versions of a verse helps me understand it more.

My journey through the pages of this story brought me to my knees more than I ever thought it would and I pray that is does the same to you. As always, I thank my family and my husband for their encouragement and support; but my deepest thanks goes to my Lord, Jesus Christ, who died for me...and for you.

Chapter 1: The Beginning

Friday, May 10, 1974

The time for the first event was drawing near. There were three of them; and they landed silently on a hill above the town to wait for it to begin. Dusk began to settle over the area, turning the sky into a mixture of pinks and blues, as a few clouds drifted lazily across the sky. Each large angel was covered in a flowing white robe with gold stitching with their wings tucked in behind them, glowing slightly in the expanding darkness. Meris, the leader, was a full eight feet tall with long dark hair and pale blue eyes; and he wore a sword that glistened in the final rays of the sinking sun, as the wind gently swayed it back and forth on his waist. A grim expression covered his face, as he looked over at the other two angels, Nardic and Galdon, who were also tall; but they were a full half foot shorter. Galdon stood directly beside Meris, his leader, and waited patiently for orders, while the younger angel, Nardic, paced back and forth. Meris shifted his weight and glanced up toward the sky, as he listened to the Father; and then he nodded in response to the orders that only he could hear. Stepping forward, he swiftly drew his sword and pointed it toward the town.

"It's time, let's go!" he bellowed, as he lifted off to go toward the place that had been chosen.

The other two lifted their wings with a *whoosh* and flew swiftly with Meris to the north end of the town, where several demonic creatures were already gathering in response to the angel's presence. They had sensed the coming change but had no idea what it would be. One of the evil creatures screamed and ducked behind a tree, when he saw the large angels approaching; and the rest of the demons crouched low to the ground, covering their faces with their gray, scaly arms. Meris took his sword in both hands; and in a single motion, he sliced through the darkness surrounding the area, fully penetrating the entire region with a supernatural light. The demons scattered and screeched in response, while Meris held his wings open to allow the glow to fully engulf the place that they needed to protect. He gently moved his wings back and forth, sending an even brighter light radiating in all directions, fully disseminating any dimness that remained in the chosen area. The three angels stood guard for several minutes and then Galdon, the second in command, took his sword and rammed the blade into the earth, sending a loud *Boom* echoing throughout the region and simultaneously scattering any lingering demons well beyond the border of the light. Meris left these two powerful angels to return to the hill to watch. Only one human in the area felt their presence and saw the light, and she was only two years old. The little girl looked out her car window and squealed and pointed. Her mom was too preoccupied to notice and her sister looked over and saw nothing.

Several seconds passed and finally the moment arrived. A truck ran a red light and slammed into the van carrying the little girl and her family, obliterating the right side. Galdon held his wings taut and braced the impact to keep the others safe, while the younger angel, Nardic, held the perimeter of light in place. Only one person was to be taken...but not at this moment. Galdon looked up to the hill at Meris, who grimly nodded his approval and acknowledged that everything was all now in place. Several minutes passed and groups of people began to congregate, as paramedics rushed to help the victims. Over in the crowd that had gathered stood a tall angel, named Flint. He turned to glance over toward the nearby hill where he knew his leader, Meris, stood and they nodded to each other, indicating that it was now time for Flint to move. Flint shifted his gaze back over to scene of the wreck to find the man who had driven the truck and was now sitting on the curb with his head in his hands. A police officer was talking to him and had the man stand and touch his hands to his nose with his eyes closed. As Flint watched this man, his newest charge, a grim expression spread across his own face, knowing this was going to be an extremely difficult job. One more glance at Meris and Flint slowly moved to stand behind the man, completely invisible to all the people in the area.

Meris stood tall and firm on the hill with his large wings slightly open and they continued to glow gently in the moonlight. Nardic landed softly beside him and addressed his leader, "Everyone is waiting. Flint is with the man from the truck and Galdon has gone with the woman and little girl to the hospital, where reinforcements are already in place. The only one left down there is the young child that they are still working with in the van."

Meris continued to stare off into the distance watching the accident scene and listening intently to Nardic's message. His face never flinched, as his voice boomed out in response, "We need to move with them. I will take the young child myself, when the time comes."

Thirty-five years later...

Sunday, June 7, 2009

The entire church was full, along with the fellowship hall, the parking lot, and even the nearby warehouse, where television monitors had been placed to broadcast the pastor's message to all who were waiting. The crowds had grown so quickly each week, that the only adjustment that could be made was to open more space and have four services each week, along with the quick technological fixes to help broadcast the message to all who had come. With the new donations pouring in, a building committee had been formed and ideas were being discussed and debated on how to handle the rapidly growing congregation.

Pastor John Miles (Pastor John as he was called by most everyone) sat in his seat by the pulpit and watched the choir sing a powerful rendition of an old song, Beulah Land. The power came from two sisters, Marian and Kathy Martin, who had plenty of wind but hadn't hit a note correctly in years. It wasn't for lack of trying, because they never missed a practice or a service, much to the sorrow of the congregation. Through the years, their made up harmonies had grown louder and more dysfunctional; but no one had had the nerve to tell them otherwise. When the choir director decided to increase the volume of the organ in response, the sisters saw this as their cue to push even harder to be heard. Within a few years of this ongoing battle, the volume of the song service had reached almost unbearable proportions. Finally, Pastor John had been forced to step in and have the organist reduce her volume and allow the sisters to belt out their off key songs as they saw fit. The congregation was so used to the way the songs now sounded, that one eight year old boy, while visiting another church with his friend, didn't recognize the songs at all, when he heard them sung in tune. Fortunately, the Martin sisters had become more subdued through the years, as their age and ailments had piled up. The newer members of the congregation seemed unfazed by the two elderly ladies and their theatrics, as they gathered to hear the latest message from the well-known preacher.

Nardic and Galdon stood guarding the doorways of each of the two aisles in the small church. Nardic smiled and gently shook his head, as the two Martin sisters proudly belted out their dysfunctional melody. Galdon frowned and looked over at Nardic, who immediately straightened in response and tried to regain his composure, knowing Galdon disapproved of any humor during an assignment. As the choir began the last verse, Kathy Martin decided to start dancing in place, while Marian marched in a circle and joined in with some excessive arm movements that had nothing to do with the words from the song. Nardic stifled a laugh; and he exchanged a secret smile with the young preacher's daughter, Rosie. Galdon cleared his throat and glared at Nardic, who simply looked at him and shrugged. How was he supposed to keep a straight face when those two women put on such a show?

The entire room, along with those in the atrium, fellowship hall, and nearby warehouse, both spiritual and human, watched as Pastor John stood and wiped his brow with a handkerchief for the third time, while he looked out at his congregation. Several were trying not to wince as Kathy Martin tried for another note that didn't exist and Marian attempted to match it with another note an octave lower, causing one small child in the front row to hold her hands over her ears. Pastor John was sweating profusely under his robe; and he again wished that the building committee would make some decisions on when to break ground on the new sanctuary. The current one was wrought with problems, including an air conditioner unit that was in bad need of replacement; and with the swelling crowds, the body heat quickly overcame the ailing air conditioner, as it chugged along trying to keep up. When the song ended,

Pastor John pushed up his glasses, turned to thank the choir, and then stepped up to the pulpit.

"I love the way that song ends! It blesses my heart."

In the second row, Pastor John's father, Roger Miles, leaned over to his wife, Terry, and whispered, "It blessed us all for that song to end!" She punched him in his ribs and shielded her mouth to hide her smile, then tried to focus on what their son, Pastor John, was saying.

"I would like to do something a little different today," Pastor John said and waited for everyone to perk up. He watched as a small wave of movement rippled through his flock; and several people even slid forward on their seats. Anticipation was added to the air of excitement to create an almost palpable silence; and no one dared to even shift in their seats for fear of missing a single word due to a squeaky pew. With the crowd nearly holding its breath, waiting for the most recent news, Pastor John wiped his face again and straightened his glasses.

"My heart is full this morning. The last few days have been somewhat unusual for our family. So much has occurred that I only know to address you all with the facts and share what we have just now learned ourselves."

Not one noise could be heard except the preacher's voice. Several people would later report that mothers were practically sitting on their own children to keep them from making a sound, because something new had happened and no one wanted to miss a single word. Listening to her son, Terry sat at her husband's side and glanced over at the church busy body, Clara Burton, who was poised to memorize every morsel of information. Clara needed a new crusade to find her purpose among the newer members. She had already placed herself on every committee she could and given herself an unofficial title as Ambassador to the growing crowds.

"All of you know my daughter, Rosie."

Several people nodded; and Clara congratulated herself for already noting Rosie was not sitting with her mom today. There was a small ripple of response; and Pastor John looked down to try to catch his breath before he continued. He knew he had a lot yet to tell them and wanted to get it right.

"You are all familiar with something that I say every week. I always start my sermon by telling you that I am here because of a gift, yet few of you know the double meaning behind those words." Pastor John paused and looked at his notes, more to gain control of his emotions than to see the words written before him.

"Most of you have probably assumed that I have been alluding to the gift of salvation, which is partially correct; but it is not the full meaning. There has been another gift, one that I was aware of but never had the curiosity or the courage to know more about it." Pastor John looked over at his wife, Lindsey, and then at his parents, who never missed a service and then at Lindsey's parents, who had only started to come over the last few weeks. He wiped the corner of his eyes and tried again to regain his composure.

"I think it's important for you all to know that what I am about to tell you all is a story that is still difficult for even me to believe." He looked back at Rosie, sitting on the seat behind him. She and her mother looked so much alike, almost like sisters. The meaning behind that thought hit him hard; and then he broke down slightly and had to take a moment to gather himself so that he could continue.

Several women began to cry, as they watched their beloved pastor struggle to tell them something that was incredibly painful. Lindsey mouthed 'I love you' and wiped the tears from her own eyes as well. Besides their parents, she and Rosie were the only ones that knew all the details of what Pastor John was about to say; and she began to silently pray for strength for everyone involved. Galdon and Nardic began to glow from the added prayer and both instinctively spread their wings in response. Galdon moved into place behind the preacher and placed a hand on him to give him added strength, although the glow in his wings was not as bright as it should have been.

In response, Pastor John stood up straight and gained some control over his emotions as he continued, "I spent some time yesterday reviewing all of this with my family and well...I'm not sure how to say this, so I think it's important for me to start at the beginning. Bear with me as I try to put this all together for you to understand." The angels in the room and outside guarding the perimeter held their wings open, glowing and daring any demon to come near.

Lindsey looked up at her husband and smiled, as her mind began to drift back and remember how they had first met and how this journey had begun that led them all to this day.

Chapter 2: John and Lindsey

October 1993

The alarm sounded for the third time; and Lindsey finally turned it off. She rolled her small frame over and planted her feet on the cold wood, while fumbling for her glasses. The bathroom was only a few feet away; and she stumbled in to survey her face and hair in the mirror.

Not bad, looks like a ponytail day.

She rummaged through her clothes to grab her favorite jeans and a sweater; but one more pass by the mirror revealed that her first look this morning was not quite so accurate. Her eyes were now better focused; and she could see that she needed more than a ponytail to pull herself together. Her thick blonde hair was not obeying her brush, as she repeatedly pulled and tugged to get it into place. This was going to take more time than she had, so she splashed some water onto her hands and slicked her hair back; and then she sprayed it down, praying her unruly hair would obey just this one day. Lindsey silently promised to not punish her snooze button tomorrow, as she hurried toward the kitchen to find her purse and keys.

Grabbing a cereal bar and a large drink cup she had saved from yesterday's late night fast food dinner, she threw her backpack and purse in the seat beside her, juggled her makeshift breakfast, and headed down the highway to her first class. As she pulled into a student lot, Lindsey realized she had forgotten to put on any makeup. For once she was thankful she hadn't washed her face well the night before, as a remnant of eye makeup remained.

My inefficiency pays of yet again!

Lindsey smiled at herself in the mirror and glanced at the clock on her car and knew she only had a few minutes to get into her seat before her professor, Dr. Letchin, would promptly begin. Gathering her backpack, she jumped out of the car and slammed the door; but right as she hit the lock button on her key fob, Lindsey saw her purse sitting on the front passenger seat.

"Crap!" She said out loud, as she pressed the unlock button to open her car door and then lunged inside to grab her purse. In one large movement, she spun around, threw her backpack and purse on her shoulder, and started to run toward the building to her class, when she collided with something large. The sudden collision caused her to fly backwards through the air, as she watched her drink cup and its final contents being sprayed into the air. Next, there was a strong impact of the back of her head against the front bumper of her car, sending her glasses as well as her purse to the sidewalk beside her. Everything went black until she heard a distant voice talking to her.

"Are you all right? Can you hear me?" Lindsey tried to open her eyes; but the light was too bright. Someone was helping her sit upright.

"What...happened...?" Lindsey could see a shape and a light. "Where...where are my glasses?" Her head was pounding from the brutal crash against the front bumper on her Honda Civic; and on the back of her head, the bump was already rising. She reached up to touch the sore area, while looking up to try to focus on the face before her. As her hand ran across the bump, she winced and let out a small groan.

"Oh, um...here they are...is that better? I am so sorry, I didn't see you." The young man handed the glasses over after polishing them briefly.

Slowly, Lindsey's eyes and the glasses began to work together; but her head was still pounding.

"I...um..what happened?"

The young man before her offered a hand to pull her up; and with little effort on her part, she was standing, still trying to make sense of it all.

"I was walking to a class and you came running out from between these cars and we collided."

The young man looked at the girl before him and caught his breath. All around her was a strange light and then suddenly, the light disappeared. He rubbed his eyes and refocused but the light did not reappear.

"Class! Oh my gosh! What time is it?"

Lindsey looked frantically at her wrist, which was empty. She had forgotten her watch. This was going to drive her crazy all day wondering what time it was during class. She loved passing the time by holding her breath or counting how many seconds passed as her Differential Equations professor walked from one end of the blackboard to the other. It usually took 8 seconds. Her other favorite activity was seeing how many seconds passed until the red headed boy in Calculus asked another stupid question. His record was usually more like 2 minutes. Now, she would have to guess all day; and that would make the day drag even longer. The young man standing before her was seemingly more stunned than Lindsey; but he quickly regained his thoughts.

"It's 7:58 AM; and we are both not going to make it this morning. I can be a little late, though. Are you okay? You hit that car pretty hard."

Lindsey dusted off her pants and tried to gather her scattered thoughts, when she finally looked at the young man before her. He had the most beautiful eyes that she had ever seen; and she also noted that he towered over her in his 6'2" frame. She was a full foot shorter, and at least 100 pounds lighter. No wonder she had bounced off of him so easily. Lindsey blushed and fumbled back on the ground for her purse, and tried to collect her dignity along with its contents.

"I'm fine...I just need to get to class. I am so sorry...I was running late..."

"You were definitely running!"

He watched her fumbling for her things and saw the Epipen among the items from her purse. He was just about to ask her about it when the strange light flickered around her again. In any other situation, this might have scared him; but he had seen this before as a child, even though the memory of the event had become like a dream--at least he had told himself that it was. The shimmery light had been around a man in his church, who quietly sat at the end of the pew every Sunday. Each week, the light had had a warm and inviting effect and had made him feel loved. Now here he was years later seeing it again; but this time it was around one of the most beautiful young girls that he had ever seen. Was she that pretty, or did the light make her more appealing?

Lindsey looked up and saw him offering a hand to help her up again; and she timidly placed her hand in his. In one quick motion, he pulled her into standing. He was as strong as he was handsome and she blushed in response.

"Thank you," she croaked and tried to clear her throat, which was knotting up more every second, as her thoughts cleared further and she realized she was not only talking to this man, but that she had met him in such an awkward way. Another wave of embarrassment washed over her, as she also remembered how horrible she looked today.

Of course I would meet a cute guy on a day that I look my worst. Well, at least he will know from the start what he is getting into! As soon as that thought entered her mind, she scolded herself for even thinking he would be interested in her.

"Well, I do need to get going; and I know you do as well. My name is John."

He offered a hand to shake; and for the third time, she placed her hand in his. The embarrassment had now completely settled in; and she mumbled, "Lindsey," then quickly ran off toward her class, afraid to look back over her shoulder. If she had, she would have noticed that he was following her all the way to the door of her building.

Lindsey hurried through the lobby of the building and caught her reflection in a window, noting that her ponytail was dangling precariously over to one side. She gingerly removed her ponytail holder and grimaced when she touched the bump on her head. Quietly, she fumbled into the classroom and found a seat, after enduring the hard glare of Dr. Letchin and the curious dead-eyed stares of her classmates. He was lumbering on about something that had Lindsey drowsy again before she could even pull out her notes and a pen. She pretended to scribble furiously to try to look as if she were engaged, hoping this would keep her awake.

Why am I so tired?

Then she remembered. She was trying to get off of caffeine again. It was an ongoing struggle to cut back on her intake of coffee and tea.

No wonder I am so out of it.

With her throbbing head, the professor's droning voice, and the lack of caffeine, she found it hard to concentrate on what the professor was saying. She ran her fingers over her head to try to stimulate her thoughts and revive her brain; but as her hand moved to where the bump on the back of her head was formally perched, a sudden burst of pain worked almost like a shot of coffee, causing her to jump slightly. Lindsey was dizzy from the new wave of pain but was quickly distracted when the door to the classroom suddenly opened.

"Great, I wasn't the only one who was late today," She mumbled to herself.

"...and so for a treat I thought we could turn our attention to one of our grad students from the psychology department, who is going to lead us through an explanation of this..."

Horrified, Lindsey watched as John emerged and took his place at the podium to began his lecture. Lindsey slid down further in her seat and buried her head behind her notebook, pretending to write furiously as he spoke. There were at least two hundred other students in the class; and she hoped he would not be able to see her among the others. Throughout the next hour, Lindsey never looked up even once but stayed buried behind her notebook.

When the class ended, she heard the girl next to her say to her friend, "He was so hot!".

Lindsey agreed. She also wanted to get out of there as fast as she could; and she ducked in behind a group of girls heading toward the exit, sneaking a peek over her shoulder to see John gathering his things and politely answering questions from some of the over zealous girls, who looked to desire much more than information. In the back of the hoard, Lindsey saw the girl and her friend, who had been sitting next to her and had made the comments about his looks. Looking over that competition, Lindsey felt herself shrink even further, as she dashed out the door.

One week later, Lindsey had already forgotten her promise to her snooze button and again found herself slightly behind schedule for the same class, despite her best efforts to get up sooner. She closed and locked her car door and turned to find herself face to face with John. He was holding out a cereal bar with a large drink, identical to the breakfast she had had in her hands last week.

"I wasn't exactly sure what you had in the cup, so I just guessed."

He looked intently for the light around her; but could not see it. Either way, he could not get this girl off of his mind. Their hands brushed slightly against each other, as he transferred the breakfast to her. Lindsey wondered if his heart was racing like hers and tried to remain calm, even though she felt herself shaking slightly. She blushed and looked down, thankful that she at least had her makeup in place today and her hair was down.

"I don't know...I mean, thank you."

"So, I know you need to get to class. I was wondering if we could meet later and maybe I could I take you to lunch?"

Lindsey took a long sip of the drink to stall for time, while her mind was reeling. The drink had a familiar taste; but she could not take her mind off of what he had just said to her. She tried to process his intentions.

Is he making fun of me? Did he just ask me out?

Guys didn't usually ask her out. It was not her looks that deterred suiters: she had a plain and simple beauty which required very little makeup to accent her large blue eyes and blonde hair. Most guys noticed her immediately; but she was excessively shy and insecure, which made her seem unapproachable. She had never developed the casual and easy manner that every other girl appeared to have with guys and seemed to be caught in a self perpetuating cycle of isolation. Her first response around any guy she thought was cute was usually to drop her gaze and walk fast; but if making eye contact was impossible to avoid, her tongue would swell and words would simply escape her, leaving her looking like either a snob or a bumbling idiot. Either way, boys always seemed to misinterpret her signals and give up on pursuing her, which seemed to feed her insecurity even more.

Today, though, Galdon, her guardian angel, was nearby and placed his hands on her shoulders to give her a sense of peace. She spoke easily and it surprised even her. "Well, I have this class and then I...well I usually meet..."

She bit her lip to stop the tears. She felt sure now that this was some sort of cruel joke. There was no way he was this interested in her, when he could obviously have his pick of the girls on campus. Galdon spread his wings and allowed peace to continue to radiate forth.

John's eyes dropped to the ground; and his face reddened as he kicked himself mentally for assuming she didn't have a boyfriend. There was something about her that had mesmerized him from the moment he first saw her last week. She was beautiful; but it was so much more than that. The glow that had appeared around her had haunted him day and night for the past week; and he was unable to stop thinking about her. He was afraid to tell anyone, for fear they would think he was crazy. His childhood memory of the old man with the glow had been easy to forget; but with Lindsey, he found her unforgettable in almost every way. He felt such a strong pull to see her again that he was unable to think about anything else and waited patiently to return to the only place he knew she would be.

Please let her say yes...

"Oh, I am sorry. I don't usually do this...I didn't mean to put you on the spot...Are you okay?"

It was a strange question, until Lindsey realized she was sinking down to her knees. She had taken only one sip of the drink; but she now realized what had happened.

"Did you...put lemon...in that tea? I am allergic..."

He grabbed her as she sank lower and she reached for her purse. She felt her throat closing as she tried her best to summon a sentence, "My purse...help." Lindsey was beginning to panic and reached for her throat.

"What do you need?" Suddenly, John remembered the EpiPen he had seen last week. He quickly grabbed her purse and rummaged through until he found the needle.

Lindsey was starting to sweat profusely and could feel her throat closing even more. She tried to speak, but nothing would come out.

Galdon blew gently into her face to help her breathe, while John jammed the EpiPen into her thigh. Looking up into Lindsey's face, John could see a faint flicker and then a shimmer; and slowly, she began to breathe normally again. Within minutes, she was sitting up and feeling better; but John was still shaking.

"I'm...sorry." Lindsey finally said, as she slowly revived from her worst reaction yet.

"Why are you sorry? Are you allergic to tea?"

"No. I am allergic to lemons."

"Lemons? I have never even heard of that."

Lindsey nodded. "It's really weird. When I was about seven, I broke out in hives from a batch of lemonade; but my parents thought that I was bitten by an insect, since I had a small bite mark on my arm. Several years later, my mom made lemon pound cake from scratch. I only had a small piece; but I broke out in hives that lasted for two weeks. We went to an allergist and they did some testing and found that I have an allergy to citrus, and particularly lemons."

"Wow, I am so sorry. So you can't eat any citrus at all?"

Lindsey shook her head. "I am usually fine with oranges and limes; but I am still careful when I eat them."

"So have you always carried an EpiPen?"

"No. I was forced to get the prescription for the EpiPen about three months ago, when I had an accidental exposure; but instead of hives, I felt like I couldn't breathe. It was much slower than this one, though. The doctor warned me that I need to have the EpiPen with me at all times, because each reaction could be worse."

"I can't believe this. I am so sorry. I had no idea."

"How would you? It's no big deal. I have known to be careful for years. It is just a part of who I am." Lindsey could not believe she was talking so freely to this guy. She felt so at ease and it made no sense to her.

"I am glad it was me."

Lindsey looked at him, confused. "What do you mean?"

"Oh, I guess I didn't explain that very well. I have been allergic to bees as long as I can remember and have carried an EpiPen for a long time. I am glad I was familiar with it-- someone else may have not known what to do."

"I guess I am glad it was you, too." Lindsey was more than glad. She smiled; but her head dropped, as her insecurity washed over her.

John watched her face and wished that he could kiss her. He had never felt anything like this before.

"I am also glad I almost knocked you out last week."

"What?"

John laughed. "I saw your EpiPen when it fell out of your purse last week. I am not sure that I would have understood what you were talking about otherwise."

Lindsey smiled and they both laughed.

Galdon kept his wings spread around them both and smiled when he thought about the accidental meeting last week, which had been orchestrated fully by the Father. He had worked hard to try to place them both together; and it had worked beautifully. Galdon looked up at the Father and smiled. The plan had been perfect, as always.

Lindsey missed class that day for the first time in four years. She and John spent the next several weeks carving out any time that they could to meet for lunches, dinners, as well as late night conversations. John simply made her feel good about everything; and she was the answer to his prayers. They both loved to laugh when telling everyone the story of how they met. His version always ended with 'I swept her right off her feet' or 'She fell for me right away.'

It was a standing joke; and one that they loved to laugh at together. The second meeting with her near fatal collapse was not one that they repeated often.

Within only a few weeks, they were not only in love, but also planning a wedding. He referred to her as the light of his life; and most people just thought it was a sweet thing to say. Only John knew that she really did bring light when she entered a room. The glow was more of a shimmer; but it became something that he treasured about her. They were married after Lindsey graduated; and she began to work, while John finished his master's degree. Within two years, he felt the call to be a preacher and took his first church in the town of Bowling Green, Kentucky. One year later, they moved to The River City Christian Church in Louisville, Kentucky, where both of their parents now lived. Throughout this time, the angels had surrounded and protected them with a steady flow of power from their prayers. Meris and Galdon both knew that this marriage was the beginning of something more...a union of spiritual significance that would begin a new and much needed revival.

Galdon volunteered to take the post to watch the young preacher and his wife; but both Nardic and Meris came by regularly to listen to the prayers and hear John practice his sermons. The angels quietly protected and served the family...and waited. Nardic could see the tension building in the spiritual world around Pastor John and his church. One day, he decided to approach Meris for information.

"How much longer? Has the Father said anything to you?" Galdon shook his head at Nardic's impatience. Meris looked thoughtfully at the youngest angel and answered with kindness and reserve.

"The Father has a plan that we all fulfill. Imagine if you were human, the time would pass even slower. There are changes coming; and we must be ready. For now, we can only build our reserve and wait. The battle will begin soon enough."

Chapter 3: Adding Numbers

During the second year in Louisville, John began to experience things that he could not explain. It was in the middle of the night when it first happened, causing him to doubt his sanity for a several days after. He was restless and woke quickly, when he rolled over in the bed to discover Lindsey was not there. He sat up and wiped his eyes, then slowly shuffled through the house looking for her, thinking she was having trouble sleeping or maybe not feeling well. The dining area of their small home opened directly to the kitchen and was lit by a terribly inefficient fixture that was in bad need of replacement--something John had promised to remedy but had never seemed to have time to do. As he neared the kitchen, he saw a bright glow and wondered how that decrepit old light fixture could illuminate the area so well. Lindsey sat at the end of the table reading her

Bible and writing some notes; but it was the light that caused John to gasp. The light was surrounding his young wife and seemed to be both behind her and a part of her at the same time. Lindsey looked up at John and the light immediately reduced to the shimmer that he was now used to seeing sometimes hanging around her like a silhouette. John stood with his mouth gaping, as Lindsey stared back at him, as confused as he was.

"What's wrong? You look shocked. I do read my Bible, you know."

"It's...it's...not that. You were *glowing*."

"What are you talking about? Are you okay?" Lindsey stood and walked over to her husband. He instinctively stepped back but felt as if someone caught him and held him up.

"Honey, are you sleep walking?"

This was a silly thing to ask; but Lindsey could not understand why her husband was behaving so strangely. An eerie calm enveloped John and he let out an audible sigh.

"I'm fine...maybe we both need to get some sleep."

John headed back to bed, confused and feeling foolish. Within days, the shimmer became stronger to form a solid glow around his wife, which would come and go on a regular basis. He had not mentioned it to anyone and feared he would sound crazy; but he started searching the internet to see if this made any sense. His first thought was a brain tumor of some kind or maybe a problem with his eyes; but if that were true, he should see the same light around everything. By the time four weeks had passed, he had started to accept the increased light around Lindsey; but then he began to notice that the glow was starting to increase again. To make matters worse, he also started noticing shadows unlike anything he had ever seen before. These dark shapes were dynamic and seemed to concentrate over certain areas. The first place he saw them was around his in-law's home. These weird anomalies began to come and go so often that John decided he needed to talk with someone; but he wasn't sure who to go to. He didn't want to worry Lindsey; and he continued to wrestle with the problem and search for answers on his own and finally decided to talk to Darron Mitchell, his associate pastor. They had become fast friends and often spent time together outside of work hours. After about two weeks of trying to decide what to do, John waited until he knew Darron was not busy and walked into his office and closed the door.

Darron looked up with slight surprise as John took a seat. "Hey, John. What's up?"

"Wow, you don't waste any time, do you?" John smiled at his friend.

"Well, I know you wouldn't have walked down here and shut the door if it wasn't important."

John loved this about Darron. He was refreshingly honest and straightforward. He had a reputation for tough love and actively seeking scriptural support for his counseling.

"I am not really sure how to tell you what is going on."

"Is it marital trouble?"

John quickly answered, "Oh no! Lindsey is wonderful. We have a great marriage." John paused.

"Is it the church?"

"No. It's...well...I think I am seeing spiritual beings."

"Like angels and demons?"

"I think so, yes."

"What makes you think that?"

"Well, I keep seeing lights and shadows."

"What kind of lights?"

John cleared his throat. "I guess I can only describe it as a shimmer or glow and sometimes it gets really bright--well, I guess only one time it became really bright."

"Tell me about that one time."

"It was around Lindsey when she was praying and reading her Bible. I came around the corner and the light was so bright; but it didn't blind me. It was almost like an amazing feeling of calm and peace. It was all around her and behind her at the same time. When she saw me, the light immediately diminished."

"Around Lindsey?"

"Yeah. I guess that is where I see it the most. She has a kind of shimmer around her."

"Where else do you see the light?"

"Well, I guess just around her mainly."

"You said she 'shimmers'? Is that all the time or just sometimes?"

"It comes and goes but seems to be staying more lately."

"You don't see that glow or shimmer on anyone else?"

"No. Well, when I was a child I saw it on an old man in my church sometimes. I always thought that I was just imagining it or something. When I saw it around Lindsey, I vividly remembered seeing it before, although I hadn't thought about it in years. Weird, huh? Am I crazy or sick?"

"Before I answer that, tell me about the shadows."

"Okay. I have seen these swarming dark shapes around my in-laws's home."

Darron smiled and answered, "Are you kidding me? You are seeing demons around your in-laws's home? Man, you can't even make that stuff up. It sounds like some kind of punchline to a joke. Like 'How many demons does it take to make an in-law?' or something like that."

John laughed. "I never thought about it like that. I love my in-laws, though."

"Are you sure? Maybe you are suppressing some type of resentment and you are imagining demons around them as a response to that." Darron's eyes danced, as he waited for John to answer.

"I promise. They are great. I mean, I wish that they would come to this church or really any church; but other than that they have been very good to us."

"See, you do subconsciously think that they need to be in church; and maybe you are imagining demons around them in response."

"Do you think this is all my imagination?"

Darron sat back in his chair and stared at his desk for a few seconds before answering. "No. I really don't. I think you may be experiencing some of the supernatural world."

"What should I do?"

Again, Darron hesitated and then answered. "John, this may be some kind of gift to you from God. Let's start by both of us praying for more guidance. I will commit to praying for you daily and both of us work on some research to see what we find. We can meet as often as you like to talk about any of it."

"Thank you, Darron. I was afraid you would think that I was crazy."

"I am still deciding that!"

Both men laughed and then they prayed for several minutes, while a group of angels around them glowed and absorbed the power. As John stood to leave he asked one last question.

"So, do you think I need to seek any medical help, just in case it is something else?"

"If that makes you sleep better, then yes; but John, I believe that it is spiritual. Otherwise you would see the glow and shadows all the time, right?"

"Right." John left his friend's office and walked back to his own office deep in thought, still not fully convinced about what he was seeing. If this was some type of gift, he had no idea how it could be of any help. That night, he wrote a sermon on the Power of God.

Before he preached each week, he spent time praying and preparing beforehand; but this particular week, he started on Saturday, praying more than usual and he asked Lindsey to do the same. There was a powerful change and he could feel it as he stepped into the pulpit that Sunday. At the altar call that week, seven people came forward and rededicated their lives, which was the most ever in the church history. The congregation numbered 212; but the average Sunday attendance was more like 100, except on a major holiday, where the numbers could swell to 150. The sanctuary had been built to seat 350 people, which John had been told had only reached capacity one time, when Clara Burton's daughter, Elana, held her wedding there. Many said that Clara invited the whole town and probably paid most to attend.

When John and Lindsey drove home that day, she reached over to grab his hand.

"I don't think I have ever heard a better sermon, ever."

"Wow! Thank you. It felt right today."

"Well, it was more than right. It was amazing. I loved all the examples you gave. I guess I never really thought about the full power available to us as Christians."

"Right now, the power of hunger has me! Let's grab some lunch."

Because he worked on Sundays, John usually took Mondays off; but his secretary, Mary, did not. When John arrived Tuesday morning, she met him at his office door.

"Pastor John! You will not believe what has happened!"

John knew Mary was not easily rattled and usually handled the flow of emergencies and requests easily with a smooth and calm manner. When John saw her excitement, he studied her face a moment, searching to see if the news was good or bad before he answered. "I have no idea." He said as he unlocked his door and entered with Mary on his heels.

"You know how we sometimes get requests for copies of each week's message?"

"Yes, and you give them the audio copy we make for our records."

"Yes, well, I usually get maybe one or two requests throughout the week; but yesterday, the phone rang off the hook."

"Really? Wow!"

"Ask me how many copies I have had requested to send out already."

"Okay, how many?"

"Seventy-nine."

"Wow! That is almost everyone that was there!"

"That's not all! So many people are talking about your sermon that I have been getting calls from people not even from our church!"

"Seriously?"

"Also...I listened to it."

John laughed. Most church secretaries do not attend the church that they work for and this was the case with Mary as well. Since John had arrived, she had been promising to listen to a sermon; but had not ever done so to his knowledge. "What did you think?

Mary blushed. "I am just sorry that I haven't listened before. Pastor John, that was the best sermon that I have ever heard!"

"That is wonderful. I am so glad that you enjoyed it and hopefully you were blessed by it."

"More than blessed. You have inspired me to pray more and to seek God more. I thought I was already doing that until I heard your message. I was way under estimating God."

"I'm so glad that--"

Mary shook her head and interrupted, "I'm sorry to interrupt you; but you don't seem to understand. Everyone feels that way! You have started something amazing."

John stared at Mary and then sank into his chair. "I have?"

"Yes, and everyone keeps asking about when you are going to preach again. I think we need to prepare for a large crowd this week."

"Oh. Okay, maybe let the staff know and my mom, so she can get more volunteers for the nursery. Let's treat it as if it's a holiday weekend and see what happens."

"That's exactly what I have done. I think everyone is getting ready for that. Everybody is so excited and we can't wait to hear your next message!"

After Mary left his office, John stared at the wall for several minutes trying to make sense of what had just happened. He knelt beside his desk and spent several minutes thanking God for his help in reaching these people. Galdon and Meris both smiled as they watched the praises go to Heaven.

"I will never get tired of that!" Galdon said and Meris nodded.

"Me either."

Chapter 4: A Growing Family

Over the next week, John prayed and worked on his follow up message on the Blessings of God. The sermon was based on several papers he had written in seminary and he had given the message before at their previous church. He worked on expanding the scriptures he used and discussed it all week with Lindsey, whom he trusted to give thoughtful insight and wisdom. They both prayed as before and committed more time than usual on prayers for the message and the service.

The next Sunday morning started like any other. Lindsey rose early to start some muffins and wrestle with her unruly hair. She normally had their clothes ready the night before; but she took one look at the dress she had picked to wear today and decided it was not right.

"You aren't going to wear that dress that you picked out and ironed last night?" John asked, as he watched Lindsey shuffle by quickly in her house shoes to put the dress back in the closet.

"I just don't feel like wearing that one today."

"I really like that one."

"Yeah, I know, but I just feel fat in it."

John had been married long enough now to know to tread carefully through his next few words. "Well, I think you look great in anything."

He walked up behind her and hugged her around the waist. He decided he needed to tell Lindsey what he was seeing; but he wasn't sure that this was the right time. Lindsey turned and gave him a kiss.

"I think I look great by your side." Suddenly she pulled away and ran to the bathroom, barely making it to the toilet to vomit.

John rounded the corner to see what had happened and found his wife laying over the commode, breathing heavily.

"Are you okay?" He grabbed a wet washcloth and did the best that he could to comfort her; but a smoke detector began to buzz in the kitchen.

"My muffins!" Lindsey cried in a weak voice.

The thought of those muffins bubbling and now smoking sent Lindsey head first back into the toilet for another round of sickness. John left his sick wife and ran to the kitchen to find smoke pouring out of the oven, so he quickly turned the knob to off and turned on the water in the sink. His thoughts swiftly darted between opening the oven and throwing the muffin pan in the sink to leaving the muffins in the oven and letting the oxygen run out. Galdon was watching and quickly stepped in to smother the fire to protect John, in case he did open the oven door too soon. John was just about to grab the oven mitt, when he noticed the smoke was slowing down; but he also saw something else. Surrounding the oven was the same type of glow that John had seen around his wife, but this time it had a shape like a...man. As soon as this realization came to John, the form and the light disappeared, while the smoke swirled in the air and the alarm continued to buzz in the background. The image of the man covering the fire dazed him for a few seconds and then John quickly opened the window above the kitchen sink and waved the newspaper in front of the smoke detector.

Within a few minutes, the smoke detector finally stopped buzzing; and John was left standing in the kitchen with the smell of smoke mixing with the smell of burnt muffins. He opened the oven door and placed the hard crusted muffins under the running water, releasing a loud sizzle along with some steam. Sinking to the ground, he tried to make sense of what he had just seen. He should have been afraid; but instead, he felt *safe*. The biblical story of Shadrach, Meshach, and Abednego came to mind. In the book of Daniel, the three men were thrown into a fiery furnace for their refusal to worship an idol. They were not burned at all, as God had provided an angel (some say Jesus) to protect them. Not one single hair on their head singed and none of them even had the smell of smoke on their clothing. John thought about that and grabbed a pen and paper to write down notes for a sermon. The words moved easily across the page as he wrote. He had never written a sermon this quickly and he was sure he was not ready to deliver it yet without prayer and some time to study the scriptures; but the image of the angel in the fire was too strong to ignore and he continued to jot down more thoughts until he had a full outline with some references to scripture as well. John looked at the paper in front of him and felt ready to deliver it, even though he had never practiced even one single line. His emotions and thoughts mixed together in a blender of ideas; but one coherent theme prevailed: God's Protection. Without any reservations, he knew that this was the sermon God wanted him to deliver today.

Thirty minutes later, Lindsey's mom arrived to stay with her, while John headed to church to deliver the sermon he had written just a few moments ago. He felt a strong urge to pray when he arrived at the church and he asked his associate pastor to lead the congregation through the first of the service, while he found a place in the back of the church to talk to God. John typically prayed in silence; but today was different.

"Father, I need focus today. I am not sure what is wrong with me or what to do. Please guide me on who to talk to or where to go for help. I don't know what these visions are for and how to use them. For now, please work through me and let me be a vessel to deliver the message today. Help me, Lord. I don't know what to do. I feel drawn to this sermon and I can't help but deliver it. Please be with me."

When he opened his eyes, John felt an enormous warmth envelope him as if wrapped in a blanket taken out of a dryer. Meris continued to hold John in his wings for several minutes and help him relax. John stood and gathered his notes and pushed open the door to the hall, almost running into Clara Burton, the busybody of the church. Fear crept over him, as he wondered if she had heard his prayer. Meris began to glow slightly and shoved the small demon aside that was responsible for the fear.

"Oh, sorry, Clara. I didn't see you."

"No worries, Pastor John. I was just overcome with the last song and went to get a tissue." The small demon of Fear crawled up her leg and onto her back, where it waited for Pastor John to doubt himself again. Another demon of Gossip sat perched on her shoulder.

"I was just praying a little. Sometimes I like to do that right before I preach." This was true; but he had more to pray about today.

Clara smiled sweetly at him; but her expression belied something deeper. He tried to determine if she had heard him praying and if there was anything he had said that might have given her some new gossip material. If she had eavesdropped, John wasn't sure how she would interpret it or what she would do. The demon of Gossip began whispering in her ear and the other demon of Fear crouched and sat ready to pounce onto John's shoulder to pester him throughout his sermon. Meris looked up at the Father and nodded. Permission was granted for additional Grace. He reached over and flicked the demon of Fear over into a corner, where it hissed and cursed. Meris dared it to come near the pastor again; but the demon simply jumped up onto Clara's shoulder, where it would stay for now.

Nardic landed behind Meris and pulled out his sword. "Should I get it off the woman?"

"No, it has not been asked. The woman is sold out to the sins of gossip and pride. That demon is one of the minions that will stay with her until she changes her ways. We can only attack if the Father asks us to or if the human asks for help."

Nardic shook his head and placed his sword back in its sheath. "When will the humans ever learn?" Nardic paced back and forth, wishing the demon would make a move so he could fight with it. His fearless nature and willingness to fight had helped him win many battles; but the angels were not supposed to ever attack first, unless provoked directly. Few exceptions existed for this.

Meris didn't answer and stayed with John, who had regained his composure and now motioned to Clara and said, "Well, let's both get back in the service before it's over."

"Yes, pastor, that is a good idea." Clara smiled and again John could tell from her expression that she was harboring something from what she had heard. As she turned to walk away, John saw something of a shadow around her right shoulder, but rubbed his eyes and it disappeared, as he turned to go through the upper door that led to the area behind the choir. When he stepped into the sanctuary, he was stunned to see almost every seat taken and several new faces. He was able to preach smoothly and easily, delivering the full message without even once looking at his outline. Even the music from the Martin sisters seemed more in tune today.

When the service ended, John stood at the door and shook some hands and greeted most of the people as they left. Clara Burton was the third person in line and she pulled him in close for a hug but then pushed away quickly, as if in a hurry. Several others seemed to have the same reaction after shaking his hand or hugging him. John looked around but could find no explanation for why everyone was in such a hurry to get out the door. He was glad, though, because he needed to get home to check on his sick wife.

John arrived home to find Lindsey sitting up at the kitchen table and feeling much better; but the glow around her body was noticeably brighter. The light made her more beautiful than ever and he smiled, no longer concerned at all about it's presence. Nardic and Meris both marveled at how the Father could shield this young pastor temporarily from worry until the time came for him to know more. The spiritual gift within him was growing; but John was not ready to know everything about it yet. Lindsey looked up at her husband, as he entered the kitchen.

"Hey, how was the service?"

"Seemed to be good...really good, actually. The place was almost full."

"Full? Wow! That is amazing!"

"Yeah, it was amazing." John leaned over to kiss his wife.

"Yuck!" Lindsey pushed him away. "You smell awful!"

"What?"

"You smell like smoke. Yuck!"

"Oh man! I didn't have time to change. No wonder everyone was acting so funny. I noticed several people step back and hurry out the door but...what?" John looked at his wife, as she bent over double laughing.

"I'm sorry. It was my fault but I can't help but laugh!"

A smile slowly spread across John's face, as he realized why he had received some funny looks from a few people who had come up to shake his hand after the service. He started to laugh and sat down beside his wife. John reached out to hold her hand and asked, "How are you feeling, by the way?"

Lindsey wiped her eyes and pointed to her glass of sweet tea. "I was very sick until mom gave me some of this sweet tea. After about an hour or so, I started to feel much better and now I am fine. Mom left just a few minutes before you arrived."

"No lemon in it, I hope."

"No, there was no lemon in it!" They both laughed and John reached in to hug her. "Yuck! You need to change!" Lindsey said and playfully pushed him away again.

"So you don't want a hug?" John's eyes danced as he pretended to hug her again and she shrunk away. "I'll go change and then I can make us something to eat or maybe we can go get something? Are you hungry at all?"

Lindsey smiled and said, "I am really craving some muffins!" and they both laughed again.

"Well, I used this morning as the sermon today. I guess that I still smell like smoke, though."

"What are you talking about?"

"Oh! Well, when I came down to put out the smoke, I saw something strange." John's mind trailed off and he stood still, deep in thought as he replayed the events in the kitchen.

"Well, what did you see?"

He looked at his wife with the glow around her and struggled with the words that would explain what he was experiencing without scaring her. "I think that I saw something in the stove. Like maybe some kind of light."

"Like a fire? I mean, the muffins were burnt to a crisp."

He studied her face and then spent the next thirty minutes telling her what he had seen and how he had changed the sermon at the last minute. He also explained how the three boys in the sermon were not only untouched by the fire but didn't smell of smoke either.

"That's what I meant. I was saved from the fire but not the smoke smell!"

"You don't smell bad, you smell horrible!" Lindsey laughed and he pretended to chase her for a hug.

Lindsey continued to call John "Smokey" for many weeks after that day; and they never looked at muffins the same again. For several days, Lindsey remained sick, but only for a few hours. She would wake up starving but end up vomiting instead. Within a week, they learned they were expecting their first child; and within a few days of the news, the glow around Lindsey began to brighten again. John noticed that the glow never blinded him; but seemed to make him feel happy. Nardic, Galdon, and Meris now all stayed with the family and set up a safe perimeter around the home, because John's gift had been noticed in the spiritual world, not only by many angels, but also by several demons in the area as well. The demons had gathered in response and had begun to prowl near the home, watching and waiting to see what it all meant.

The church was growing rapidly and holding two services on Sundays and one on Saturday night. John was happy but concerned that Lindsey's parents would not come to a service. John's mom and dad had raised him in the church, since he was a child. Lindsey, on the other hand, had been to church some; but her mom had been cold and distant and eventually stopped going at all. By the time Lindsey had reached high school, her dad took her with her sisters; but her mom had always stayed home. John and Lindsey had talked about this through the years; but Lindsey didn't really know why her mom would not go.

When they moved to Louisville, John had assumed that Lindsey's family would at least come and hear him preach occasionally. It hurt him slightly that they wouldn't even come on a holiday. Lindsey had tried every tactic from asking them directly to offering to bring them. Finally, her dad had gently told her that they would come soon; but he never gave her a specific time. The weeks had passed and eventually, Lindsey had given up asking them. There was a distance between her parents and God; and it seemed to come mostly from her mother.

As a preacher's wife, it should have been obvious to turn to prayer; but for some reason, Lindsey had rarely done so in this situation, until she found out she was expecting a baby. Because the maternal instinct stirred within her, she needed her mom now more than ever and began to pray regularly for her family and especially for her mom. A strong surge moved through the spiritual world; and the angels absorbed the added prayer and waited for the right time. Meris gathered the angels around the home and set up a perimeter that no demon was allowed to cross unless it was affixed to a human already. The demonic presence grew in response and several would challenge the perimeter, only to be beaten down, usually with a single blow. Within days, this attracted the attention of more powerful demons, who were wise enough to stay back and wait.

One evening after several weeks had passed, John sat on the couch holding Lindsey in his arms, while they both watched the growing lump in her belly move. John also noticed that the glow was now brighter over Lindsey's abdomen than anywhere else. He wanted to talk to Lindsey about what he saw; but he didn't want to worry her or scare her, especially with her expecting a baby. Feeling the need to talk to someone, he made a mental note to talk to Darron again soon.

"Wow! Do you see that?" Lindsey pointed to one side, where the baby was kicking so much that her stomach rippled up and down like waves on an ocean shore.

John immediately placed his hand over the area to feel the small baby push and tumble around inside his wife. "That is unbelievable! He...she is going crazy!"

"Some people say it's from eating something spicy; but this baby just likes to move!"

"I can't believe it. It's like an alien from a movie."

"Great, we are having an alien." Lindsey teased.

"You know what I mean. Does it hurt?" John thought about the words as he said them. He couldn't imagine something moving like that inside his own body.

"No, but I mean sometimes the baby kicks very hard. I can't wait until Friday to see if it is a girl or a boy!"

"Do you really want to know?" John held back a smile, knowing that the wait was killing Lindsey. He really did not care either way. The thought of fatherhood was enough for him. To try to determine more was almost too overwhelming. He loved watching Lindsey's belly grow; and she was more beautiful to him now than ever. Besides, he had a growing concern about his own health or sanity.

"Ha ha. No, I really don't care at all!" She rolled her eyes and reached over to kiss him. "My mom called today. She has been so strange since she found out about the baby."

"What do you mean?"

"Well, it's hard to explain. She just calls every day and wants to know how I am feeling. She keeps saying not to drive and to stay home."

"I'm glad she is at least calling you some. Usually you are the only one who calls her." John never did understand that. His family was very open and loving; and they all called and talked regularly. Lindsey's sisters called; but Lindsey had to do the work to keep in contact with her own mother.

"Yeah. I don't know what to think. I talked with Millie and Sarah and they both said she was weird when they were pregnant as well."

"So, it didn't stay the same with your sisters after they had their babies?" John watched as Lindsey stared off into the distance and thought about her response.

"Well, both of them said that she stayed very involved until their children turned around two. You know Lexie just turned two and mom hasn't called at all, since the party over two months ago. Millie was upset until Sarah told her that was just the way mom was."

"Lindsey, why do you think your parents never come to our church?"

Lindsey sat in silence and rummaged through her mind for an answer. "I honestly don't know. No one in my family will really talk about it. I did hear my parents arguing one night when I was probably around seven. They were trying to be quiet; but I was thirsty and came down for some water. They didn't hear me, so I sat on the steps and listened. My dad kept telling my mom that she had to let it all go; but my mom kept saying she could never do that and to just leave her alone about it. I don't know what she was so upset about; but Millie and Sarah and I have always thought it had something to do with our dead sister."

"Do you think she hates God because of the accident?"

"Maybe; but I think she blames herself for some reason. Somehow, she is stuck in that pain. She was a good mother in many ways; but she was not happy."

"Do you think we could ever help her change that?"

"I have tried everything. I think we all did through the years. I am hoping that one thing might bring her to church." Lindsey turned to look John in the eyes, while holding her hand over her belly.

"I hope you are right. Her other grandchildren didn't do it though."

"I have an idea, though. I am not sure it is a good one; and I need your input. I have been praying--I mean really praying hard. John, I think we are having a girl."

John smiled and grabbed Lindsey's hand. He couldn't wait to hear her reasons. For as long as he had known her, she had completely captivated him with her ideas and stories. Lindsey always seemed to see the world in a slightly different way than everyone else; and it was one of the many things he adored about her. She was so different from the shy introvert that he had met not so many years ago.

"Now why do you think the baby is a girl?"

"Are you making fun of me?" Lindsey's face pinched slightly; and she was truly hurt. Her hormones were surging again; and she felt the tears before she could stop them. "I...I just know...I mean...I..."

John hugged her close and tried to comfort her. "I wasn't making fun of you. I promise." Now he had to hide his face, as he stifled a laugh. She was more precious to him than she could ever know. How could he convince her, though, when he couldn't stop laughing?

She pushed away. "You are laughing! Why are you laughing?" Lindsey cried harder.

"Honey, I love you so much. I'm sorry, but you are so darn cute."

"Then why are you are laughing, John?" Lindsey continued to sob as she spoke.

"Okay, I am smiling and sort of laughing, but not at you. I just think you are perfect."

Lindsey sobbed and folded into his arms. "I am not perfect. I'm fat and ugly; and now I am a joke to my own husband!"

John held her tight and rocked her side to side. He had learned that these outbursts were short lived and they usually laughed and joked about them later. He was hoping she could recover quickly from this one. Within a few minutes, he got his wish and they were laughing together.

Suddenly, Lindsey sat up and looked at John. "I never got to tell you what I wanted to tell you before."

John held her hand and stroked it slightly as she spoke. "Go ahead and tell me. I really want to know."

"I'll bet you do! You can't wait to laugh again!" Lindsey was smiling this time. "Well, I have been really praying about this, so don't shoot me down too quickly."

"I'll try my best."

Lindsey's eyes were sparkling. "Well, I just know it's a girl. I just feel it. I have a name that I want to use. Please just hear me out on this."

"I'm listening."

"I want to use at least one of these names. If you don't like the whole thing, you can pick one too; but I really want to call her by the name I picked. I mean, the whole name should sound good and of course we have to think about the initials and if they spell a bad word. I also want to try yelling the name out a few times to see if we like it when it's yelled."

"Yelling it out?" John was intrigued.

"Yeah, like we are really, really angry with her so we have to say her full name. I think that it should sound really good that way too."

John was completely amused and wished that he was recording her right now. How did she always manage to make him laugh, even when she was being so serious?

"Are you laughing again?" Lindsey stopped in mid-sentence and stared at him.

John stifled his smile and tried to look as serious as he could. "No. I am just wondering when I am going to hear this name."

Lindsey sat up on her legs and a huge smile spread across her face. "Are you ready?"

"Yes, of course."

"Well, you don't sound ready!" Lindsey frowned.

John braced himself for another mood swing and tried to sound convincing. "I'm ready!"

"Okay! How about Rosalyn Theresa Miles?"

John stared at his wife for a minute and could not believe what she had just said. Nardic looked over from his post outside the door. He was not sure that he had heard it correctly either. Meris landed next to him on the front lawn.

"What are my orders?" Nardic said to his leader.

Meris spread his wings to test their strength. "When they tell her the name of the baby, the demon will attack with all that he has. I can hold for a short time, but I am afraid the strength of the Bitterness demon that holds Lindsey's mom is going to be very difficult to fight unless we get some help. Send out the call when you see it coming. We will all rally together, if the prayers don't come. The strength of our numbers will at least hold the family together for now. This demon is very strong; we have fought him for years. Prayer is the only hope we have to save Lindsey's mom and preserve the family."

Chapter 5: Making Friends

The ministry is a lifestyle more than a profession; and the duties at each church vary depending upon the size of the church and how many associate pastors are available to help distribute the work. When John first arrived at the River City Christian Church (RCCC), the congregation was small with only about ninety faithful members and the church had only one associate pastor, Darron Mitchell, that shared the load of visiting with the homebound or sick. During his early ministry, Pastor John had developed a passion for the shut-ins at nursing homes; and in Louisville, he had picked The Sunshine Nursing Home, located a few blocks from the church, as his focal point for this ministry. The routine of pastoring a church is a personal pilgrimage for each pastor, although there are some basic similarities. Besides developing relationships through visitations and assisting people through different types of counseling, there are a myriad of events that cascade through the schedule that involve church planning and basic church business. On top of these events, a pastor is expected to develop fresh and appropriate sermons, not just for Sunday services but for additional church events as well. In many churches, a pastor might also be expected to write and produce books or some type of study materials; but at RCCC Pastor John's main responsibility revolved around the weekly sermon. The search committee that had interviewed him had made it clear that the church was in need of someone in touch with God's word and who would preach it boldly. John was thrilled to be called to such a place and easily transitioned into the new congregation. Now that the numbers had grown so rapidly, the church had formed a committee to determine how to handle the new people. Most were leaning toward buying a large tract of land and building an entirely new building; but John wanted to make sure that the church did not take on too much debt and wanted to move slowly, saving money through a special offering.

One of the first strategies that Pastor John implemented for improving his sermons was a Thursday ritual of visiting the nearby nursing home to deliver an abbreviated form of that week's message. He had a twofold reason for doing this. One, he truly had great compassion for these residents and felt the need to visit and share with them. His second reason was slightly more self-serving, as it gave him a chance to practice his sermon before delivering it the next Sunday. He started this right after the explosive growth at the church; and after a few weeks, he began to gain a following at the nursing home too with several residents that attended every week. Pastor John loved being able to do this service; but it was the time he invested afterward to visit with the residents that became his favorite activity each week. He began to look forward to Thursdays so much that he often wondered if he was being blessed more than the residents. Most of their conversations remained lighthearted; but several of the residents touched him deeply with their stories and their appreciation of his visit. One resident in particular became one of his closest friends; and John would later even credit him as his official sermon editor.

The first encounter with this man occurred after John had been coming for a couple of years. He had established a good routine of arriving right as the residents finished lunch, so that he could walk through the dining hall and remind them of the service, as well as invite some of those who had never been. John walked into the dining hall and began to greet several familiar faces, when he noticed a man in a wheelchair that he had never seen before. He watched the man for a moment and noticed that he was eating alone and seemed about finished with his lunch. As the man pushed away from the table and began wheeling himself toward the corridor that led to the residential area, John weaved his way through the room to intersect the man's path and politely introduced himself.

"Hello, I am Pastor John Miles; but everyone just calls me Pastor John."

"A preacher! I should have guessed. I'm Doug Roberts. I will answer to anything close to that."

John smiled in response and continued, "Are you new here?"

"I was just dumped off here this past Saturday."

John liked the man immediately and appreciated his quick wit. "Were they nice enough to leave you with some of your things?"

Mr. Roberts quickly retorted, "They pretty much cleaned me out; but they did leave me some clothes."

"That was generous of them. Did you leave you some furniture too?"

The old man returned John's smile. "Well, they didn't want to; but I guess they had to. I have a bed and a dresser. It really should be considered some type of abuse."

"I believe you have a group of comrades here at the home. Maybe you could start a support group or some type of petition."

"I am fairly sure that few here could read it much less sign it. I am not sure I could sign it either, with these arthritic hands." He held his hands up and John could see the painful looking contortions of his fingers. "Anyway, it was nice to meet you, son."

"You too. If you are not busy, I would love for you to come to the activity hall and listen to my sermon."

"Here it comes! Next you will want ten percent of what I have. Let me tell you that you couldn't buy a cup of coffee with that."

"I don't know, I drink pretty cheap coffee."

Mr. Roberts tried to hide his smile as he responded, "I am sure you would like to add me to your body count. Something about churches, preachers, and their numbers.

It's like you guys are not happy unless you can brag about your numbers."

"Well, I--"

"Now don't get offended. What I said was absolutely true and you know it. I will come, though, so you can add another name to your roster. I would love to hear what you have to say. I just hope it isn't crap."

"I will try to keep it at least one level above crap."

"That would be at the 'it stinks' level."

"What if I try for the level above that?"

"Then you would hit 'barely survivable'"

"I think I would like to see this scale of yours. How many levels are there?"

"Oh, I don't know. I will tell you that very few get above the 'I stayed awake through it' level around here."

John laughed out loud and shook his head. "I hope I can at least hit that one for you."

"I'll let you know. If I snore, then you know you are below that."

John watched Mr. Roberts roll away toward the activity hall and was both amused and intrigued by this man. He definitely wanted to get to know him better.

The room began to fill up with the collection of walkers and canes along with their owners. On the far side of the front row, Pastor John saw Mr. Roberts anchored between the last chair on that row and the wall, waiting intently on the young preacher to begin. The service went smoothly and the residents began to file out the door; but Mr. Roberts remained in his spot and sat motionless until only he and Pastor John were left in the room.

"What did you think, Mr. Roberts?"

"I have to say that the sermon was not crap."

"Thank you for that assessment. I don't think that I have ever had a review quite like that. I see that I made it at least to the 'I stayed awake through it' level."

"Hmm. Well, you are at least at the 'I will come and try it again' level."

"That is quite a compliment."

"I am not sure it was a compliment; but I do think you are worthy of another try."

John was growing more fascinated with each exchange between them. "I come every Thursday."

"Do you give the same message again on Sunday at your church?"

"Most of the time, yes."

"So we are your practice round--kind of a dress rehearsal?"

John's face turned red with embarrassment; but he remained composed as he answered. "I guess you could say that; but I also enjoy visiting with everyone here."

"I guess that is okay. Do you really enjoy visiting with everyone? I can't get more than a grunt or two from most of them. Some of the people here don't even seem to know that they are alive; and I wouldn't be surprised if they weren't."

John fought back a smile and responded, "I can get a few of them to talk to me; but I have noticed that several people here are not very responsive."

Mr. Roberts snorted in response and then added, "I have to tell you. I witnessed something that I never thought even possible here yesterday."

"What?"

"I just started my time here on Saturday."

"You make it sound like a prison sentence."

"It is. I was absolutely sentenced to this--against my will. No matter, though. I will get them back."

"How?"

"Someday I may tell you, if I live long enough--which I plan to do. Anyway, I was watching this little nurse girl training with a supervisor. I heard the supervisor give the girl an assignment to bathe this woman in a room down from mine. About an hour later, the girl came out of the room as I was rolling by; and I could see the woman sitting up in her bed. The woman was all fixed up with her hair combed; and she even looked like her nails were freshly painted--at least I think I smelled nail polish. The young girl was carrying old bed sheets, so I think she even changed the old woman's bed. I was thinking that the girl did what seemed like a great job and that made me happy, because I had been worrying what kind of care I would get here when I finally get old and can no longer do things for myself. I rolled further down the hall and saw the supervisor coming to check the girl's work; but then I remembered that I had left my medicine in my room and needed to take it with my lunch. So when I went back by the room, I heard the supervisor fussing at the girl. Apparently, the girl had bathed and changed the woman as well as made her bed; but the woman had been dead the entire time without the girl even noticing."

"Wow. Seriously?"

"Yeah, I guess the girl had no idea."

"That is quite a story. Maybe the woman was alive but died when the girl left the room."

"No, I heard the supervisor telling her that the woman was stone cold and had to have died before the girl even worked with her."

"At least she was all clean for her family."

"Now that might be the saddest part. She had no one. I went to her room and said a prayer after they took her. There was not a single person who even came to collect her things. The staff came in later last night and boxed it all up and took it away. It was not my favorite day here."

"That is very sad." John stared at the floor and wondered about the woman who had died alone.

"It will be me someday, only my family will come to get that bed and dresser for sure."

"So it's that valuable--maybe I do need my ten percent?" John tried to hide his smile, but failed miserably.

Mr. Roberts laughed and he shook his head. "No, they just don't have it yet; and I am sure it bothers them. I would bet that they would have taken the boxes from that woman's room, if they could have."

John wasn't sure if Mr. Roberts was teasing or trying to be funny. There was a faraway look in the old man's eyes and John thought he might have even seen the beginning of a tear; but Mr. Roberts shook his head suddenly and sighed.

"Anyway, I need to go to my room. All of this excitement is getting me tired."

The old man headed toward the door and continued to talk as he exited.

"I'm going to go to my room now. Thank you for inviting me. I will be back as long as the Lord let's me."

"I'm glad you came. I will see you next week."

Pastor John followed him out the door and stopped to watch him roll down the hall. As the pastor turned to head toward the front door of the nursing home, he stepped back toward the hall again.

"Hey, Mr. Roberts? What has been your favorite day here?"

Without any hesitation, the old man answered,

"Today!" He said and continued on to his room without looking back.

Chapter 6: The Birth

Both sets of grandparents stood in the small hospital room as John let each one hold the tiny baby girl for the first time. Lindsey sat up in the bed watching her precious daughter in the arms of so many people who loved her. Lindsey's sisters, Millie and Sarah, both lived out of town and had called several times each to talk with her about the labor and delivery; and both promised a trip to Louisville soon to meet their new niece. John's brother and his wife had also been unable to come in town, since they lived on the west coast. Several of Lindsey's friends had helped coordinate the meals and gifts from all the well-meaning parishioners so that when the new family came home, they would have a refrigerator and freezer full of meals for the next couple of weeks.

Lindsey silently prayed for peace and courage, as she waited on the moment that she and John would announce the name of their new baby girl. Only Millie and Sarah knew what Lindsey was about to say; and both had promised to pray for Lindsey as well. They knew how hard this would be for their mother, Ellie; but both agreed with Lindsey that the name was absolutely perfect. John had been harder to convince; but he had finally agreed as well.

"Well, I guess we need to let you know the name we have chosen." John looked at Lindsey and she nodded for him to continue. "We prayed about this and want you all to know that we very much want your blessing on this and hope you will be honored by the name that we have chosen. Lindsey, I want you to do the honors."

Meris, Galdon, and Nardic all stood with their wings enveloping the room. "Here it comes. Stay strong!" Meris ordered.

All eyes in the room turned toward Lindsey, as she smiled and looked from John to her small daughter. "Like John said. We wanted to honor you all and hope that you will love the name as much as we do. First, we wanted to use a middle name to honor John's mother, so Terry, our daughter's middle name will be Theresa, after you."

Terry and Roger grabbed hands and smiled. "Thank you, Lindsey. That's wonderful!"

Lindsey paused and looked at John, who nodded for her to continue. "We thought about the first name for a long time. We wanted to honor my family too and finally decided on…Rosalyn in honor of Rose Louise, my sister who passed away years ago. We want to call her Rosie for short."

Lindsey's parents, Ellie and Mark, stood frozen and unable to respond. The demon from the hoard of Bitterness that had clutched onto Ellie for years began to whisper into her ear as fast as he could talk. Meris stepped forward and placed the blade of his sword between the demon's lips and Ellie's ear, stopping him from spreading more venom. The demon screeched in frustration and lashed out at Meris's arm, leaving a wide gash; but the angel never flinched and instantly swatted the demon to the ground, where he scattered to a dark corner to wait for the prayer surge to slow. The gash on Meris's arm had already healed to a pearl colored scar that was barely noticeable against the glow of the angel's wings.

"Mom and dad," John said as he turned to look at his parents, "I don't think you all know that Lindsey had a sister named Rose Louise that passed away when she was a small child." John kept his eyes on his parents and could not bring himself to look at his in-laws, because he knew that they must be struggling with this. All of his training as a counselor and pastor was not helping him at all right now, as he tried to soften the words. "We wanted to pass her name along to our daughter."

Lindsey was unable to gauge exactly what her mom was thinking and timidly watched her mom's expressionless face. It had been over twenty-five years; but Lindsey's mom, Ellie, seemed frozen in time when it came to Rose Louise. From the corner near Ellie, the demon from the hoard of Bitterness began to creep toward her and tried to move around the sword; but Meris flicked him back again. The angels knew that they needed more prayer to continue; but each one glowed and carefully guarded the peace and calm in the room for the next few minutes.

"Mom, what do you think?" All eyes turned to watch Ellie, while her husband, Mark, grabbed his wife's hand and gently squeezed.

"We are honored that you would do that, Lindsey and John. Thank you." Mark answered as he leaned in closer to Ellie to help steady his wife and hoped that his strength would somehow help her stay stable.

The demon screamed, "She's dead! She's dead! It's your fault!"

Nardic could not restrain himself and he stepped forward toward the demon; but Galdon held him back. Meris looked up to the ceiling and nodded; then he slowly moved his sword until it touched the demon's mouth. A loud screech and then a sizzling sound followed; and the demon fell silent. His mouth had been sealed shut for now.

Nardic spread his wings high above his head and said, "He's mine when the time comes!"

Meris nodded. "Not yet, but soon."

No one in the room was aware of this spiritual struggle; but they were all fully aware of the uncomfortable silence building around the announcement of the name.

Trying to salvage the moment, Terry exclaimed, "Well, Rosie is simply beautiful!" She reached over to hold her new granddaughter again. "I think she has your eyes, Lindsey."

"Really? I mean, I thought maybe she had John's nose, but I wasn't sure," Lindsey answered and looked up as John grabbed her hand. She glanced over at her parents, who seemed to be struggling with the news. She silently prayed,

Please let them be okay. I didn't mean to hurt them. Please, God, please help them.

Immediately, the angels moved toward the demon, who moaned, then he retreated back to the corner, while the angels remained positioned to shield Ellie as long as the power from the prayer would last. The moan from the demon caused Rosie to suddenly cry. Nardic and Galdon both looked at the baby and then at each other.

"She can hear us!" Galdon said and Nardic nodded.

"Yes, I believe she might see us soon." Meris said.

All three angels felt the power of the prayer surge begin to fade throughout the room; and the demon's mouth began to open again, allowing him to start to chant. He jumped and stomped as he continued to speak; but his words bounced off the powerful wings of the angels, causing him to yell and curse.

Rosie cried harder and Meris touched her gently on the forehead, instantly calming the young baby.

Nardic looked back at the demon and said, "Having fun?"

Even Galdon smiled and the demon immediately reached out and scratched Galdon's arm.

"That's all? Really?" Galdon answered and then he shoved the demon, sending him tumbling into the hall, where he seethed and groaned as he paced back and forth, dragging his talons along the wall in frustration.

Visiting hours would be ending soon and both sets of new grandparents lingered to take turns holding the new baby. Ellie seemed somewhat more distant with her mind tumbling through a variety of emotions until she finally looked over at Lindsey and sighed. Galdon had taken the lead of placing his wings around Ellie, trying to soothe her and keep her at peace as long as the prayer support lasted; but he could feel the strength fading fast. The demon slowly moved into the room and touched the edge of Galdon's wing, singing it slightly and causing Galdon to flinch. The burning sensation spread throughout the lower half of Galdon's wing; but he held his position. The demon continued to burn small places on Galdon; but the angel continued to hold his protective circle.

Finally, Ellie found her voice and walked over and kissed Lindsey on the forehead. "I love you, honey. You are going to be a wonderful mother." She turned toward her husband and said, "I'm going to go down and get something to eat. Does anyone else want anything?"

Mark looked at his wife, puzzled, knowing that they had eaten right before they arrived. He wisely decided to follow her and not say a word. Out in the hall he put his arm around Ellie, as she crumpled into his embrace. The demon flew beside her and began whispering into her ear, as tears began to flow quickly down her cheeks. Mark escorted her as fast as he could out of range, so that no one in the room would know what was happening. The three powerful angels all followed them into the hall. Galdon's wounds healed quickly; but left small scars where the burns had been. He stayed near Ellie; but his power continued to fade and he was forced to just watch, as the demon smiled and drew close to her again.

Mark held his wife close and whispered in her ear. "Are you okay?"

Ellie looked up into his eyes and said, "I don't know!"

"Is it because they named her Rosalyn?"

"Of course it is! I can't stand it! How can they do this?"

"I don't think they mean anything but respect for her. It's a wonderful gesture and a wonderful way for us to all heal and remember her."

"I know they mean well. I feel horrible. It's just difficult for me still. I still feel like it was my fault. She was too young. It's not fair! I still hate… I mean…I'm still mad…"

Mark grabbed his wife and held her close. "It's okay honey. Remember I lost a daughter too. We all miss her. It's been a long time now though; and we have got to let her go and enjoy our life and our time with our new granddaughter."

"I can never let her go! Why would God take my baby? What good could it have possibly done to take that beautiful child out of this world?"

The demon lurched at Ellie and grabbed onto her again. The angels stood by helplessly, only able to keep him from doing any physical harm to her. As he chanted more lies into her ear, he looked over at the angels and smiled.

Meris barked orders, "Nardic, go back to the hospital room to try to remind the humans to pray. Galdon, you stay with me to guard Ellie and Mark." Both angels nodded and immediately responded.

Mark stood holding his wife in his arms and let his wife's words fall silently around them for a few seconds, like a cold blanket. Finally, he pushed back to look into her eyes and spoke in a soft voice, "I don't know why we lost Rose Louise; but I do know that God loves you."

The demon chanted "God doesn't love you...God doesn't love you!"

Ellie's heart stiffened and she blurted out, "Well, I don't love him!" Her hand flew to her mouth, as she realized for the first time in over twenty years that she really did hate God. In her heart, she had always known that she was angry over losing her child; but she had never verbalized it like this before. The demon snarled and laughed, then leaned in to whisper more lies into Ellie's ear. Galdon spread his wings; but the last of the prayer surge was gone and he was unable to be effective. The demon's venom slithered through Ellie's mind and she felt a renewed sense of anger and bitterness. In frustration, Meris looked up and waited for the Father to intervene.

"He doesn't care! He took your baby!" The demon continued to say, over and over.

Ellie's thoughts flowed freely through the sea of bitterness, as the demon continued to whisper into her ear. She stood shivering from the waves of hatred lapping at her soul. *I know it's wrong; but I don't care. I can't stop being angry. Why did you take my baby, God?*

Ellie looked up at Mark. His eyes reflected a strange expression, somewhere between confusion and fear. As he watched his wife, he knew something sinister lurked beneath her eyes. She was physically shaking now and her words had crushed his hope that Ellie was just depressed. This was something much deeper and much more personal. His wife blamed God and worse than that; she had said she doesn't love Him. There were few things Mark could not accept; but this was one of them. Where did that leave him or their marriage for that matter?

He fought back tears as he reached out to steady her, "Ellie...you can't stop loving God. He will never leave you--"

"--or forsake me?" She blurted out, as she pulled away violently from his touch. "What do you call taking my baby? He did leave me and He did forsake me!" *Now my own husband has to hate me. He finally knows my secret. I never meant for him to know. I don't care...I can't stop myself from being angry. It's not fair!*

Mark sighed and tried to gather his thoughts. He closed his eyes and tried to form a coherent thought; but the demon saw his chance to attack and began to chant to him too. Thoughts were swirling in Mark's mind and he couldn't seem to make any sense of them. Galdon could take no more and he looked at Meris.

"No, Galdon, you can't keep taking on scars!"

"I can handle it." He said as he stepped forward and allowed the demon to burn and claw at his wing, sacrificing some of his glow to temporarily block the demon's words and allow Mark to clear his mind as well as mute the words going to Ellie. It was a bold move and he would pay with a large scar.

The block worked and Mark suddenly found the words, "Ellie, I love you. I know God loves you too, I just know it." Galdon held as long as he could; but the pain forced him to pull back his wing and he fell down to the floor to recover. Another small angel immediately landed beside him to help him heal. The pain was intense; but fortunately, the smaller angel was able to reduce it quickly. The injured area on his wing turned from a singed black to the shiny pearl color of an angel's scar within seconds. Galdon was known for his selflessness in battle, as evidenced by his many small scars along both wings. In the angel's world, a scarred area could no longer glow; and once enough glow was lost, the angel would no longer be able to fight in a direct battle. The angels love to glow and allow the glory of God to shine through them; and the loss of glow is an enormous sacrifice and is never expected of them. Galdon's heroics were widely known and respected; but Meris was concerned that at the rate he was going, Galdon's warrior days were numbered, which would be a great loss to them all.

The temporary block from the demon worked to soften Ellie's heart temporarily too. She blinked and seemed dazed; but her anger was gone. "I know that you don't understand. You probably hate me now. I'm so sorry; but I can't help it. I have been so mad at God for taking her!" There were no more tears; but she was still struggling with the battle raging in her mind and the anger began to rise again from the influence of the demon, who was now back whispering in her ear again.

Galdon knew he had to get prayer support now. The pain in his wing had subsided; but he could feel the tug of the scar, as he stood and moved toward Mark, who was in a state of shock, silently watching his wife. Mark had never realized how deeply Ellie had buried those feelings. It crushed him to know that he hadn't been there for her; but he was also confused.

Why hadn't she told me how she felt? I could have helped her.

"I know one thing. I know God does not hate you. I know God loves you and he loves me and he also loved Rose Louise." Mark's words seemed hollow, even to him. He was still trying to process what had just happened. He pulled Ellie in close again to hug her. "It's okay. I just never knew you were hurting that deeply. Maybe we should go get some help for you." Mark said a small prayer of only four words, but they were enough.

God, please help us.

The prayer was short; but the emotion was deep and a connection shot to Heaven and back instantly. As the last word left Mark's mouth, Galdon moved swiftly to pierce the demon with a shot of light, causing him to scream and release one arm. The hideous creature was forced to stand beside Ellie with Galdon blocking him from reattaching the arm. The prayer gave Galdon a choice to either blast the demon off completely for a short time or to hold this position for a while, which is what he chose to do. Again, Meris shook his head. Galdon always chose the more daring way and Meris again wondered how long his friend could last. Mark and Ellie continued to stand by the elevators sobbing and holding each other tightly for several minutes, while the angel and the demon continued to hold their positions.

In the hospital room, Nardic waited intently for someone there to pray. John asked them all to bow to pray for little Rosie and a myriad of other things. During the prayer, he finally referenced the intense need by praying for Lindsey's parents and their pain from the loss of the baby so long ago. Meris felt the power and Nardic landed beside him to confirm the news.

"That should give us what we need. I'm going to help Galdon, you go back to the room. We will all feel it, if more comes. The Father promised some extra help as well." Outside, small battles for position had begun; but the prayer shifted the momentum of the battle and a shard of light from Heaven pounded the air, sending the demons tumbling to the ground and scurrying away. A large cheer arose from all the angels and they began to sing and praise God.

Meris moved into the hall to be with Mark and Ellie. The demon was still standing beside Ellie, greedily hanging on with one arm and growling violently and hitting Galdon with his free hand, when Meris stepped in to take over and surround Mark and his wife with his wings, leaving only a small opening where the demon stood. Galdon fell back and drew his sword, waiting for the right moment to strike. His wounds from the demon healed instantly; but left a few more scars.

"I'm sorry God I'm so sorry. I don't hate you. I thought I did but I don't. I love you. I'm so sorry. Please take away this pain."

Ellie shook in Mark's arms and began to cry softly, as Mark held her tightly and tried to calm and console her. Galdon struck the demon with a blast of light from his sword, sending the demon careening out of the hospital, where he desperately clung to the outside of the building, howling and screaming, but unable to return. When Galdon turned around, though, he was met with a surprise. Another demon had moved into the edge of the room. This one was larger and glared at both Galdon and Meris. The years of bitterness from the other demon could not be erased in a single fight. Galdon and Meris both knew that this new demon was very powerful and dangerous. He was from the hoard of Pride. His lips curled and snarled as he paced back and forth at the edge of the room. Galdon and Meris never took their eyes off of the beast and both moved to shield Ellie and Mark.

"No wonder that demon of Bitterness has been so bold! He has had help from that mangy beast!" Galdon boomed as he signaled to the demon to attack if he so dared.

Meris held Galdon's arm and spoke with authority, "Not now, Galdon. We will defeat him when the Lord is ready."

"I will gladly wait! You hear that demon! You need to turn from your wicked ways and seek God. Only His love will reign!"

The demon showed no response and simply lingered in the shadows with his red eyes locked on Galdon, who continued to glare back at him.

Back in the hospital room, Lindsey held her new daughter again, while John took some more pictures. A nurse entered the room to check on the new family and turned to leave.

"Hi, I am Ann. Please let me know if you all need anything."

"I feel fine. I guess I just want to go home."

"Oh, I think you will be going there tomorrow! The doctor should be by first thing in the morning to check on you. Do you want me to take your baby back to the nursery so you can get some sleep?"

"No, I would really like to keep her here with me tonight."

"That is fine. You are nursing her, correct?"

"Yes, she seems to be doing great."

"Wonderful. We have a great lactation consultant, if you have any questions. I will be here all night, so call if you need me."

Ann paused slightly, as she scanned the room and noted the grandparents. Something triggered a distant memory; but she could not remember what it was. She headed back to the nurse's station to do some notes; but something continued to tug at her memory. Those grandparents looked so familiar, but why? It would be a long time before she remembered who they were.

Ann left the nurse's station and started to walk down the hall; but as she neared the elevators, she could hear part of a hushed conversation and someone crying, so she stopped and ducked into a small vending area to give the distressed people some privacy. The anguish in the woman's voice was so compelling that Ann instinctively began to pray fervently for her without any knowledge of why the woman was so sad. As her prayers soared toward Heaven, a flurry of activity in the unseen world began to occur.

Nardic, Galdon, and Meris all felt the swell of intensity to their skills immediately from the fervent prayer. The new dark demon of Pride cowered in the corner of the room, ready to strike until the prayer power subsided; but the influx of strength was too great this time and Nardic boldly stepped forward. He moved swiftly, flashing his sword at the new demon, who could only curse and scream, as he was forced to retreat out toward the hall. The angels began to glow from the surge of prayer; and for the first time in years, Ellie felt a peace wash over her. The angels could only help free her--she had the choice to allow the demons back into her life. Now that both demons were gone, Meris looked around to find the source of the prayer surge. He saw Ann, the nurse, who had simply prayed silently for God's help and he went over to her side.

"It was her."

Nardic sheathed his sword and landed beside Meris. "If the people only knew how important prayer was."

Galdon landed next and quipped, "They should. It has been explained in so many ways."

Meris moved back toward Ellie and Mark. "It will need to be explained again. That is our mission and why this is so important."

"I will stay with Ellie." Nardic said as he pointed his sword toward the demon of Pride, who shrunk back further into the hall. "Why do these people not understand?"

"Free Will. It is what the Father wanted." Meris watched the couple gather themselves and enter the elevator. "Stay with them and I will bring more help to surround their home tonight. We can at least give her one night to heal. I hope more prayer comes by tomorrow."

"Me too. We have plenty for tonight; but that demon of Pride is very strong."

"We do have the baby. Hopefully, she will make a difference. She has the gift. She heard us in the room, when we were fighting the first demon." Galdon stated in a low voice.

"Did you all notice if anyone else seemed to hear?" Meris looked to see if any demons were close enough to hear them talking.

Both Galdon and Nardic shook their heads. Meris's face remained grim, as he weighed all the information carefully. He looked up to Heaven for several long seconds.

"We will have to stay closer than ever. The demons will spread the word as well. I will send more help; but I need you two to go on now to your assigned posts. The Father has sent power to help us through the night."

As Galdon turned to leave, Nardic saw the large new scar and the smaller burn scars on Galdon's wing. "What happened?"

Meris looked at Galdon, who answered, "Nothing. Just a demon that needed a lesson."

Nardic and Galdon turned to leave to follow Ellie and Mark; but Meris grabbed Galdon's arm, "Hold on for a minute." Galdon nodded to Nardic, who continued on without him.

Galdon waited for Nardic to leave. "What is it?"

"Galdon, you have one of the bravest and most selfless attitudes of any angel I know."

Galdon looked puzzled. Angels generally don't understand praise unless it is given to God. "What do you mean?"

"I mean that you are doing a good job protecting and helping; but I need to talk to you about something."

"Yes, Meris. What do you need?" Galdon immediately snapped to attention, anticipating another assignment.

"I need you to be careful."

Galdon relaxed and looked at Meris. He was confused by not only what he said but also how he said it. There was a sad tone in his leader's voice. "What do you mean?"

"I know you love to fight for God."

"More than anything, sir!"

"That is why I need you to be careful. You are too bold with your moves sometimes. Be patient and wait on prayer or scripture to help us. You are taking on too many scars too quickly."

"Meris, I can't stop. I was given the gift of boldness and I must use it."

"I think you should use it. I just need you to work through the situation carefully. Tonight the prayer support came and would have been fine without your sacrifice. Just choose your sacrifices carefully so we can keep you on the battlefield longer. I would hate to lose you. You are also rubbing off on Nardic and Flint. Both of them look up to you. They are much too small and not experienced enough to fight like you."

Galdon's powerful legs rippled as he walked back and forth, listening to Meris. He stopped and looked at his friend and leader. "I would not want to see either of them get hurt; but I never want to stop fighting. Do you think that the Father would heal me, if I were to go too far?"

"It has never been done before so we can't assume anything. Please just be careful."

Galdon nodded and then left for his assignment.

The news of the child's ability to hear the angels spread quickly in the spiritual world and was almost overwhelming. Time is not the same to an angel and the years ahead would pass quickly. All the angels felt a renewed energy just knowing that the baby brought new hope.

Ellie and Mark spent the rest of the evening together talking and praying; and the increased power from their prayers kept the demons more than a block away from their home. The perimeter glowed with light, as the angels kept watch; and by morning, Ellie woke with more energy than she had felt in years. She was up early and made breakfast in bed for Mark, something she had not done since their first year of marriage.

"Wow! What a treat. Thank you sweetheart."

"I guess I just wanted to thank you for helping me yesterday."

Mark looked up at Ellie and they both knew the truth. Mark had tried everything to help her in the past. Neither of them realized the spiritual battle that had been raging for years to control Ellie. The demons would not give up this easily and would try to simply wait until the prayer surge subsided. Within a few weeks, life slipped back into a normal routine and the prayers had slowed. The demons crept back closer to the home and eventually made their way into the room with Ellie again. Neither the demon of Pride nor the demon of Bitterness were ever able to latch on again, but they stood behind her and kept her in a state of gloom as much as they could. Nardic could only watch until more prayers arrived; but he was craving the moment that he would be able to fight those demons head on.

Chapter 7: Long Nights

Rosie was a beautiful baby but she had a difficult time determining day from night. Lindsey was unsure of how far to push her small daughter and struggled with getting her on a schedule, as all of her friends had suggested. She could not bear listening to her tiny little girl cry in distress; and many mornings John would find his young wife asleep in a chair holding their baby girl.

"Lindsey, you have got to get some sleep. Call your mom to come over and help you. My mom would come too. You need some help."

"I know. I just hate to bother them. I mean, we should be able to handle one little baby."

John laughed and scooped up his daughter, "Well, this little goose is quite a handful." He held her on his shoulder and rocked side to side. Rosie yawned and cuddled up to go back to sleep.

"Of course! Now she goes to sleep!" Lindsey smiled and stretched. "I have been up since 2:00 AM."

"Call your mom. She would love to come and help, if you would just let her."

"She has been helping some. I mean she has helped with organizing all the meals people have brought over. I just can't get her to hold Rosie very much. She seems so sad every time she is here. Dad said it is because Rosie looks just like Rose Louise."

"Well, my mom would be happy to come over too."

"I might call her. I know she has that bad knee; and I just hate to bother her."

"I don't think it would bother her at all." John kissed his wife on the forehead and handed little Rosie back to Lindsey. "I have to head in to a meeting and then a few counseling sessions. How about I come home at lunch and let you take a nap?"

"That would be great! I can try to have her ready and fed by then."

John grabbed his briefcase and keys and headed for the door. "Please call my mom or your mom. I really think either one would love it if you needed them."

"Okay, I will." Lindsey swayed side to side and cuddled Rosie close.

As she heard the garage door close, she decided to lay Rosie down and grab a quick shower. Right as she got her hair full of shampoo, she heard Rosie screaming. Quickly she rinsed what she could and grabbed her towel and robe.

Rosie was red faced and kicking when Lindsey scooped her up. There was a terrible smell and as Lindsey placed Rosie on her shoulder, she saw the source. All over the bed and now smeared along her robe was what John called a diaper blow out. Now, instead of a long hot shower, the baby bed, Rosie, and Lindsey were all covered in poop.

"Yuck! For someone so cute you sure make a nasty mess." She spent the next thirty minutes juggling a screaming baby, changing sheets and cleaning up, all while freezing and still loaded with shampoo in her own hair. Maybe it was time to call John's mom or her own mom. She definitely needed help. Within an hour, reinforcements arrived. Lindsey had decided that her own mom was a better choice, because she didn't want to admit failure to John's mom yet.

"Hey mom."

"Oh, Lindsey, you are a mess! What can I do?"

"Well, can you move the clothes over to the dryer? I had to wash a bunch of stuff covered in one of Rosie's blow outs." She saw the confused look on her mom's face. "Rosie pooped everywhere; and when I picked her up, it got everywhere. It was really gross."

"Oh. Well, I will be glad to do that. Where is the baby?"

"Well, she just fell sound asleep on my bed and I came down to let you in."

"You left her on your bed?"

"Yeah, I didn't want to move her and wake her up."

"Lindsey! Never leave a baby on a bed! She could fall off!" Ellie ran up the stairs as if to save her granddaughter.

Lindsey rolled her eyes. "Mom, she hasn't ever rolled over at all."

As they both entered the bedroom, they saw little Rosie awake and alert and at the edge of the bed. She had rolled all the way over to the edge on her own. Ellie grabbed her and looked at her daughter.

"See! She almost fell off!"

Lindsey collapsed to the floor in tears. "I am a terrible mother! I almost let my baby die!" The words had spilled out before Lindsey realized what she had said.

The demon of Pride had been lurking nearby and he immediately laughed and began to dance and chant, "You were a bad mother too! You were a bad mother too!"

Ellie had not prayed in the last few days and her defenses were weak. Galdon and Nardic were both in the room; and before Galdon could stop him, Nardic moved to put a wing over the demon's mouth. The burn was instantaneous and Nardic fell back in pain.

"Nardic! You know you can't do that! We have to wait on prayer!"

Both angels watched the two women, while a few small angels tended Nardic's wound.

Lindsey stood and walked to her mom. "Oh mom, I am sorry. I didn't mean..."

Ellie's face was ashen and she gently handed Rosie to Lindsey. "I have to be going now. I will...I will call you later." She calmly left the room and walked toward the front door.

"Mom, please. I am so sorry. I didn't mean you. I..." The front door closed and Lindsey watched from the bedroom window as her mom backed her car out of the driveway. She picked up the phone and quickly called her father to explain what had happened.

"I'll take care of it, Lindsey. Don't worry. She has had worse days than this."

Mark hung up the phone and walked to the den to wait on Ellie to come home. It was going to be a long night. There had been many in the past.

"I will stay here, you go to Ellie's home to warn the angels there. I will talk with Meris about how to handle this." Nardic nodded and flew quickly to reach Ellie's home before she arrived. Within a few minutes, he quickly spread the word to all the angels there what had happened and helped them set up a perimeter to protect the home. Now the only thing to do was wait and hope that Mark and Lindsey would start to pray soon. Nardic reached over and rubbed the new pearl colored scar along the side of his right wing that no longer glowed. He didn't know that it would feel different from the rest of his wing. The wing of an angel serves to give strength and power for flight and the glow helps to defend and strike during a battle with a demon. The surface of the wing serves as a shield to protect all that are inside as well. Nardic could feel a distinct numbness where the glow was missing and he knew that his wing was now slightly weaker. The rest of his body could be struck repeatedly and it would heal almost to perfection; but the wing was different. Too many insults and it would be useless in battle, causing an angel to have to give up his place in battle and serve in another way. Although Nardic was glad he had helped the woman, he knew that his actions had been foolish. Standing on the porch of the home, he watched and waited for Ellie to return home, as several dark foreboding demons lurked around the street waiting for whatever was coming. Somehow they had been alerted to the pain that was swelling within Ellie.

More angels had now arrived and joined to protect the perimeter that had been formed around the home. The demons had grown in number as well and huddled in dark masses, watching the angels to see what would come next. When Ellie's car rounded the corner, all heads simultaneously turned to watch as she moved toward the house. Meris flew low over the car with his wings fully expanded and glowing. Suddenly, he pulled out his sword and pointed it toward the largest group of demons near the home and a beam of light flashed forward and scattered them in a screaming rage, leaving a clear pathway for Ellie to get to her home. The rest of the night was a standoff in the spiritual realm around the home, as Mark and Ellie talked and prayed together. The surge from these prayers along with the Father's protection allowed the angels ample strength keep the demons from attacking. There was nothing the angels could do to keep Ellie from inviting her personal demons into her life, though, so the demons of Bitterness and Pride were allowed into the home.

"Stay with the woman, while I talk with everyone out here." Meris looked around the yard and then turned back to Nardic. "Good job on the perimeter."

Nardic stiffled a smile and nodded, then disappeared into the home. The two demons were nowhere to be seen;

but he could sense that they were near. The prayers of the couple were keeping them away; and Nardic felt the surge and smiled again. He was happy that he was serving the Father and that everything was going smoothly so far. Even though he was young, he was not naive enough to think it was over for the night; and he patiently waited for the demons to try to intervene in some way.

After Ellie and Mark had exhausted their prayers and conversation, Ellie excused herself to take a bath. In the privacy of the bathroom, the demon of Bitterness attacked; but she resisted. Somewhere in the conversations and prayers of this night, Ellie had given up on being angry with God and now only felt sorry for herself. With his assaults ignored, the demon of Bitterness writhed in anger and cursed her repeatedly. From a corner of her closet, the demon of Pride slowly emerged and reached over to beat the demon of Bitterness until he ran away screaming. The large demon of Pride that remained moved slowly around Ellie, as if deciding where to attack her first. His hunched shoulders and large red eyes blazed with hate, as he flexed his talons open and shut in a sickening cadence. His reputation for being both cunning and bold were well known; and Nardic could only wait for more prayer support in order to help. He didn't want to make another mistake. He stretched his wings, but they only flickered with some of his remaining strength; and the demon merely glanced over at the young angel and then continued his methodical movements. For a moment, Nardic again considered attacking without help; but he knew that the only result would be injuring himself and little relief for the woman.

Ellie sat on the side of the tub in her robe and tears formed along the creases of her eyes. She watched the water swirl down the drain and felt her energy being pulled away with it. An incredible sadness enveloped her and the only clear thought she could hear was coming from the demon of Pride, who whispered it over and over into her ear, as he reached out to grab her shoulders.

"Your baby is gone. Your baby is gone."

A strong beam of light showered the room and Meris landed beside Nardic. The demon had to cover his face and stop chanting, as the glow from Meris enveloped the room. Both angels surrounded Ellie and worked to keep the light between her and the demon of Pride.

"That's cheating!" Yelled the demon.

"We haven't touched you!" Boomed Meris. He had saved a little of his glow for this moment, knowing that this night would be hard for Ellie.

"You have to let her go! She wants to be sad!"

Meris did not answer, but pushed with all of his strength to complete a full sphere of light around Ellie. When he finished, he looked over at the demon, whose red eyes were tucked behind his claws and he groaned in pain.

"Turn it down! I will stay away if you will turn it down!"

Meris kept his eyes on the demon and stretched his wings high to release the last of the glow. Within a few seconds, the glow subsided and returned to a steady soft glow around his wings; and Meris grabbed Nardic and pulled him back to the edge of the room across from the demon.

"What--" Meris held up his hand to keep Nardic quiet. Together, they watched as the demon slowly lowered his arms and looked at them both. Along the edges of his arms was now a slight glow and the demon screamed in anger.

"You made me glow! I will never glow with the Glory of God! Take it away!"

Nardic's mouth dropped open and he looked at Meris, who remained calm. "You can't touch her ever again. None of you mangy creatures can. A direct order from the Father."

"You can't tell me what to do! I don't serve Him!"

Nardic instinctively placed his hand on his sword as Meris continued. "She is covered by the blood."

The demon's face dropped as he flew over to Ellie and looked at her face. Around the edges there was a faint glow; but only noticeable now that he was looking for it. She had been without praise for God for so long that she no longer had an obvious glow.

Meris looked at Nardic, who had many questions; but he wisely waited until the demon retreated to the outside of the house, too afraid to go back inside and unable to cross the angel barrier around the perimeter of the property.

Nardic looked at Meris, who began to explain. "Ellie was saved years ago. She has not lived that life for years and her glow has almost disappeared; but it never goes away. The Father has allowed the demons to touch her but never harm her."

"I thought they could not touch a believer!"

"They can't physically harm them; but they can touch them. Only a few demons are strong enough to do so. Most can't stand to be near them for fear of starting to glow. That is a terrible insult to a demon."

"I have only heard of it. I never dreamed that I would actually see a demon glow."

Meris dropped to one knee and winced in pain.

Nardic instinctively grabbed his arm and several small angels appeared to help Meris.

"Why are you hurting?" Nardic watched as his leader struggled to compose himself.

Meris began to heal and stood up straight. "The transfer and the surge of the glow...it makes us weak for several minutes. I have only done that one other time."

"Will you recover fully? I mean, is it like the burns?"

"No, the burns are forever. This will go away; but my glow will take time to restore to full power."

"How long?"

"I don't really know. This transfer was minimal. The last time I had less transfer and didn't regain my full power until the next day."

"Why did you do it?"

"It needed to be done. That demon is very powerful and it was worth the sacrifice. He won't be able to touch her ever again, no matter what. The glow will drive him crazy and the other demons will taunt him. It is possible that he will be severely punished by his superiors."

"So we win! He has to leave her alone."

Meris shook his head. "No, he will be more determined than ever to get her or someone in the family. Revenge is a powerful force in their world."

Nardic thought through all that had happened. Ellie was now in her bed asleep and Mark was with her. The angels around the home had begun to sing and the demon of Pride was howling in response. Nardic and Meris flew to the roof to watch the glow from the angel perimeter. In one dark corner of the yard they could hear the demon and see the faint glow that tormented him. Nardic turned to Meris. "Will that glow last?"

Meris watched the demon and turned to Nardic. "It will." He turned away and Nardic could not determine why Meris was so serious. The idea of the demon having glow made Nardic smile.

"Good! He will be easy to spot and can't hide in the shadows!"

Almost as soon as Nardic finished speaking, the demon flew up to the roof to face them both. All the angels around the home watched the sight of the strange bold demon that dared to face two angels alone. The sight of his glow caused them all to stop singing and stare. The hush lasted but a moment and then a murmering began as they all pointed and watched the glow.

"You have not won! I will never quit!"

Meris calmly stood and let his wings open slightly. The demon stepped back but tried to hide his fear. "I have a right to her! She has a choice!"

"So do you! You can chose to stay and fight or you can leave!" Meris's voice boomed through the air and all the angels fell silent again.

The demon of Pride looked from Meris to Nardic. He turned and flew to the ground and then entered the home.

Both angels followed. Inside, they found Ellie awake and by herself at the kitchen table. Her face told the story of a woman still tormented by her past and in her hands she held a picture of Rose Louise.

The demon of Pride was working on Ellie as hard as he could, knowing that prayer could change his advantage at any minute. He was careful not to touch her but whispered in her ear over and over. Nardic looked at Meris who only shrugged.

"He is using her pain. I have only faced him a few times; and each time he was extremely good. We did defeat him, though."

"Always!" Nardic shouted and pointed his sword toward the creature, who looked up and smiled with a nasty grin. "We will defeat you!"

Meris had to hold Nardic back from the challenge of attacking, as the demon hissed and snarled to taunt him. The glow around his arms did not seem to bother him anymore.

"Not yet, Nardic. There will be a day for him."

Nardic continued to point his sword at the demon until the demon turned away. "Why can't we take him now?"

"We need prayer, you know this. By the way, what is this new scar?"

Nardic's head dropped and he balled up his fists, knowing that Galdon had had to report the incident to Meris. "I couldn't let the demon say those things to that woman. She has to have time to heal and know how much God loves her."

"I know. We all feel the frustration of why the humans won't believe and trust in God. You can't take chances like that over small battles. We need you to stay strong for the bigger war in front of us. We will prevail, it is written so; but you have to make better choices."

"I will do better; but I am ready to defeat that demon when the time comes." He pointed at the demon of Pride, who smiled and hissed.

"How is the wing?" The demon laughed.

"Nice glow!" Nardic answered and drew his sword. The demon growled and stepped toward Nardic, who stood firm, hoping the demon would attack. After looking from one angel to the other, the demon of Pride turned back to Ellie.

Meris whispered in Nardic's ear. "Good job distracting him. That is a great tactic; but make sure they don't do the same to you." Meris continued out loud, "Our battles would be easily won, if the people will only pray and use scripture."

Nardic nodded and seemed deep in thought; and he began to pace back and forth. He was significantly smaller than Meris; but he was strong and quick and was becoming a fierce warrior. Although he was new to Meris's command, he had quickly earned the respect of his leader in their first few battles together. Meris only worried that Nardic followed Galdon's lead too much; and that was not a way to stay in the warrior ranks for long. Finally, he answered, "Why won't the humans pray? They have so much power and they won't use it!"

"They don't use the scriptures either. At least not enough. Putting these two powerful weapons together is one of the Father's best gifts; and very few either know or try to use them."

"Why? Why don't they want to beat these foul creatures? We could win every time!"

"The longer I work with humans, the less I understand the answer to that question. They seem to not know or care. Some are listening, though. We only need a few. God has tried to make it as simple as possible. One of the shortest verses in the Bible is 'Pray without ceasing.'"

Nardic nodded and continued to stare at the demon, watching the ripples underneath his scaly skin as he slithered from one ear to the other, tormenting her with his words. "What is he doing to her?"

"He is a demon of Pride; but he uses sorrow, which is a form of pride that makes the human think more about themselves and how horrible their circumstances are."

"How is that pride?"

"Pride by definition is when you think of yourself more than others. Even when someone is feeling sorry for themselves, it is an act of extreme pride. They put more value on their own thoughts and feelings instead of concentrating on the Father."

"Demon of Pride...using sorrow," Nardic repeated to himself. "I have not seen him or any like him since he appeared that day in the hospital. Most of my battles have been with pride in a more traditional form."

"There are many forms of pride, my friend. Humans are easily swayed to think of themselves first. I believe that the demons and Lucifer himself love exploiting this area the most."

"Well, let's see what he does when a little prayer comes his way!" Nardic spread his wings and winced. "I'm weak."

"Yes, I feel it too. We need more prayer. The Father will help keep a level of protection because they are believers; but we still need prayer.

The two angels worked with the others that were surrounding the home until late into the night. The demon of Pride was able to stay within the same room as Ellie and the angels could not stop him.

Chapter 8: Weekly Visits

Thursdays were quickly becoming Pastor John's favorite day of the week. He felt almost guilty about it sometimes. The overall service was a fun way for him to play with the wording of his sermon to get it just right and he did feel as if he made a difference in the lives of several residents; but it was Mr. Roberts that made it so appealing. Today's service had gone well; and Pastor John was excited to see what his friend thought about it.

"Hey Mr. Roberts, wait up!" Pastor John had to jog slightly to catch up to his friend, who was almost to his room. "Sorry, I got caught in a conversation."

"Oh, that! You mean Ms. Mitchell? You'd better watch it, Pastor John, she is on a hunt for her next husband."

John laughed while he followed Mr. Roberts into his room and then closed the door and found a seat. "Well, I will be sure to let her know that I am happily married."

"I'm not sure that would work, if she's after you."

"A cougar, huh?"

"More like a cougar, a lion, and a tiger all wrapped up in one. I am not sure what she plans to do with you; but I promise that if she is after you, trouble is coming."

"I think I can handle her. I will just preach about lust at the next service."

Both men laughed and then John continued, "What did you think about today's sermon?"

Mr. Roberts grew solemn and looked at his hands. "It was fine. I think it was at least the 'Good enough to keep your attention' level."

"You are one tough critic! Anything you would change?"

Mr. Roberts looked up. "Son, did you really understand what you were saying today? Have you ever been through any real suffering?"

"I basically chose to concentrate on suffering this week because my next message is 'When God Says No' and I used today's message of 'Why Do God's People Experience Pain' to lead up to it."

"That's not what I asked. I asked if you had ever experienced real suffering."

John opened his mouth and then sat back in his chair. "I have worked with many people...I guess the only personal suffering that I have experienced was back when I was child and I was very sick."

"Do you remember being sick?"

"No, not really."

"Then that doesn't count. I think that you might want to bring in some good news in the next sermon before you do that one about saying no. If you have never experienced any real suffering, then you wouldn't understand. It is a soul searching and character shaking experience. Most people are just never the same afterward."

Both men fell silent and then Mr. Roberts continued. "I have seen some terrible things and all of them changed me to some degree or another. It's the change that makes or breaks you."

"What do you mean?"

Mr. Roberts's eyes glistened and he fell silent for a few seconds before he finally spoke in almost a whisper. "Suffering brings change that creates a new you, someone that you may not recognize or even like; but it is what you do with that new you that matters."

John was not sure what he meant and replayed the words again in his mind. "I guess it is kind of unconvincing to talk about something that I have not really experienced. Did it seem uncaring or unrealistic? I would never want to confuse anyone. I just want to preach the truth in God's word."

"Yes, that should be the goal; and no, it was not wrong what you said. I think what was missing was the pain. There was no pain in your words, like when someone who has been tested and found God's Grace describes that feeling of being released from the pain. Real pain...real suffering, well, it can't be faked."

"Do you mind sharing some things from your life? Maybe I should include some stories."

"I don't mind sharing; and I do think that a story or two from real life examples might help. I guess my first exposure to real pain was during the war. I was 24 years old the day that we landed on the beach at Normandy. Within just a few seconds, most of my friends either drowned trying to get out of the boat or were shot dead as they exited the boat. I only remember complete chaos and blood mixing with water, as I tried to dodge the bullets." Mr. Roberts put his hand to his eyes as his voice broke slightly and then he continued, "My best friend at the time was a boy from Mississippi named Marty. We both somehow made it out of the water and onto the beach. Bullets were flying all around us; and I saw things that day that no man should ever have to witness. Anyway, we were laying flat and trying to decide which way to go, when I felt something burning in my leg. I had been shot and didn't even know it. I looked back and saw that I had been shot in the right lower leg about an inch below my knee right there." Mr. Roberts pointed to his leg to show where the bullet had hit him. "Anyway, I never knew when it happened and the doctor's later decided it might have been a bullet that ricocheted off something. I know it hurt and I couldn't move fast enough, so Marty grabbed my shoulder and began to tug me toward the next group of men. There was so much noise and some smoke provided us a little cover to move forward.

Mr. Roberts paused and seemed to be lost in another world. Finally, he continued, "I thought that I had suffered in my life when I didn't get something I wanted or got cut from the basketball team in high school. Nothing prepared me for what happened next." Mr. Roberts stopped again to gather his emotions. His frail hands rubbed along the edge of the wheelchair as if he could roll back time to change what had happened. Finally, he found the strength to continue his story. "My first experience with true suffering was when Marty, my best friend that I had ever had on this earth, leaned over to dress my wound and took a bullet through his jaw. Blood and tissue splattered all over my face and before either of us could react to that, another bullet caught him directly in the side of the head. I watched my best friend fall forward across my own chest and die. It was the worst day of my life until that point." Mr. Roberts had to stop to regain his composure. "I can still see him in my dreams." Silence wrapped both men in a dreary fog that left them staring at nothing yet both seeing the vision of that poor boy, dead on the beach with his best friend underneath his corpse.

John spoke first in an almost inaudible whisper. "That is unbelievable."

"I have never told anyone back here that story. I left it over there when I was sent home."

John thought about that for a second and then answered, "I had no idea you were a veteran. You should write some of your stories down to share."

"No, pastor, that is one story that I don't want to tell again. I will give you other examples, but that one is off limits."

"Sure. I understand. Is there a story you could tell me that I can use?"

A wave of sadness gripped his expression and held it as he spoke. "There are many things that I have seen in my lifetime that are examples of true suffering. Going through The Great Depression provided daily suffering for everyone when I was a child. I think that pain is difficult to share without creating more pain. I think losing my wife ranks up there..." Mr. Roberts paused and wiped his face, then gently folded his hands in his lap. "Pastor John, suffering is not something that you can explain; and it is even more difficult to explain why it happens. I think you are trying to help people who can't identify with you."

John was slightly hurt but appreciated the honesty. He thought about ignoring this advice and just continuing on with his plan to deliver that sermon this week. Something in Mr. Robert's expression made him rethink all that he thought he knew. Finally, he cleared his throat and sat up on the edge of his chair. "What if I had you come and speak?"

Mr. Robert's laughed and shook his head. "No, son, I am not the one you want. You are on the right track, though. You need someone to give a testimony to give credibility to your sermon, since you don't have one for yourself."

"That is exactly it. I do need someone. I'm not really sure who to get, though."

"Pastor, put that sermon in a file and wait. God will bring the right person to you and you will know."

John thanked his friend and drove home in deep thought. He had a couple of days to change his sermon or to find someone who could give a testimony on suffering. He drove on through the traffic in silence, praying that God would lead someone to him that would be able to help give some credibility to his sermon, not knowing the he had someone very close to him that would be perfect.

    Meris smiled as the prayers lifted up to Heaven. He absorbed the power and thanked the Father for his love and perfect plan. Everything was moving along well.

Chapter 9: Baby Dedication

February 2000

   Rosie was now a bustling 8 month old and Lindsey was finally getting enough sleep to feel normal again. The sun was bursting through the light cloud cover and beginning to gradually warm the morning air, as Lindsey headed to the car juggling Rosie and her diaper bag. John half chuckled to himself watching his wife checking to be sure Rosie had shoes and matching tights and all the things that seemed important at the time. He decided it was best to let her vent and stay quiet, as they jostled all the items into the car. How could so much be needed for just a simple baby dedication day? He looked down at his phone and saw a message from his parents saying they were already at the church. Lindsey's mom and dad were supposed to be there as well.

The church had been growing steadily over the last few weeks in response to a new youth program on Sunday nights and an outreach program for new mom's that Lindsey had started. Some people had originally been against all the changes; but no one could argue with the expanding new members. John handed Lindsey a tumbler of fresh coffee and started the car.

She looked over and smiled and said, "I love you. Sorry I was grumpy this morning. I had really wanted Rosie to wear those ruffle tights; but they had a run in them. I didn't want her to wear plain old tights."

"Me too! I can't imagine her in just plain old tights!" John tried hard to look serious.

Lindsey punched him in the arm and laughed. "Yeah it is kind of stupid isn't it?"

John reached over and kissed his wife on the cheek then started to back the car out of the driveway.

"Not if it's important to you, babe!"

He sneaked a glance at baby Rosie in her car seat snuggled in tight and shaking a rattle. How had eight months gone by so quickly? She was growing so fast and getting prettier every day, like her mom. Before he turned around, he thought he saw a slight glow around his young daughter; but instead of concerning him, he smiled. Meris, continued to calm the pastor with his touch, until he was ready to learn more about his gift.

As they arrived at the church, both sets of grandparents stood outside waiting nervously, as if the president were arriving. John and Lindsey had quickly learned that they were of little importance in their parent's world anymore, since Rosie had arrived. Something special existed between a grandchild and a grandparent and Lindsey suspected it had to do with perspective. She and John were so busy trying to complete tasks and keep up with schedules that she sometimes wondered if maybe they were missing some of life's most precious moments.

Lindsey looked up and squealed, "Millie! You made it!" then ran to hug her sister.

Behind her Sarah came with her husband Roy. They all headed inside the church; and Lindsey helped everyone find a seat close to the front, while she scurried off with Rosie to the back of the church with the other new parents. John took his place in the pulpit and the service begin promptly at 9:00 AM.

Ellie leaned over to Mark as Lindsey came out on stage carrying Rosie in her arms.

"I don't think Lindsey has ever looked more beautiful! Look at Rosie. She is the most beautiful baby I've ever seen!"

Mark squeezed her hand and leaned over and kissed his wife on the cheek. "As beautiful as her grandmother!"

John had his assistant minister, Darron, reading the names so that he could go stand with his wife; and when the ceremony ended, he took his place back in the pulpit to begin the message. He had warned his mom, Terry, in a long phone call the night before that his sermon would be emotional and had asked her to pray. Everyone knew it would be emotional for Lindsey's mom because of losing a daughter with the same name so long ago; but the prayer surge from Terry's prayers provided the power that the angel's needed to keep the demon of Pride outside in the parking lot. He paced back and forth snarling, but there were too many prayers at this time for him to get near enough to Ellie to torment her.

"No matter, I hate that place anyway!" He snarled.

Nardic stood outside by the door and hoped that he would be able to face this demon in a battle soon. He wanted to send him away for good. Meris had warned him to hold his ground and that there would be plenty of time for battle in the future. For now, the greatest need was to keep helping the humans. Even so, Nardic watched the demon carefully and kept his hand close to his sword. He had a large amount of prayer support and had no fear of this detestable creature.

The rest of the day was spent together as a family at John and Lindsey's home. The grandparents took turns playing with Rosie until time for her nap. The grandfathers retired to the den and the grandmothers to the living room, while Lindsey rocked Rosie and then took a nap herself. John sat in the den trading stories with the two men.

Terry Miles and Ellie Henley had not forged much of a friendship as many in-laws do. They didn't dislike each other; but they each had a set of different friends and just never seemed to really need time together. With the birth of Rosie, though, they had been spending more time than usual around each other to see the new baby.

"Lindsey looked so pretty today," Terry stated.

"Well, I thought John did a wonderful job with the service." Ellie turned to look out the window, hoping Terry wouldn't see her deceit. In truth, Ellie had been unable to concentrate on her son-in-law's message at all and struggled to keep from crying. Every time she saw Rosie, the resemblance to Rose Louise was remarkable. Somehow, she was going to have to get past this and let it go.

"I am proud of them both. They have done a wonderful job at the church."

"I know they work very hard." That was really all that Ellie had to say about that. She still refused to attend most of the time, claiming some ailment or another; but Mark was now going as much as he could.

Terry had thought and prayed about how to talk to Ellie. She really thought that maybe working through the pain would help her more than ignoring it; and she decided to tell Ellie what they had been through. "Ellie, do you know about John? Did you know we almost lost him?"

Ellie tensed up and tried not to snap. Of course she knew. "Yes, Lindsey told us that."

"Well, I guess I just wanted to say that I can't imagine what you all have been through. We struggled for months afterward just to relax and enjoy him again. Every time he did anything, we were afraid we would lose him to some accident or something. We were always on edge when he was sick. It was horrible."

"Well, he is still here." Ellie stared out the window and tried not to sound angry. *Why would Terry bring this up? Everyone always assumes I want to talk about this and I don't!*

Terry ignored the harsh answer and sighed. She said a small prayer and then softly continued. "Anyway, today must have been hard. I guess I just wanted to say--"

"Say what? I mean, don't you realize there is nothing anyone can say? You still have your child. I will never see or touch mine ever again."

They sat in silence as Terry continued to pray and tried to salvage the conversation. She felt terrible but couldn't understand why Ellie still harbored such intense sadness after all these years. Of course, it would be understandable to be like this initially; but it was as if Ellie were caught in a state of sadness and she couldn't get out of it. She had heard Lindsey reference her mom's fragile state; but Terry had never witnessed a breakdown. Neither woman understood the spiritual battle for control of Ellie that had raged on for years. Galdon continued to soak up the power from the prayers and worked to increase the feeling of love and peace in the room.

Please, God. Help her break free. Please help that poor woman let the pain go.

Galdon's wings spread wide and glowed, filling the room with light, forcing the demon of Pride to stay outside. The newest scar left a large dim area on one wing. Galdon looked down at it; but he had no regrets.

Terry leaned forward to speak, "Ellie, I am sorry. Let me tell you something my grandfather used to say. He said that when you first lose someone, it is like a terrible cut that bleeds and hurts all the time. Over time, the wound will start to close; but it will still hurt and open up and bleed. Within a longer period of time, the wound will scab over. Again, though, it will remain tender and sore and may even break open again. Sometime later, the wound will scar. The memory of the event will be there and maybe some type of tugging sensation from the scar tissue. Overall, though, the intense pain will subside and be gone forever. For some reason, you have never been able to reach the stage where the wound has been able to fully heal. Have you ever talked with anyone about that?"

Ellie looked down at the floor and then directly at Terry. "I won't let it heal. I can't let it heal. I need to feel the pain to remember her. I am so afraid to get to a point where I don't. That would make me an even worse mother than I already am."

"Oh, Ellie. You are a terrific mother. Look at Lindsey and your other two daughters. All of them have stable and happy marriages. Lindsey talks fondly of her childhood and the memories you all made together. Letting the pain go only helps you. It doesn't mean you love Rose Louise any less."

"Thank you for saying love and not loved. I get so tired of people talking about her in the past. She is still so alive in my memory. I...I don't want to lose that."

"Letting yourself heal will not reflect at all on your love for Rose Louise. She will always be your little girl. I am afraid that you are missing the joy right in front of you now. Lindsey, Millie, Sarah, and Mark need you; and now little Rosie is going to need you too."

"I know you are right. I guess I just don't know how. I have been sad for so long that it is all that know."

"Start by not blaming yourself. You have not done anything wrong. Just start there and let God help you put together all the pieces. He is an expert at that, you know."

Ellie nodded. She wasn't sure God still wanted her. The demon behind Ellie at the window cursed the other grandmother, as his red eyes watched the women through the glass. Pacing back and forth, his foul breath curled in the air, as he panted and growled and waited for a chance to get near Ellie again. Nardic moved from his post at the front to watch the demon. He pulled his sword out of its sheath and waited for any reason to blast the foul creature. Galdon continued to keep his wings around the two women, as he thought about what Meris had said to him. As Nardic walked past the window, Galdon felt a tinge of pain at seeing the fresh scar on the young angel's right wing.

He is too young to have that scar. I have got to be careful with him around.

"Terry, I would like to hear your story. Maybe that will help me in some way."

Terry tried not to seem too excited; but she knew that Ellie was trying. Silently she thanked God for the opportunity to help in some way. "Well, it was a long time ago...but it was the most difficult time in our lives. John had been very sick and I mean very sick. He just couldn't get well. We tried everything to help our little boy. Finally, the pediatrician sent us to the hospital for some tests. We still lived in Florence at the time...I was working and trying to juggle all the doctor's appointments. It was really crazy. I remember the week we found out seemed so long, because he had been sick for several days and we didn't get any sleep. We were not going to church then either. It seems like so long ago now."

"What was wrong with him?" Ellie perked up slightly, trying to remember anything Lindsey had told her about John's past. She couldn't remember what Lindsey had said, having spent most of the time always reflecting on her own loss.

"Well, I kept thinking he would just get better. I mean, who would think that their child has cancer? It was the worst day of my life when we found out."

"Oh, I didn't know that he had cancer! How old was he?"

"He had just turned three. I remember at his birthday party he didn't even want to eat his own cake. I thought he was just excited. Within two weeks, though, he wasn't eating much of anything and his stomach was bloated. I took him to the doctor several times; but they thought he just had a virus.

"That must have been so frustrating."

"Oh, it was. The day that we found out it was more serious was so strange. He had seemed fine that morning, so I thought he was getting better. I was only at work a few hours when I got a call from the daycare to come get him because he was running a fever. I really thought he was fine and maybe just not over the virus. I used to say that my kid's noses would run from October to April and just thought he had some normal thing and never dreamed that this was related to his decreased appetite either. I just never would have put it all together."

"Did you go straight to the hospital?"

"Oh, no, we had to go to the pediatrician again and wait forever because they had to work us in. I remember when I got to the daycare, he was just laying on his side in the room, while all the other kids were playing. I was sort of mad that they hadn't told me how sick he was. Anyway, he was burning up with a fever; and by the time the doctor saw us, his fever was 103.6. None of the nurses were particularly worried, though, until the doctor started feeling his belly. I will never forget the change in demeanor and the look on that doctor's face."

"Did he tell you that he thought John had cancer?"

"Well, that may have been easier; but no, he had no diagnosis yet. He left the room and returned with another doctor, who also felt John's belly. I was thinking maybe he had appendicitis, because that runs in our family. Within a few minutes, though, the look on their faces was very clear that something very bad was wrong. I couldn't get them to tell me directly; and they just sent me straight to the Children's Hospital in Cincinnati. It took about two hours to locate Mark and get him there too. By then, the emergency room doctor had told me that he suspected a tumor in John's liver."

"That must have been awful."

"It was more than awful. They immediately sent us for blood tests and a CT scan. If you can believe it, I had never heard of a CT scan back then. It was relatively new at that time; but the tumor showed up easily. The next few hours were a blur; and by the next day we had our answer: the tumor was cancerous. I always thought that cancer was supposed to only be in someone older--someone who had lived at least part of their life, not a three-year-old. There weren't many things in the world that could scare me. I had lost both of my parents to a car accident when I was only 15 years old and had had to move in with my Aunt Betty, until I was 18 and left for college. I was so lonely for my parents; but it made me tough. In my mind, I reasoned that I had already suffered enough for one lifetime and felt that I was due a fairly good life from that point forward. Aunt Betty had introduced me to church and I was so thankful for her; but it was still not the same not having a mother or a father. I did give my life to Christ when I was only seventeen; but through my college years, I began to have some doubts and drifted away a little. It was about then that I met Roger, who had never been very religious himself. We sort of clicked and never looked back."

"Did you guys marry right away?"

"Yes, we were married six days after graduation!"

They both laughed and then Ellie asked, "How did they treat John? Did he have to have chemotherapy?"

"Not immediately. What would normally take months to accomplish, the doctors were able to squeeze into just a few days. Roger and I watched as the doctors poked and prodded John and put him through a battery of tests and examinations only to come back and tell us what we had already feared. The tumor could not be taken out by itself. They wanted to try to shrink it with chemotherapy; but they were afraid to wait too long and decided that John needed a liver transplant. The only good news was that they were fairly certain that the tumor had not spread."

"How did you all handle that news? I would have crumbled."

"Well, we wanted to. I remember turning to Roger and asking him what to do. He looked so helpless that it broke my heart even more. I had always leaned on him for strength; and there he was leaning against the wall and sobbing like a baby. I wanted to hold him and he wanted to hold me; but it was almost too much for either of us."

"I actually understand that feeling. That was exactly how we felt when we lost our Rose Louise. It was like we both wanted to be brave for the other; but neither of us knew how."

"Exactly. The pain we both felt was doubled by watching someone we love hurt as well. I had been married to Roger for ten years at that point; and I had never seen him break over anything. He was always so calm and easy going. He cried so loud that even the nurses were all sobbing. It was horrible. I couldn't help him; and I couldn't help my John. In all reality, I couldn't even help myself. It seemed like we cried for an eternity. I remember a nurse helping us with tissues and bringing us something to drink. All I could think about was I needed to call work and let them know. Why in the world that would even matter, I didn't know. I never really understood what the term rock bottom meant; but I found myself face down on the floor crying out to God. It was such a lonely and horrible feeling to lay there and not know what to do to help my child."

"I know that feeling and I know rock bottom too. It is a very lonely place."

"I almost didn't make it back out of there."

Ellie looked at Terry in surprise. She had never guessed that Terry had been so low. A new realization hit Ellie: she was really not the only one who had been that low before. So many times she felt like no one really understood. Maybe Terry did.

"Later, I was told that many people go into a robotic state under extreme stress. Anyway, I somehow gathered myself and went to the pay phones in the hall and called both Roger's office and mine."

Ellie watched Terry in silence and then sighed. "I remember the robotic stage. Sometimes I feel like I am still there."

Terry studied Ellie's face for a moment. "You know, I can really understand that. I was stuck like that for about two years. I mean, John was better; but I still felt like I had to be so guarded with everything. I found myself feeling very alone and scared."

"Why, though? You had your child. I was alone because all of my friends with children Rose Louise's age continued on without me."

"What about Lindsey? Didn't that help that you had her just a few months later?"

"I guess it should have helped; but I felt like I was in a dark fog all the time. All of my friends still seemed to care; but no one knew what to do or say."

Terry nodded. "They were the same with our family. Even though John lived, no one knew what to do or say either. I think everyone was afraid because the cure rate was so low back then. They only gave us a 40% chance; but I think the success rate is now around 70% when the tumor is contained in the liver."

"I didn't know that. I thought...well...I guess I didn't think about it. I hate to admit this; but I was jealous of everyone and mad that God took my baby. I have been very selfish, I guess."

"Of course you were! Who wouldn't be? I was jealous that all my friends had healthy kids and they could go do anything they wanted. I was stuck at home because of John's low immune system."

"Really? How long did you have to do that?"

"I can't remember when I finally felt safe again; but it seemed like forever. Poor Michael couldn't do much either. We all had to stay home."

"I didn't realize it was so involved. I guess I thought once you had the surgery, your life went back to normal."

"No. I don't think we have ever been normal again. Listen, Ellie, you have got to give yourself permission to grieve. I think you are still punishing yourself."

Ellie folded and unfolded her hands in her lap and looked down at her feet. She felt so foolish, having admitted so much to Terry, whom she barely knew. Looking back up at Terry, she realized something: she wasn't crying anymore. Were her tears finally all dried up? Was that even possible? "Terry, I don't know if I can."

"You can't do it alone. You need God to help you. Do you want to pray with me?"

"I should, I know that. I...I am just not ready. I guess I need to think about a lot of things. Can you tell me more about John? How long was he in the hospital?" Ellie had no idea how serious John's sickness had been.

"We were in the hospital for about five months to start with--"

"Five months! Oh my gosh! How did you all do that?"

"The Ronald McDonald House became my home and Mark traveled back and forth from our house. We had to move our older son, Michael, who was only six at the time, in with Mark's parents."

"Why did you all have to stay there so long? Does it take that long to heal from removing the tumor?"

"They don't remove the tumor, they remove the liver and replace it. We had to wait on a donor so he could get a liver transplant. Some of the time was for doing chemotherapy to prepare for transplant, then the actual transplant, some time for recovering, and then we stayed for post surgical chemotherapy as well. By the time we left, the weekly trips for blood work seemed easy. His immune system was always such a concern too; and it was over three years before we let him venture out to either play grounds or to play with other children again."

"I had no idea that you had been through so much. A transplant...that is amazing that they could even do that for a small child."

"I know. We were amazed too. We probably didn't relax until he was around seven and all of his scans continued to be clear. It was a terribly long time and it felt even longer than it was."

"I had no idea that John had once had cancer. I just remember Lindsey mentioning that John had some surgery as a child; but I had no idea it had been that serious."

"We are so thankful every day, even still. During that time, I became very close to Jesus and eventually Roger did as well. A nurse at the hospital would pray with me every day. Believe me, I would have done anything to save my son; but I was already a believer. I just wasn't really living the life that I should. Roger and I rededicated ourselves to living the Christian life every day for the rest of our lives. In a way, John saved us all."

Ellie stared at the floor and a sadness came over her. "I wonder if Rose Louise could have saved us. I wish there had been a surgery that would have saved her."

Terry came over to the couch and sat beside Ellie and put her arm around her. The two women sat leaning into each other, as Terry said, "I wish there had been too. God's plan doesn't always make sense. Rose Louise could never save you, though. I really said that wrong when I said, 'John saved us.' Only Jesus can do that. Only the love of God can get you through the tough times. Lean on Him. He will never leave you or forsake you."

Ellie pushed away and looked at Terry.

"Everyone says that. I feel like He did. Why would God take away my baby and not yours? What could He possibly need Rose Louise for? He could have left her here just a little longer! Time doesn't really mean much to Him! Why did He take her?"

Terry looked directly at Ellie and silently prayed for strength. A thought came to her and she simply said, "I have no idea why He took your baby and didn't take mine. You are right, He could have left her."

Ellie sat up straight and her mouth dropped open slightly. This was the first time anyone had ever agreed with her. Most people had only tried to explain the Will of God or tell her that it would be okay. No one had ever seen Ellie's side before. Maybe because Terry had almost lost her child, she had a unique perspective.

"Thank you. Thank you for saying that. I get so tired of people saying that I will be okay and that God's Will is perfect and we shouldn't question it."

"Well, I do believe it is perfect; but I have a LOT of questions to ask him someday."

Ellie was stunned again. She had never heard a Christian talk like this. "Do you question other things too?"

"Of course! I would have to be crazy not to. The Bible says to 'Work out your salvation with fear and trembling' and I think God wants us to come to Him and shake our fist sometimes, as long as it's respectful."

"Really?"

"Think about it. When your girls were teenagers, how many times did you get the sense that they just needed to vent. You had to learn not to say much and just let them rant and rave and then they would calm down and talk, right?"

"Yeah. That took me a few screaming fits to figure out. I remember Mark pulling me aside to explain that I shouldn't argue with them. They just wanted to hear themselves vent. When I stopped arguing and allowed them to tell me what they thought, our relationships blossomed."

"I would bet that they actually obeyed better as well."

"They did. We talked about it a lot and couldn't believe how well it worked."

"Well, God is our Heavenly Father. He wants us to come to Him when we are happy, sad, scared, upset, and even when we are mad. Don't you want your family to feel like they can come to you for anything?"

"Yes, I do."

"God loves you so much, Ellie. He would never want to lose you and never want you to feel like you couldn't come to Him."

The two women sat in silence for several seconds thinking through the conversation, when Ellie asked, "Did you ever meet the other family?"

"What family?"

"The donor family for the liver. Did you ever get to meet them?"

"Oh, no. They keep that information very private. It's too difficult for everyone. I did write the donor family a letter and sent it a year after the transplant, which is what they allow."

"Did the family write you back?"

"No. I guess it was just too much for them."

"I know I would not have been able to write back. I can't imagine getting a letter like that."

"Ellie, can I ask you something?"

"Sure."

"Did you donate Rose Louise's organs?"

"Oh, no. We were much to traumatized. I was in the hospital and in a coma for two months and even missed the funeral. I think that is part of the reason it has been so hard for me. I practically lived at her graveside for several weeks afterward because I felt so guilty."

"I don't think I knew that. I am so sorry. No wonder you have struggled. You had no closure. You should talk to a psychologist about how to do that. I think that would help you."

"I'm not crazy, Terry. I don't need a shrink."

"I know you're not crazy. If I thought that, I would suggest you lock yourself in an asylum."

Both women laughed and then Terry continued, "I had to see one for several months."

"A shrink, I mean, a psychologist?"

"Yes, it was so traumatic for us all. Roger went too."

"Really? I would have never guessed."

"Ellie, it is nothing to be ashamed of and you should embrace help, if you need it. She helped me so much."

"She? I guess I always pictured an old man with a couch."

"I see where Lindsey gets her humor. No, this was a sweet lady doctor; and I don't think I could have managed to return to a normal life without her."

Ellie sat in thought and then asked, "Do you think I could find a woman like that here in Louisville?"

"Absolutely. I will help you, if you like."

"I think I would like that."

"I think you would like Dr. Gaines at our church. Her office is not far from here either."

"Oh...okay."

The two women sat in silence as Ellie thought about the story of John's sickness. She had never known the details of the events before and was shocked to hear about the horrible long days that followed his surgery.

"Is John short for Jonathan?"

"No, we were very adamant that he be John. For some reason, we thought that that was a big deal. Our perspective on what is important has changed a lot through the years. It's funny what you think is important when you aren't facing anything important."

Ellie's hand went to her mouth suddenly; and she looked at Terry. "I just realized that in order for John to live, someone else's child had to have died. I never really thought about that before."

Now it was Terry's turn to be silent. Her face clouded over, as she tried to gather her thoughts. "There is not a day that goes by that I don't thank God for their unselfish act. We owe them everything and can give them nothing."

"How...how in the world would someone even know to do that--donate organs? I know that adults have the choice to check a box on their driver's license; but I have never thought about my children as potential donors. How in the world does anyone ever sign up for that? That sounds like the parents are morbid or crazy or have a death wish."

"No, it's not like that at all. We learned so much about this. The hospital calls in special counselors, when there is no hope for a child to live. The counselors talk with the family and help them understand how important the donation would be. Through a series of steps, they guide the family to help them decide to do it or not."

"Wow. That's amazing."

"They told us that a person is six times more likely to need a transplant than to be a donor."

"Really? I had no idea. I guess I never thought about it."

"We have always signed our driver's license to be a donor but never knew what it meant until we needed a liver for John. Did you know that there are approximately 120,000 people on the list waiting for an organ donation?"

"I had no clue there were that many. I guess it's hard to think about what will happen after we die. I mean, I would bet many people would do it; but they die before they actually sign up."

"I'm sure that does happen. I think they told us that somewhere around ninety-five percent of people support organ donation but only forty percent are actually signed up to do it. If I remember correctly, I believe every ten minutes someone is added to the waiting list. Did you know that there are some organs you can donate while you are still alive? Of course, you can donate a kidney; but bone marrow is something you can give and it doesn't really cost you anything. We all signed up and have our information available in case we are a match for someone."

"Really? I never thought about bone marrow before."

"We didn't know anything about any of this before John was sick. We met so many other families at the hospital when we were going through all the treatments and surgery. It was a humbling and eye-opening experience for us."

"I'll bet."

"Ellie, you don't have to; but if you want to tell me your story, I would be glad to listen."

Galdon perked up and instinctively opened his wings slightly. The demon of Pride stood outside the window behind Ellie and immediately began to scream to get Ellie to hear him. Galdon stepped forward and slapped him across the yard, where he seethed and growled.

Ellie looked down at her hands again and simply answered, "I guess it wouldn't hurt to tell you."

Galdon blocked the demon and spread his wings slightly, allowing some protection as long as it would last. He looked up to Heaven and the Father sent some added power.

Ellie sighed and her mind began to wander. "I remember the last day I had with Rose Louise--I remember every detail. It was such a beautiful spring day; and I was five months pregnant with Lindsey. I had taken the girls outside to play, not knowing it would be our last day together. I remember that I sat down in the grass watching my Rose Louise investigate a caterpillar. Part of me was wondering if I should sit in a chair instead of the ground because I was pregnant; but I just couldn't stop watching those soft blonde curls bounce around, as Rose Louise went from one activity to another. Rosalynn Louise Henley. I loved saying her name. She was only two years old that day and full of life. She was the youngest of my three girls so far and was so spunky. Mark and I had labored over her name more than the other two girls and finally settled on two distant aunts, one from each side. Sitting there in that warm sun, I can still remember how it felt with Lindsey kicking and stretching inside my body. I also remember wondering if

Rose Louise really understood that she was going to be a big sister."

Galdon continued to block the demon to allow Ellie tell her story. He placed his hands on her shoulders to add comfort and peace. Terry sat motionless and watched Ellie, as she continued talking. A strange expression spread across Ellie's face, as her mind drifted back to that last day together in Florence, Kentucky in 1974.

* * * * *

"What do you think we should name the caterpillar?" Ellie waited for her Rose Louise to come up with a name. Millie came bounding up.

"Fuzzy!" Millie cried and tried to grab the soft bug from her sister, causing Rose Louise to turn away screeching.

"Be careful girls. You can hurt him. Why don't we put him down so he can find some more food?"

Ellie grabbed both of her little girl's hands and helped them into the house. Millie was a petite five-year-old girl with large brown eyes and hair that had once possessed the golden tint that still glistened in both Rose Louise and their oldest sister, Sarah's hair.

"Mommy, why can't we keep him?" Millie looked up at her mom with large sad eyes full of concern, waiting for an answer.

Rose Louise clapped her hands and said, "Keep keep!"

"Well, girls we have to let him eat so that he can turn into a butterfly. Remember we have that book that talks about how the caterpillar eats everything and then turns into a butterfly?"

Both girls nodded their heads in response.

"Can we read it now? Millie stopped and stared up at her mother.

"We sure can. Sarah is going home after school with her friend Molly."

* * * * *

Ellie's mind drifted back to the present and she looked over at Terry and then down at her own lap.

Galdon strained to keep his wings around Ellie, hoping Terry or someone would pray again. As his strength began to fade, the demon of Pride eased back into the home and began to whisper in Ellie's ear. Slowly, tears filled her eyes and anger began to build in her heart as well as a strange jealousy toward others who still had their daughters, including Terry.

"It's not fair!" The demon whispered.

Ellie immediately echoed the thought in her own mind: *It's not fair!*

Silence draped over the room. Terry was unsure whether to stay quiet or prod her for more information. Galdon leaned toward Terry.

"Come on, pray for her." Of course she couldn't hear him; but he couldn't help but speak out loud.

Before Terry could decide what to do, Ellie spoke again in a small, weak voice.

"I remember it so well! Why did that day have to end? Why didn't I have Sarah come home from school that day?" She covered her face with her hands and wept. Terry instinctively moved closer and pulled Ellie into her arms.

Ellie crumpled into a ball and the tears flowed freely. The demon licked his lips and continued to chant softly. He leaned in close and whispered more venom into her thoughts. "Why did God let you down? You did everything right and what did it do for you? You deserve to always be happy!"

Galdon could stand it no longer. He gathered every ounce of strength that he had and placed his sword between the demon's lips and Ellie's ear for several seconds; and then he collapsed. Meris suddenly landed in the room and strode over to the demon, where he thrust him back against the wall and then leaned over to check on Galdon.

"I'm fine. How did you--"

"I saved a little power just in case." Meris answered and he stood and walked over to listen to the two women.

Terry pulled back from Ellie and grabbed a handful of tissue from her purse. "I am so sorry. I just thought it might help to talk about it."

Ellie took some of the tissue Terry offered and wiped her eyes. "It does and it doesn't. I guess it is just me. I guess I am ready to talk about it. I need to. It was so long ago; but I still try to remember it so that I won't forget. I don't ever want to forget."

"What do you remember about the accident?"

"Not much. I remember waking up a few times...images. There were so many lights. It hurt too bad to open my eyes and I just remember being in pain. I could hear a familiar voice...it sounded like Mark..."

"I can't imagine how confused you must have been. Did you know where you were or what had happened?"

"No, not at first. I thought I was dreaming. It was very confusing."

Again, Ellie's mind drifted back to the hospital, right after the accident in 1974.

* * * * *

Ellie tried desperately to focus; but she hurt everywhere. Her head was throbbing and her right leg felt weird. She tried to reach down; but her arm was strapped to something; and when she opened her mouth, no sound would come out. Someone was leaning over her, then everything went black again. Within what seemed like seconds, she felt like she was floating and someone was saying her name. Galdon had been with her since the wreck; and he stood nearby stroking her head, invisible to all in the room. He spread his wings around the walls of the room to protect and fill the room with peace, as had been the prayer request of several of Ellie's friends through the prayer circles. There were so many gifts that the Father had authorized Galdon to give; and he patiently awaited for the prayers to allow him to release each one. Nardic, was in charge of the new baby girl; and he stood beside Ellie with wings wrapped around her belly.

There were many plans that depended upon that. No angel was permitted to know all the future or the complete plans that the Father had designed; but Galdon had been told that this one was special.

Dr. McGill, the neurologist, greeted the family and positioned himself by Ellie's side and grabbed her hand.

"Ellie? Can you hear me? If you can understand, squeeze my hand."

Why won't my hand move? Am I paralyzed? Where am I?

Ellie willed her hand to move; but everything was hurting. Her eyelids were so heavy; but finally, she found the ability to focus hard and push them open. In front of her she saw a blinding light and then a strange face. There were...white wings...she could see something surrounding the strange man as he spoke. He had a light behind him; but it didn't blind her like the other lights from the room. Then the pain hit hard. She moaned and quickly shut her eyes again. Galdon continued to work with Nardic to keep her and the baby safe. He could sense her confusion; but he knew she was not ready to hear everything yet and needed her rest. Ellie drifted back to sleep for a few more hours.

The next thing she remembered was someone squeezing her hand. Ellie opened her eyes with less effort this time and tried to focus. There was the strange man in front of her again.

"My name is Dr. McGill. You were in a car accident and are now at Loudin Hospital. If you understand, can you squeeze my hand?"

Ellie tried to concentrate.

Did he say he was a doctor? What happened? Where are Mark and the girls? Ellie tried to look around; but she couldn't move. *Did I lose the baby?*

Finally, she could feel the touch of his hand holding hers again. A strange warmth spread through her body, as she willed her fingers to squeeze his hand; but she couldn't tell if they moved.

"Okay, Ellie. I felt you move your fingers. Let's try again. Can you squeeze one more time?"

This time, Ellie felt her fingers tighten around the doctor's hand and something hurt terribly bad in her shoulder, causing her to wince. The warmth continued to move through her and the pain eased. Galdon continued to stroke her head as Nardic continued to surround the baby. Both were sending as much peace through her as they could at the time.

"It's okay. You broke your collar bone, it may hurt a little. Can you try squeezing the other hand?"

Ellie felt the doctor grab her other hand and then noticed someone standing beside him. It was Mark. Her eyes tried to focus; but they continued to hurt. Tears were forming, as she tried to make sense of what was happening.

What had the doctor said? I was in an accident. Where are the girls?

She desperately wanted to ask but couldn't make her mouth work. Finally, a hoarse whine emerged from her throat.

"Girls...baby" was all she could manage to say. She saw the two men look at each other and Mark was crying.

Oh God, NO! Please don't take my baby!

This time a loud moan rumbled through her throat she heard a strange voice emerge.

"My baby!"

Galdon felt the sorrow and the panic. He tightened his wings slightly; but he needed much more prayer power to overcome what was next. He looked up and heard the Father's answer. A strong surge filled his body; and he let the power engulf Ellie and Mark to help them endure what was coming.

Please, God. Help me wake up. Please don't take my baby.

She felt Mark grab her hand; and she tried hard to listen to what the doctor was saying. Her thoughts tried to find some sort of truth. What was the last thing she remembered? Next she heard Mark's voice.

"Hey sweetheart. You are going to be fine. I love you."

Ellie tried to focus on his face. He was crying. She must have lost the baby. Her head was hurting so bad but she tried to remember.

I was heading home...no I was on my way to pick up...Sarah! Sarah was okay. She was not with me in the car. Thank you that Millie and Rose Louise are okay. How will we explain to them that we lost the baby!

More memories started to emerge. They were leaving to go get Sarah and it was almost dark outside. The Wheels on the Bus was playing on the CD when the light turned green.

I remember...there was a loud sound and the feeling of an explosion--like something catching me as I was shoved to the left. Oh God! I lost my baby! Ellie could feel herself start to panic and somewhere in the background a monitor began to beep.

"Ellie, can you look at me? I need you to relax." Dr. McGill was leaning over her and trying to look into her eyes; but she was too frantic to relax. She needed to see her girls. Her eyes were suddenly too heavy again and she had to let them close; but she was awake and could still hear.

Mark reached over and touched her arm. Ellie heard his voice like it was in a tunnel. "When do we tell her everything?"

Another voice was in the room. It sounded like the doctor; but Ellie was not sure. "I think the sooner the better. She is going to have a lot of support here. We have counselors and pastoral support, if you need it."

"We will all need it."

"I will check on it for you."

Ellie could hear everything that they were saying, even though her eyes remained shut. She tried hard to wake up again; but she was so tired.

"I don't know what we are going to do." Mark started crying. After what seemed like only a few seconds, Ellie heard Mark's voice again, this time much steadier. "We had to go ahead with the funeral."

Someone answered, "Let us know if there is anything we can do."

I did lose the baby! How long have I been here? Ellie tried hard to listen to the other sounds in the room. She could hear footsteps and a door closing; but sensed someone else in the room besides Mark. Someone was stroking her head.

All the events seemed meshed together; yet they didn't seem to go together. Mark was now holding her hand and seemed to still be crying. Ellie wanted to open her eyes again and tell Mark it would be okay--they were still young and had plenty of time to try again. A sadness enveloped her for a moment, as she mourned for the loss of the precious baby that had been growing inside her.

Poor Mark! He was so excited about this baby.

The thought of losing the baby was overwhelming; but a part of her was thankful that the rest of her family was safe. She would help Mark understand that eventually. Suddenly, she felt it. There was a thump. Ellie had just started to accept that the baby girl inside her was gone, when she felt her kick.

Oh God! Oh God thank you! Thank you for sparing my baby!

Ellie willed her eyes to open and slowly focused on her husband, who was leaning across her and quietly sobbing. She squeezed Mark's hand and smiled, as he looked at her with intense hurt in his eyes. She wanted to tell him it was okay--that the baby was still alive. He needed to know, so he wouldn't have to be sad. She knew the truth! They were all okay. Mark tried to say something; but Ellie fell into a slumber again.

The next time she woke, it was very dark in the room. A small light on the wall illuminated the area enough for her to see that it was night in the hospital. She looked around and could see that she was in a room with cords and machines all around her. There was a call button to her left that someone had clipped onto the side rail about three inches from her hand. Her arm felt like it weighed a hundred pounds when she tried to move her hand over toward the button. Too much energy was required for her to hold up her head and watch her progress while trying to move her hand, so she was forced to lay flat and work her hand slowly toward an unseen target. After working up a sweat, she was able to move her hand over just enough that her fingers could touch the edge of the device. Frustration was replaced by excitement when she felt the cold plastic against her hand; and she uttered a weak, "Yes!" She walked her fingers slowly up the edge and felt for a button to push.

The first button required three tries before she had the strength to press it down. In response, her TV came on but with no sound. She rested again but kept her fingers on the first button so that she wouldn't waste time pushing it again. The second button moved the head of her bed up slightly and caused her to lose her touch on the controller altogether. Now, though, she could see it and she strained in the pale light to determine which button she needed to push. After battling for several more minutes, she finally found the button and pushed it, causing the light above her to blink. Shortly after, a nurse came to her room. From that time forward, her memories began to line up some.

Over the next two days, Ellie was alert more of the time; but she struggled with the energy to stay awake and concentrate on what people were saying to her. Talking was too hard and she preferred to nod or just listen. Moving was terribly difficult and painful as well. The doctors filed through her room, ordering a variety of tests and having discussions that left Ellie feeling dizzy, as she tried to keep up with the conversations. The baby growing inside her continued to kick and Ellie tried desperately to point and show Mark. He would just smile and tell her that he loved her.

Why doesn't he understand? He must think that I am confused.

Throughout the next week, Ellie's time with Mark was minimal, as Ellie was whisked through a variety of therapy sessions and a barrage of more tests. Within ten days of her being fully awake, she found it easier to stay awake and could begin to understand more of what was being said around her. When Mark came to visit her, Ellie was able to grab his hand and put it on her belly. She wanted so desperately for him to stop being sad. She smiled and watched his face, as the baby kicked over and over. He leaned in and kissed her on the forehead. Ellie grabbed his hand and again placed it on her belly.

"Baby...alive." She croaked. She waited to see the change on his face.

"I know, sweetheart. She is growing well."

Ellie's face dropped, as she tried to understand why Mark was still so sad.

He must be exhausted and so worried about me.

Ellie grabbed his hand again and said, "I'm okay."

Mark put Ellie's hand up to his mouth and gently kissed her fingers. "I know, honey. You just keep working hard in therapy. We love you so much." He looked so sad; and Ellie could not understand why.

Maybe he is just overstressed.

Several days passed and finally they had some time together. Ellie had been sleeping and when she woke, Mark was sitting beside her on the bed. He stroked Ellie's hand over and over and she looked up and smiled.

"I love you. You are such a fighter."

"I love you too." She was starting to remember more every day but still did not have a clear picture of it all. "How long have I been here?"

"You have been in the hospital for two months. It is July."

Ellie could not believe what he had said. No wonder he has been so stressed! He must be overwhelmed at having to take care of the girls with his wife in the hospital for the last three months. She loved him so much. He was an amazing husband and father.

"The girls. When can I see them?"

Mark looked at her with deep concern. "We are trying to keep them away until you are more like you. We thought it might scare them. I think that it would be okay, though. Let me talk to the doctors first."

Ellie smiled and sank back onto her pillow. By the end of the day, the doctor's had approved the girl's visit and Mark agreed to bring them soon. Ellie was so excited; but she was also very nervous. In the accident, she had suffered three broken ribs and a broken collar bone and her right knee was badly bruised; but she had healed from these injuries. The most devastating injury had been her head injury, which had left her in a coma for two months. Fortunately, she was recovering quickly, now that she was awake; but there was an understanding that she would need to continue rehab for a couple of weeks to gain her strength back enough to go home. The cognitive damage had not been fully assessed; but she was remembering more every day. All she could think about was her family; and she just wanted to see her beautiful girls again.

Ellie awoke again, this time in less pain. She wasn't sure how much time had elapsed, as she worked to focus her eyes. Mark was sitting in the chair beside her bed; but he quickly jumped to his feet and grabbed her hand. Ellie squeezed his hand and tried to remember what she could. An accident...she was in the hospital...Mark was sad...the girls were fine. The girls--they are supposed to come see me.

Why does Mark look so different?

Slowly, she realized the difference: he looked happy.

"Hey sweetheart. I love you." Mark held her hand and brought it up to his lips and kissed her fingers.

Ellie opened her mouth; and this time she could hear words coming out clearly. "Where are the girls?"

Mark squeezed her hand gently; and she could see the pain in his eyes. He turned to look over his shoulder and that's when Ellie first noticed that his parents were also in the room. She could hear Mark's mother, Leah, say, "Mark you need to go ahead and talk with her. We will wait outside."

"What is it? When can I see them?" Ellie felt a sudden pain in her side as she tried to sit up, causing her to catch her breath.

"You need to rest. I will bring them soon. The doctor said we could bring them soon."

She instinctively felt her belly, which felt bigger than she remembered. A small kick fluttered in her abdomen, giving her a strong sense of relief. "I need to see them."

"Sarah is with her friend Margaret."

"Please bring them."

"I will."

"No, I want them today!" Ellie felt so much stronger now. She wanted to hug her babies and couldn't understand why they were not here.

"Let me talk with the doctor. I need to make sure."

"I'm ready. Please." Ellie watched as Mark turned toward the window. He seemed to be in deep thought.

"Okay. I will do my best." He turned back and she could see he had tears streaming down his face as he choked out the words, "I love you so much."

As he came to her side, Ellie reached out and they hugged for several seconds, until she felt her strength waning again. Mark sat back on the chair beside her bed and began to talk. She tried so hard to listen; but he was talking so fast. Ellie concentrated as hard as she could; but Mark's words were blurring together.

"Millie...bruises...so happy...scared...mommy..."

Ellie tried to put those words together in her brain and could not find the other pieces of the sentence to put with them. She heard him continue but only caught one phrase.

"...our baby...they tried to save...she's gone..."

Ellie's mind was fuzzy from all the pain medication and she had great difficulty concentrating on his words and then she heard Mark say,

"I had to do it."

"It's...okay." Ellie finally said. She knew Mark had been through so much. He must still think that they lost the baby. Ellie smiled and looked at her husband and patted her belly. He moved close to her and kissed her gently, while he placed his hand on hers. "We are blessed."

Mark answered, "You are amazing. We can do this together."

Ellie smiled again and fell asleep. The next morning, the nurse's told her that Mark was bringing the girls. Sarah was the first one through the door; and she ran to her mom's side. The physical therapist had positioned Ellie in a chair so that she would be able to visit with the girls and seem more like the mom that they knew. Sarah grabbed her mom's neck and hugged as hard as she could, while Mark came through the door and reminded her to be gentle. Sarah jabbered on and on about a variety of things and twirled around in the new dress that she had put on to show her mother. Millie stayed with Mark and eyed her mother suspiciously, until she recognized Ellie's voice; then she moved closer and also began talking and laughing. Ellie smiled at Mark, who smiled back; but she began to look around for Rose Louise. Mark saw her searching and did not understand.

"What is it, honey?"

"Where is Rose Louise?"

A look of horror crossed Mark's face and both girls stopped talking at once. Before anyone could react, Millie simply answered,

"She is with Jesus."

A tsunami of emotions swept through the room. Mark had thought that Ellie understood Rose Louise was gone when she kept saying, 'My baby!'. They had told her several times about Rose Louise; but she had not understood what they were saying. She had responded as if she understood and so everyone, including the doctors, thought Ellie knew.

"What...How is she? Please, Mark!"

"They did all they could..." Mark grabbed his wife's hand.

The meaning behind Mark's words was slow to divulge itself to Ellie's foggy mind. She tried to get out of her chair; but she was so weak. Mark held her hand firmly, as Ellie slowly began to realize what the words meant.

They did all they could...

Ellie closed her eyes and shook her head violently. "NO! God NO! Please Mark! Please just go get her! Where is she? I need to see her!" Ellie felt faint and weak and she was forced to lay back in the chair. The room swirled around her as she remembered Mark's words.

I had to do it...They did all they could... She heard the words tumble from her memory. Now it began to make sense.

Sarah and Millie both began to cry; and Mark's mom entered and scooped her two granddaughter's hands and lead them away, while Ellie continued to sob. "It's okay, come with me." The two girls went out of the room, while their grandmother tried to console them.

Mark answered Ellie through her sobs, "Ellie, you have been in a coma for two months. We had to make a decision. I had to make a decision."

Ellie released her husband and sobbed violently. "Where...Where is my baby? Please, Mark! Please, God! Please! It's my fault! It's my fault!"

"Ellie, it's not your fault. We had to let her go. There was nothing more they could do. You can't blame yourself."

Mark leaned forward and laid his head on her hand. He prayed and the power filled the room. The prayers of family and friends swelled through the hospital; but the angels carefully conserved the power for the upcoming months. Galdon braced himself and allowed the pain to spill out, as he pulled on the prayers from friends and family to embrace both Ellie and Mark. The Father had provided an enormous amount of support as well. Nardic stood with his wings spread around the room to try to fill the room with peace. Both Mark and Ellie had no idea that these two powerful angels watched over them and could not have endured the pain without the help of the Father through them. Nardic and Galdon exchanged a look and relaxed, as more prayers arrived.

For the next several weeks, even with all the power that was reserved for her, Ellie invited the spirit of Bitterness into her heart and the demon moved in close. The angels could not help her if she didn't want help; and the more she gave in to the whisperings of this demon, the more difficult she became to protect and soothe. Even the knowledge that a drunk driver was responsible and was eventually convicted and sent to prison did not help her overcome her pain. Ellie was completely entrenched in her sorrow.

* * * * *

When Ellie finished telling Terry about her memory of the ordeal, Terry could not find any words. The two women sat in silence, each reliving the other's words as well as their own memories. Galdon and Meris both blocked the demon of Pride and willed the women to pray. Terry spoke first.

"Ellie, I think you are amazing."

Both the angels and Ellie all looked at Terry, while the demon stopped hissing and listened.

"I can't think of a single person who would be able to get through what you experienced without some severe emotional scars. I would have been a basket case."

Ellie sniffled and then answered. "I was. I guess I still am."

"How could you not be? You were in a stuper for so long and then misunderstood that everyone was talking about your unborn child. I can't imagine the emotional blow, when you realized it was Rose Louise. On top of that, you had to recover yourself, deliver a baby, and return to a life that was drastically different. Then add to all of this that you were never able to attend the funeral. How you did that without extensive emotional support, prayer, and counseling is a mystery to me. You should understand that you are an amazing woman and have unbelievable emotional strength."

The words washed over Ellie and bathed her in a strange new love. No one had ever admired her or praised her for how she had endured. Everyone always seemed frustrated with her and most of her friends and family simply wanted her to be resilient and return to her life. So many well meaning friends had visited or sent cards with Bible verses--all with the same intent: God's Grace is sufficient. Many would even tell her it was all God's Will and she should just accept it. Ellie did believe in God's Will and his Grace; but what no one ever did was make her feel like she was normal for feeling so bad. No one even asked.

"Thank you. Thank you for saying that. I don't even think that I have ever told that whole story before."

"You should tell that story as much as you can. People need to hear what you went through from your side. I should thank you. You have made me realize that people who are grieving need love and not judgement."

"That is exactly it. I have always felt judged. I know everyone meant well."

"Maybe they did; but I can say that I remember people saying some of the dumbest things to us too. Anyway, I think you are amazing and you should never feel bad about missing Rose Louise. You never said anything about Millie. Was she hurt in the accident?"

"Millie was mostly okay except for some minor scrapes and bruises."

"I'm glad to hear that. I am sure that Mark was scared to death. It must have been a terrible time for him too."

"I can only tell you that he has been amazing through it all. The poor man had to take care of Millie and Sarah, the funeral, and me all at the same time. We did have great support from our church and family. By the time I woke from the coma and did a few weeks in rehab, I was only about two weeks from my due date. I came home for a short time and then went right back to deliver Lindsey. I think the church was really tired of praying for us."

"I would bet that they were not. I know I never tire of praying for anyone who needs it. I forgot that you were that far along in the pregnancy. That is crazy that you were only home for a couple of weeks and then went back."

"I was only there a short time to have Lindsey."

"I don't see how you did it."

"We had some wonderful friends and they all pitched in to help. I was really out of it for about a year. Thank goodness Lindsey was a great baby."

Lindsey heard her name as she came into the room.

"So, I was a good baby?"

Ellie smiled and responded, "Yes, you were. You have always been wonderful."

The rest of the evening, Ellie remained quiet as the men joined the women and the conversation danced around current events, baby Rosie, and basic family conversation. Galdon and Meris quietly watched as the demon of Pride seethed in the corner and waited for another chance. The glow along his arms made Meris smile.

Chapter 10: The Nursing Home

Several years passed with Rosie now 4 years old and full of life. John still occasionally saw the glow around Lindsey; but there was now a constant shimmer around Rosie. He met with Darron several times about it; but neither preacher could see any pattern to this weird phenomenon; and since John had no other symptoms to indicate a medical problem, they both agreed that it was a spiritual gift of some sort, even though neither man could see how it was useful. John just came to accept it; but he also decided not to talk about it until he understood it more himself for fear of sounding crazy.

One Thursday afternoon, John was picking up his Bible and notes to leave his office, when he heard a commotion outside his door. He cracked the door slightly to see Marian and Kathy Martin, the outspoken and off key matronly sisters that monopolized the song service, marching down the hall wearing long white robes that were cinched together with a belt made from what looked like plastic grocery bags tied together. They each wore a crown made from aluminum foil with long streamers of crepe paper hanging down their backs. As the two women turned to continue their march, John almost lost his glasses in surprise from the sight of the bright blue eyeshadow and painfully red lipstick that each woman had layered heavily over their pale complexions. In one hand, they carried large scepters that they had made from broom handles and silver duct tape. There was nowhere for John to hide now and his mouth hung open in both shock and disbelief.

"Hello Pastor John, would you like to see what we are working on?" Asked Kathy.

"Oh--"

"Look at our costumes! We made them ourselves out of recycled materials! We are going green!" Marian brimmed with pride as she twirled to show off her outfit.

"Yes, the only splurge was the crepe paper! The grocery bags we saved from the last two weeks and this foil is from last night's dinner!" Kathy held the scepter up to John's nose and the scent of something disturbingly familiar caused him to step backward.

"I--"

"I thought we could have used a new piece of foil; but Kathy insisted that we be good stewards. Do you want to see our dance?"

"Oh, um, I can't. I am just heading over for my weekly visit to the Sunshine Nursing Home."

"Oh how wonderful! We were just here working on a duet that we are going to perform this Sunday."

Both women looked directly at him and the full effect of the smell from the aluminum foil and sight of the abundant makeup made John queasy. He tried to repress a look of fear, as he remembered the last time the sisters had performed one of their infamous duets. The two had arrived in matching red, white, and blue outfits, complete with hats with large stuffed eagles perched on top. They performed for the Memorial Day weekend service and did a version of God Bless America that was complete with sign language, marching, and of course their horrible voices. The performance was so bad that everyone applauded when it was over, simply because it was over. The sisters believed the applause was for their efforts and immediately began petitioning to perform again. After months of holding them off, the choir director had simply caved in to their insistence; and so the congregation was bracing itself for the next onslaught of horrendous theatrics.

"I really need to get going, otherwise we could chat. Come by anytime." He tried to make a dash for the door, while wondering exactly what theme they would be promoting in their upcoming show. He had purposefully asked the choir director to assign them a non-holiday weekend, hoping it would tone down their flare for theatrics.

Kathy gently tugged on the Pastor's arm, "We would love to go with you. We really don't have much else to do today."

Marian jumped up and down, her red lips wagging, "I have an idea, why don't we practice our duet by singing it for the people at the nursing home?"

"Oh yes! It's a perfect way for us to work on our staging!"

John's mouth dropped open; and his face turned white, as he tried to think of an excuse that would prevent them from being able to go. His secretary, Mary, heard the exchange and came running around the corner.

"Oh Pastor John we might have an emergency. I don't think you'll be able to go today." She half-winked and he quickly caught on to her cues.

"Okay ladies, I hate to excuse myself in such a hurry; but something needs my immediate attention."

Both sisters perked up and tried to hear the hushed conversation that followed; but Mary quickly pulled Pastor John down the hall and out of ear shot.

"Okay, there's no emergency except that you needed to get away from them. I'm so sorry if that's a sin."

"No, you said there *might* be an emergency. I guess the only emergency would've been having them scare the life out of someone in that home." John wasn't even trying to be funny; but Mary couldn't help but laugh out loud.

"I'm sorry. I know that is not really funny; but I guess I was just trying to figure out exactly what song they were going to sing in those outfits."

"So you haven't heard them practicing?"

"Oh, I didn't say that. You know as well as I do that there is no way to recognize anything that they sing.

Sometimes even when I know, I can't make out the words either."

"I was wondering about the song too. Anyway, thanks for your help. Somehow I have to get past them to get to my car; and I'm already running behind now. I usually try to spend time with a few of the residents beforehand and now I don't think I can squeeze that in. It's kind of my way of drumming up business to get them to come and listen to my service."

"Don't worry, I've got this; but you owe me for this one." Mary took off down the hall; and John could hear her say, "Kathy! Marian! I was wondering if you could let me hear your song?"

John listened to the sisters squeal in delight and waited for Mary to lead them to the sanctuary; and then he darted down the hall, out the door, and to his car. As he turned onto the road for the nursing home, he was still thanking God for his narrow escape from the Martin sisters.

I have got to get Mary a gift card or flowers or something. She must be in some type of torment that I can't imagine right now.

John arrived at The Sunshine Nursing Home on time due to his quick exit from the church. As he pulled into the parking lot, he noticed some dark clouds gathering in the distance and he wasn't sure that he had an umbrella with him today. He put his car in park near the door, grabbed his Bible, and then hurried toward the entrance. Coming here had become a ritual for over three years now; and he had grown to enjoy it very much. He strolled down the halls, waving at some of the staff members and shaking hands with several residents along the way. As he entered the main dining area, he walked around the different tables, greeting people that frequently attended his service; but he was slightly worried when he couldn't locate Mr. Roberts, who was now one of Pastor John's friends. Linda, one of the administrators saw John looking around with a puzzled expression and walked over to find out if she could help.

"How are you today, Pastor John?"

"I'm good, Linda, and yourself?"

"I'm still chugging along! Who are you looking for?"

"I don't see Mr. Roberts, is he alright?"

"His son picked him up and took him to lunch. They should be back any moment."

"His son?"

Linda nodded and answered. "Yes, his son. His daughter and son-in-law are the ones that admitted him here. They never come around. I don't think that they get along. His son, Carl, is who came to get him. He felt bad when his sister and brother-in-law brought Mr. Roberts here; but he didn't have much say in it because he has been in some trouble--I think maybe even some jail time. Anyway, he lumbers in here occasionally. Today, he took Mr. Roberts to lunch and that is rare."

"I can't imagine not spending time with my father."

"Me either. You will soon see, though. That family is a little dysfunctional"

"You said they will be back soon? I was hoping to see him today. I brought him a new CD of one of his favorite gospel groups."

"I am not sure exactly when they will get back; but it should be any time now. I can give it to him for you if you want."

"That would be great--"

"Wait a second--here he comes now. That's his son with him."

John looked where Linda was pointing and saw Mr. Roberts rolling in with a thin haggard man pushing him.

Linda leaned over and spoke softly. "His son is not one for words. He is a bit strange. You will see." She stood up straight again and continued, "I guess I will see you in the service! Break a leg or something like that!" Linda left to start helping move the residents into the activity hall to wait for Pastor John.

John laughed. "I hope I don't. That is for actors. I hope to keep both of my legs in tact."

Linda laughed and continued on her way.

Mr. Roberts and his son had reached the opening to the hall and John walked toward them. As he approached, he reached out his hand to Mr Robert's son, "Hi, I'm Pastor John."

Before the son could respond, Mr. Roberts reached up and grabbed Pastor John's hand and a broad smile stretched across his weathered face. His son watched the two men and then timidly reached out to shake hands and quietly spoke, "I'm Carl."

"Glad to meet you Carl. Your father and I have become good friends over the last few years."

Carl kept his eyes downcast and shifted back and forth on his feet, obviously very uncomfortable. John noted that

Carl's clothes were filthy and hung loosely on his thin body; and he had a slight body odor that mixed with a faint smell of alcohol.

Mr. Roberts answered, "I am stuffed. We went to that new hamburger joint over by the mall."

"Now, aren't you supposed to be watching your cholesterol?" John suppressed a smile, as he heckled his good friend.

"Shhh, don't let that crazy Linda hear you. She will fuss at me all week long. Let an old man have a simple pleasure." Mr. Roberts's eyes danced and John smiled back, then he held out the CD he had brought as a gift.

"Look what I found the other day." He handed the CD over to Mr. Roberts, who inspected it carefully and smiled again.

"I can't believe you found this! This is the album I was telling you about!"

"It's not an album dad, it's a CD." Carl rolled his eyes. He really wanted to get out of here as soon as he could but didn't want to be rude.

"I know, I know but I always called it an album--old habit, I guess. Anyway, let's get it back to my room and listen to it. You've got to hear some of these old songs!"

John said, "Sure thing, but I've got to give my message first. Come join in the service with me and then we'll go to your room and listen to some of the songs."

"Wow, it is that late." He turned to Carl and said, "You have got to stay and hear this young man preach!"

Carl felt a small panic building, as he tried to figure out a way to leave. The last thing he wanted to do was hear someone preach. The demon on his shoulder began to whisper into his ear and he grew more uncomfortable. The first instinct he had was to just run.

John sensed the hesitation and said a silent prayer that this man would stay and just hear at least today's message. The small prayer created enough movement in the spiritual world to help. Flint, Carl's angel, shoved the demon back and surrounded Carl with his wings; and with very little effort, Flint was able to keep Carl from leaving. As Carl tried to think of something to say, his thoughts were so scrambled that nothing made any sense. Finally, Mr. Roberts reached up to his son's arm and said, "Carl, can you take me into the activity hall to hear the service?"

Carl looked from his father to the preacher and back and then nodded and began to push his father's wheelchair into the room where several of the residents had already gathered to wait on their weekly minister. Flint and the demon both positioned themselves beside Carl; but the prayer support was low, so Flint had to reserve some of his power and step back. The demon laughed and dug his claws into Carl's shoulder and Flint could only watch.

There were several people in the room in wheelchairs like Mr. Roberts; and a few others were being led in by staff members in a slow parade of walkers and canes. The staff members helped the walking patrons find a seat; and then pushed the others up to the front row. By the time the procession ended, several of the people in the chairs had already dozed off. One elderly lady in a wheelchair in the front row sat slightly hunched over a Bible that she clutched in her tiny bony fingers. She smiled at John; and he nodded and smiled back, noting that he had never seen her before.

As the music began, a powerful spiritual presence began to build in the room. Carl's demon sat snarling and panting, as his sharp claws clung to his shoulder. The sound of praises rising to Heaven was too much for weaker demons; but Carl's demon was able to withstand it easily, which concerned Flint. He watched as the demon slowly released one claw and began to stroke Carl's head and whisper into his ear again. Several angels materialized inside the room and took their places along the wall with their wings and robes starting to glow and their hands on their swords, ready to strike at any moment; but they were also there to hear the Word of God and listen to the praises that were lifted up in song. Flint moved over beside Nardic, who was watching the people in the room, as they mumbled the words to the first song along with Pastor John. Outside in the halls, some smaller demons were clutching onto several other people that they were trying to control, while other demons in the region around the nursing home sensed something happening and began to gather around the outside of the building in response to the increased number of angels.

Meris landed outside to check on the angels standing guard around the perimeter; and then he strode into the building to make his presence known. The demons in and around the building were noticeably shaken at the sight of Meris. His size alone was enough to shred even the boldest of the demon's plans; but his reputation as a warrior was what made most demons cower even at the sound of his name. Only Michael and Gideon were above him in rank. His muscles rippled in his legs and his wings glowed, as he walked boldly through the halls, his hand resting on the sword that swayed in cadence at his waist.

There was a distinct movement of demons to the outer edge of each room he walked through followed by hissing and snarling as he passed. One demon shoved another younger demon out into the path of Meris, where he froze in place in front of the approaching angel. Meris merely smiled and then blew on the demon, sending him tumbling into a wall, while the older demon howled with laughter. Next, Meris turned to look at the older demon, who tripped and fumbled as he ran outside.

When Meris arrived at the activity hall, he immediately joined in the songs and waited to hear the message from young preacher, while he constantly surveyed the room for signs of trouble. Although Meris always enjoyed watching the power of God flow from Heaven through any preacher, Pastor John was especially good at it. Tension grew into a thick and strange mixture of love and hate throughout the area inside and around the nursing home as the demons and angels watched each other carefully.

The old woman from the front row listened intently to the songs and tried to join in when she could. She was the only human in the room that was fully aware that something more was happening. She noted the large dark shadow hovering over the new man with Mr. Roberts. This demon seemed larger than the ones she was accustomed to seeing and it concerned her. The large presence of angels was another indication that something was happening. She could see only light at this time; but it radiated with such strength that she knew that the room was full of angels. Clinging to her Bible, she worked hard to concentrate on the songs, while continuing to offer a prayer intermittently.

Meris's large frame engulfed the room, so he stepped out into the hall briefly to watch the entrance and glare at the evil minions that pestered and prodded their victims in a variety of methods. The angels could not understand why humans did not turn to the Heavenly Father, who loved them more than they could understand. They also marveled at how these humans could be at the end of their lives and yet still be so stubborn and calloused. Through the years, Meris had watched countless individuals struggle against the powers that pulled at their souls without their knowledge. Free Will was difficult for the angels to understand. To them, it was painfully obvious which choice to make. Then again, even the demons had made their choice. After all, they were simply angels that had chosen to serve Satan as their master instead of God.

Pastor John continued with another song, which he belted out to try to keep the rhythm; and a chorus of mumbles and sounds accompanied him by the few that stayed awake long enough to listen. One voice was stronger than the rest and it belonged to Mr. Roberts. He sang right along with Pastor John; and Carl was surprised at how steady and true his father's voice was and how his father knew the words to all the songs. Growing up, they had never attended church as a family; and he distinctly remembered his father being rather indifferent toward religion as a whole. How and when this had changed was something of a mystery to Carl; but then again, he had missed so much over the last 20 years.

Mr. Roberts closed his eyes for the next song and tears formed as he sang the words that were dear to his heart. Carl had been watching the clock above the door and wishing the service would end so that he could leave; but the words of this song stirred something inside him that he didn't know existed. As the old woman's prayers continued, Flint was able to pull the large demon back to allow the full effect of Carl's emotions to wash over him, leaving him feeling exposed, yet somehow he also felt...safe. Pastor John led the group to continue to sing the chorus one more time; and Carl began to feel warm, as the words coursed throughout both his mind and his soul.

Jesus paid it all,
All to Him I owe;
Sin had left a crimson stain,
He washed it white as snow.

Carl had to close his eyes to stop the tears and he squeezed his eyes shut in desperation to keep from being embarrassed. The demon writhed and screamed as Flint held onto him, allowing more time for Carl to hear the words unfiltered and raw; but some of the demon's words slipped through to Carl's mind.

The demon snarled and yelled out, "You are unworthy. Remember what you have done!"

Carl hung his head, as his mind reorganized the demon's words. *I am not worthy. I have done too many things for God to want me.*

He continued to stand beside his father, but he had no idea about the battle for his soul that was being waged around him. The old woman in the front of the room with the Bible heard it all and knew that the man was in trouble. She closed her eyes and prayed vehemently for help. The demon shook violently, screaming out as Flint stepped forward and pierced him with his sword, forcing him to let go of Carl's shoulder but not before he reached over and slashed Flint on the arm. Flint winced in pain but used the reserve of power that he had been trained to save and lunged forward to strike the demon in the head, sending him careening to the corner of the room. The other angels stood ready and waiting; but they nor any of the other demons were allowed to interfere. In the battle for a single soul, the demon and angel assigned must use the power available to fight. If anyone else prayed for the man or if he made a decision to accept Jesus, the balance of power would tip in favor of the angels and they would be allowed to rally and fight the demon. Most demons would leave and only return after a few days, when the newness of the decision would fade; and they had a chance to torment the new believer with memories of their past. Their days of fully enveloping that human would be over. There was also the matter of their punishment for losing a soul. Many would flee to hide from the master demons, who were in charge of doling out such punishments. On the other hand, if a human determined to wait on salvation or push aside the offer to accept Christ, then it was the demons who won that battle for that moment; and the angels would merely retreat and wait for another chance. For now, Flint stood poised to strike the demon again, as he watched Carl's face, waiting for Carl to break.

"Let it go, Carl," Flint said out loud.

Only the old lady heard the angel's voice; and she looked over toward Carl and smiled. Meris returned to stand with Flint and they both watched her, willing her to pray; but she seemed caught up in the spectacle of the scene in front of her--a trick that some demons used. Meris looked around the edge of the room and saw the demon that was working on her. He was carefully whispering something to her that she obviously heard. All she felt was the light in front of her, which the demon used to distract her from praying. He whispered over and over, "It's so beautiful, so bright." As she concentrated on the light, her focus of prayer was lost.

"I'll take care of that!" Meris moved swiftly behind the small demon and spun him around. The demon screamed when he saw Meris and ran out the door, where he was met by another larger demon, who grabbed and punched him for running away. With the small demon gone, the old woman shook her head and seemed to regain control of her thoughts. She silently began to pray and the room began to glow. All the angels instinctively spread their wings. Outside, the light radiated onto the lawn and the angels on the perimeter began to sing. With the surge of light and the song of the angels, thousands more angels suddenly appeared in the sky, hoping to witness a human soul being saved.

Carl continued to struggle with his emotions and quickly wiped his face clean, while the preacher stopped singing to begin his sermon. Flint and the other angels all kept their wings open to protect the room, while Pastor John gave a powerful and earnest sermon on the prodigal son. The demons in the room were forced to retreat to the hall, not being able to stand hearing the Word of God. Flint kept his hand on his sword and he continued to pace the back of the room, itching to leave and fight the demons out in the hall. He looked over at Meris, who nodded to finally give him permission to leave the room and chase down the one demon that had been tormenting Carl. Within seconds, Flint had found and grabbed that demon by the throat and then thrust him out of the building. By the time Flint returned, Carl was regaining his composure.

"Please...just trust Him," Flint said out loud again; and again the old woman looked over and smiled.

This time, she echoed the words, "Trust him."

Pastor John heard the words and looked around; but he could not find the source, so he continued preaching. It was not unheard of for someone to speak out during a sermon; but it was usually with an "Amen." He could not understand what he had said that would warrant any response right now; but he shrugged, knowing that the Holy Spirit moved in mysterious ways sometimes.

Carl did not budge when the preacher gave an altar call; but Flint knew something had changed, he could feel it. Carl's demon would have a hard time latching back on again right away. More prayer would be needed to make sure that it never happened again; and Flint was worried that Carl would not get it.

After the service, Pastor John greeted a few of the people and Carl hurried to get his father back to his room, so he could leave. He was uncomfortable with the new feelings he was having, so he slipped out to his car before Pastor John was able to get to Mr. Robert's room to spend some time listening to the CD he had brought for his friend.

All the angels in the area slowly retreated, disappointed that the man had not chosen Jesus today. Flint felt an enormous frustration at coming so close but not being able to see it happen. He rode on the roof of Carl's car, contemplating how he would handle the demon when he returned. There would be nothing he could do to stop the demon from reattaching himself to this man; and Flint knew that the demon would work harder than ever to deter this man from ever getting so close again. Prayer was the answer; but who would pray for Carl?

Chapter 11: Prayers for Carl

John's ministry at the nursing home continued to grow. His weekly visits became a treasured time for him to stay and talk with Mr. Roberts, who had now become his unofficial critic. Several years passed with Carl continuing to attend occasionally; but he seemed distant and uncomfortable. Mr. Roberts offered little information and John did not want to pry. There seemed to be a very large wedge between the two men; and John began to pray that both men could find peace in their relationship.

Around the time that Rosie celebrated her eighth birthday, things began to change. The change started one week when John arrived early to the nursing home for his weekly visit. The room was beginning to fill with a few patrons, while he greeted a few people and continued to look through his sermon notes. There was a noticeable drop in the number of residents that were filtering into the room today due to the flu sweeping through the home, causing many of the people to fall gravely ill. Pastor John was making a note to ask for prayer for those battling this illness, when he noticed Carl move into the room along with his father, Doug Roberts. John noted that the old woman from the front row was there and already smiling as well. She had been gone for several years and John had thought she had passed away. As John smiled back, he caught a glimpse of what looked like a slight glow around her, similar to the way Lindsey and Rosie sometimes glowed. This was the first time in several years that he had seen the glow at all and now it was around someone new and it startled him. John rubbed his eyes and tried to focus on his sermon; but the image of the light around this old woman caused him great concern. As everyone started singing, John silently prayed for help.

Please, God, help me with whatever this is. Please heal me if it is an illness. I am scared and unsure about what to do. Please let me stay focused today and help me deliver your Word to Carl and anyone else here who has not accepted you into their life. In Jesus' name, Amen.

John lifted his head to join the songs, when he noticed a faint glow around the edge of the room. His knees weakened and he would have collapsed, if Meris had not provided unseen support. John's head was spinning, as he contemplated the ramifications of what he was now seeing. He had done enough research to know that this light could be a very serious neurological problem like a brain tumor or might signify some type of impending but major eye problem. In his heart, though, he believed it was from God. Either way, it scared him. He and his associate pastor, Darron, and talked through so many of these scenarios and always felt that it was not medical; but they both remained confused about what this gift meant or how it could be used.

How in the world will I even tell my church what has been happening? What if everyone just thinks I am crazy? How could that possibly help my ministry?

Keeping quiet seemed like a better choice. A small demon of Fear was near the window behind Pastor John, chanting these thoughts loud enough for John's mind to register them and file them away.

Meris heard the small demon and saw the affect that he was having on the pastor, so the angel stepped forward and glared at the demon, who backed up, until he was at the edge of the street. Pastor John rubbed his eyes again and the glow in the room remained; but now he only felt peace. Meris gently laid his hands on the pastor's shoulders and spread his wings to protect him. The residents who were not sick and wanted to attend were in place and now waiting on Pastor John to begin. He glanced over at Carl, who was looking down at his feet and seemed miserable. Pastor John had no idea that Carl's discomfort was from the internal struggle between his past, which continued to torment him, and the Holy Spirit, who continued to work on him every visit to the nursing home. Carl's past haunted him; but something about his time with Pastor John made him feel better. John had no idea what could be so bad that this man could not forgive himself.

Why does everyone always think that they have to be perfect to come to God?

John watched Carl and silently prayed to be able to reach him. This question often pervaded his thoughts; and he had preached about it many times. He opened his mouth to sing and suddenly stopped. Galdon and Meris looked at each other and felt the surge from the silent prayers of the preacher, as he struggled for words. Meris again reached forward and placed his hands on John's shoulders, this time sending a strong beam of light from Heaven onto the humble man. John straightened up and folded his notes and returned them to his notebook, while he looked around at his tiny group of faithful attendees.

The song service today seemed slow and endless to Carl, who found himself bored and losing interest. The demon was able to creep back in and sit beside Carl. Meris and Galdon glared at the demon, who only smiled and sneered back at them. The battle for Carl would only be won if Carl wanted to be saved; and until then, the demon was allowed to pester and torture him. Prayers were effective to help; but not in the same way that they did for the saved. The demon whispered doubt and fear into Carl's ear; and Carl began to listen.

Why am I here? It's too late for me anyway. God could never want me after what I have done.

The demon jumped onto Carl's back and stroked the side of his head, while he continued to whisper more thoughts into the poor man's ear. Outside the room, several angels arrived, hoping that this was the day for Carl's transformation. In the spiritual world, news of a possible new believer reverberated throughout; and angels were drawn to the area to try to witness the event.

"I just don't understand why they don't all come to the Father. Come on, Carl!" Flint said, watching helplessly, as the demon desperately continued to scramble ideas and thoughts into Carl's mind to keep him from hearing the songs.

Pastor John stepped forward, as the last song ended. "I stand before you today, because of a gift. A gift of life that I am forever indebted to. I want to tell you about a gift of life that you can receive. It's never too late and you're never in too bad of a place that Jesus will not take you. In fact, the Bible tells us that Jesus wants to come to you wherever you are. All you have to do is call on him. He's ready, are you?"

Carl slowly lifted his head, as he tried to avoid eye contact with anyone in the room and especially that preacher. The demon continued to whisper and then noticed Carl looking up and scrambled to insert more thoughts into his mind. Carl noticed the preacher looking directly at him and he immediately began to squirm, then dropped his head.

Was he looking directly at me? Why was he looking at me?

John began to survey the others in the room; but Carl could not shake the feel of the stare pouring over him. The demon that had engulfed Carl for years whispered feverishly to keep his thoughts away from the pastor's message; but there was a strong power emanating from John's mouth and the light from his words punctured the darkness that entangled Carl.

"Stop!" The demon screeched and the old woman from the front row looked over. She searched and could finally see the dark force and feel it's presence, causing her to begin to pray. A large surge of strength from the power of her prayer emanated to Flint, who plunged his sword straight through the demon, causing him to screech and fall to the ground simultaneously releasing Carl. Carl suddenly felt something change; and he raised his eyes one more time to look into John's eyes. This time they seemed inviting instead of threatening. For the first time in years, Carl felt loved.

John noticed Carl looking up again and he seemed *lighter*. It occurred to him that Carl had always seemed darker before and now he just looked normal. He cleared his throat and began, while Meris held him steady. "Well, I have a prepared sermon that I had planned to deliver today; but the Lord has laid it on my heart to give a different message. I always start my sermons the same way by saying, 'I stand before you because of a gift,' which is true. Today, I want to talk to you about this gift of salvation."

John delivered a short but powerful explanation of salvation and tied in several stories and verses with the theme of not waiting to be perfect and that God wants you to come to Him just as you are. For the song, he chose a simple and popular altar call song with a similar message.

Just as I am, without one plea,
but that thy blood was shed for me,
and that thou bidst me come to thee,
O Lamb of God, I come, I come.

John watched as Carl squirmed and seemed to struggle with the words of the song. The glow around the room might have been slightly brighter; but John could not keep his mind off Carl. Meris leaned in close to the preacher and willed him to pray.

"Come on...pray for him."

John felt an overwhelming urge to pray and closed his eyes and knelt by the makeshift altar to pray. The sight of the pastor kneeling was a powerful signal; and all the angels immediately opened their wings and began to glow. A strong and powerful wave of strength swept the entire nursing home purging every demon in the home and all the ones within several hundred yards of the property, blasting them to more than a mile away. The raw and earnest prayer of the humble Pastor John ripped through the building and the grounds and drew a large army of angels to assemble to protect the area. Carl's demon was struck by several blows of light and Flint stepped forward, grabbing the hideous creature to personally drag him out of the building. By the time the song ended, every person in the room could feel the love that radiated there, including Carl.

John could see the hurt in Carl's eyes and could not understand why that man clung to his pain. When the residents began filing out, John walked toward Mr. Roberts, but felt a tug on his arm and turned to see the elderly lady from the front row. She stood and hugged John and thanked him for the sermon. She leaned in close and said simply, "The glow was fantastic today, thank you!"

The words hung in the air, as she sat back down in her wheelchair and rolled it out the door before John could answer. He was confused and captivated by what she had said; but he needed to find Carl, who had already left with his father. As the elderly lady moved her wheelchair carefully down the hall, John noticed that she had a faint glow around her again; but he did not have time to consider this for long. He rushed to gather his things and get to Mr. Robert's room; but by the time he arrived, Carl was already gone.

"I'm sorry, Pastor John. I am not feeling well today. I hope that I am not coming down with that awful flu."

"Me either. It seems to be bad. So many people were absent today."

"Yes, several are in the hospital. I have tried to keep up with praying for them; but now I just pray a general prayer to cover them all."

"I am sure that it helps."

"Well, I doubt few of them know their own name anyway, so God will just have to keep up with it all. By the way, I give you a 'Good enough to hear again' rating today."

"That one is new! Thank you, I think. Is that a compliment?"

"Oh yes. It means what it means. I liked it enough that I'd love to hear it again sometime when you are stumped for a new sermon."

"I will remember that!"

"In all seriousness, I want that preached at my funeral."

The two men locked eyes and John spoke first. "I guess we will have to find someone to deliver it because I am sure you will outlive me."

"I'm planning on several more years. Anyway, I'm going to go lay down awhile."

John smiled and thanked his friend, promising to pray for him and be back the next week. "Please call me if you need anything, Mr. Roberts."

"Can you beat up my son-in-law and get him to let me out of here?"

"I can't; but I can probably find someone to do it."

The two men laughed and John shook his hand in farewell and made his way to his car. In his heart, John silently prayed for Mr. Roberts to be okay and that he would get to see Carl soon. He had noticed that Mr. Roberts looked particularly pale today; and it worried him. When he reached the parking lot, he fumbled in his pocket for his keys while juggling his notebook and papers. The keys slipped from his fingers and fell under his car.

If I were a cursing man, I would be letting it fly right now!

Balancing his notebook and papers on top of his car, he bent down to search for the keys, when he heard a faint sound that caught his attention. John froze and listened; but couldn't hear anything except the occasional car passing by on the street. Just as he started to stand up, he heard it again; but this time, the sound was more localized; and he was easily able to follow it to the car parked directly behind his in the next row. John could see someone slumped over in the driver's seat and he walked toward the car to help;

but he suddenly stopped, when the man sat straight up and started crying and talking to himself. John wrestled with what to do and then decided to try to help. He took a few more guarded steps and the man's words were easy to decipher and so was his identity--it was Carl.

"Okay I'm here! What do I do? I don't know what to do. I'm here and I'm trying God. What do I do? I want to be forgiven; but I don't deserve it!" Carl hung his head on the steering wheel and openly wept for the first time in years.

John stopped and prayed a simple prayer for wisdom, thanking God for the opportunity to talk to this troubled man. Cautiously, he approached the window and knocked. Carl sat up quickly and seemed conflicted about what to do as well. He lowered his window; and the two men faced each other, both trying to gauge what to say and how to say it. The demon that had been with Carl desperately tried to grasp onto him again; but Flint stepped in and blocked the dark force from getting near.

"Hey Carl, I wanted to thank you for coming again."

"Um, yeah, it was...I enjoyed it." Carl tried to wipe his eyes inconspicuously; and John pretended not to notice.

"Your father seemed to be feeling pretty bad--I hope he isn't getting the flu."

"Oh, I think he is just tired. We did some shopping today; and that usually wears him out." Carl's demon growled and hissed at Flint, then worked his way toward the tormented man; and Flint was forced to let him go. The demon jumped onto Carl's back, causing his demeanor to immediately change, while the demon laughed. Flint needed John or Carl to pray again but had enough power left from the last prayer to grab the demon and tug on his back. The demon let go with his arms and began punching and screaming; but Flint held on to his shoulders and strained to give Carl at least partial relief. The spiritual battle waged on as the humans continued to face each other unaware.

John looked at Carl and saw that he was not ready to talk. "Let me know if your father needs anything. I would be glad to help him, if you are busy."

Carl nodded and looked away and seemed relieved that the preacher was ending the conversation. "Sure. I will."

Carl sat in his car watching, as John pulled away. Again, he bowed his head on the steering wheel. "I want out of this! I can't live like this anymore! I would make a deal with the devil to get rid of this pain!" Immediately, Flint let go and flew back a few feet.

BOOM

The sound was accompanied by a jolt, as if someone had hit his car. Carl sat up quickly and looked around; but the parking lot was empty except for a couple of parked cars several spaces over. Fear was replaced by confusion; and he shook his head, scolding himself for his imagination. Just as he put his keys in the ignition, his car began to rock violently side to side and he screamed, grabbing the steering wheel to keep from pitching over in response. His first thought was that maybe it was an earthquake; but nothing else in the parking lot was moving. The rocking continued for several seconds; and he instinctively lowered himself to the seat. Abruptly, the rocking stopped and Carl remained trembling on the seat for several more seconds before he had the nerve to raise up and peer over the edge of the window. A horrible smell suddenly permeated the car, causing him to gag and choke, forcing him to quickly fumble for the keys try to open a window; but as he raised up, a large black shadow appeared hovering over the front window of the car. Carl opened his mouth to scream; but fear seized him and he was unable to produce any noise at all.

Time seemed to stand still as he sat frozen, staring at the sinister form that began to shift and move until it took the shape of a man. A blinding light flashed as Flint used his remaining strength to slash at the demon and then everything disappeared, even the smell; but Carl was so terror-stricken that he sat there for another few minutes before he could regain his motor functions enough to be able to drive. Flint remained on the ground for several minutes after Carl had driven away, while smaller angels ministered to him. Before he was fully recovered, he stood and whipped his wings to fly quickly to catch up to Carl, who was speeding home as fast as he could. The demon flew low over the car and sneered at Flint as he approached. For the rest of the night, both the demon and Flint remained with Carl and waited for him to make a choice.

John decided to use the sermon he had used at the nursing home the following Sunday instead of his prepared one. He was sure that God had laid it on his heart Thursday and the response had been so good that he wanted to deliver it to his church. The attendance for the last two years had been steadily declining, although he worked hard to develop his messages and felt like he poured his heart into every one. Something had changed, though, and it was related to his gift. The more he had doubted it, the harder time he seemed to have with his sermons. The connection to this had never occurred to him, though, and he felt much better when he didn't have to worry about a gift that he had no idea how to use. The return of the glow and the response of this week at the nursing home had brought new life to him in the pulpit; and he couldn't wait to deliver the sermon once more, hoping God would use him and allow him to see the light again. With polished precision, he preached that Sunday with twenty-five people coming to the altar to either re-dedicate their lives or accept Jesus as their savior. He knew now that God was somehow wanting him to use this gift and he began to pray harder to learn how.

    As Pastor John experienced an amazing weekend at his church followed by an outpouring of requests for copies of the sermon, Carl was struggling harder than ever just to concentrate on even the most mundane tasks. No matter what he tried to do or where he tried to go, he continued to be tormented by the memory of that dark form towering over his car and the violent rocking back and forth. In his mind, he reasoned it off several times as hallucinations from the years of alcohol and drug abuse; but he couldn't shake the bone chilling fear that the memory of that day evoked each time he replayed the events over in his mind. By the time the next Thursday arrived, Carl could not decide whether returning would help the fear go away or make it worse. He tried every excuse he could come up with not to go but felt so drawn to the nursing home that he couldn't resist and then drove around the parking lot three times before he had the courage to go in.

What will my father say when I show up again?

All he could think about was what he needed to do. He strode in through the atrium and straight to his father's room. Mr. Roberts was sitting in his chair facing the door when his son entered and walked toward him.

"Hey Carl, what brings you here? I didn't expect you today."

Carl cleared his throat and tried to think of what he could say. He couldn't be honest and tell him the truth without sounding crazy.

"I was just in the area and thought that...well...maybe I should come by and maybe see you again."

"I'm glad you did. I was just visiting with my friend here; and it's almost time to go down to the service."

Carl looked up and for the first time noticed the preacher sitting in the corner. The demon on Carl's back eyed Pastor John carefully and then began to whisper in Carl's ear. Immediately, Carl felt uneasy and overcome with a desire to leave.

"Oh, I'm sorry. I didn't know… Maybe I should just go." Carl said and started to back up toward the door.

"Absolutely not--of course you're welcome. Let's go ahead to the service." Mr. Roberts motioned for them both to come. Carl jostled in behind his father and began to push him down to where the service was held, while the demon crouched on Carl's back and dug his claws in tight, continuing to whisper and implant apprehension and discomfort, as they approached the activity hall. Flint,

Carl's guardian angel, kept his distance and was forced to wait until Carl asked for help this time. The prayers of the preacher had allowed him to block some of the demon's words; but Carl could only be free, if he chose to be.

John watched Carl closely during the beginning of the song service. The man was obviously struggling with something; and it puzzled John that this man could be Mr. Robert's son. How could such a spiritual man have a son that was so lost? There had to be an explanation for it all; but neither man was willing to share it just yet.

As the last song ended, John silently prayed for his sermon and for Carl. The light from the prayer burst forth and filled Flint's sword until it glowed. Flint moved toward Carl and held the blade between the demon's mouth and Carl's ear to block the venomous words through the beginning of the service to allow Carl to only hear the preacher. Within seconds, Carl's body began to relax and he felt an immediate peace envelope him as his doubt and fear subsided. The demon cursed and moved over to avoid the light from the angel's sword that was burning his feet. He screamed, "That's not fair!"

Meris locked eyes on the demon, who immediately cowered and clung to the edge of Carl's shirt, awaiting the prayer power to subside. The heat from the sword was causing the demon to wince and squirm; and Meris noted that this particular demon was willing to endure more pain than most. Meris moved closer to watch, but allowed Flint to take the lead.

John decided to use the message from last week that he had prepared and not used. He finished his message and gave a short invitation, Carl felt a strong urge to go forward; but by this time, the prayer power had subsided enough to allow the demon to begin to dig his sharp claws back into Carl's shoulder and press hard. Tears welled up in Carl's eyes, as he struggled with his desire to be free, while his guilt tormented his mind. The demon smiled and leaned in to whisper and chant; but as he did so, he bumped Flint's arm. Flint took this as an invitation to fight and smacked the demon full across the face, sending him flying into the nearby wall; but as he moved toward the demon again, Meris held him back. "Not yet. Not until Carl calls on God."

"That's not fair! You can't touch me!" The demon screeched.

"You touched him first! I am a witness! He is allowed to retaliate!" Meris boomed. The demon immediately fell to the ground and slithered over to Carl. Meris turned to Flint, "You have to let the man decide."

"I want to decide for him!" Flint boomed and the room was immediately illuminated by a bright white light.

Pastor John saw it as soon as it happened. There was a white flash and in an instant he saw the room filled with angels; but just as quickly as the flash had come, it all disappeared. He rubbed his eyes and tried to regain his composure; but the majesty of the moment was too much for him. Emotionally, he was torn between praying for Carl and falling to his knees in awe. The demon laughed.

"Flint! You have caused the preacher to lose his focus! You can't lose it like that! The demon wins if we don't receive more prayer!"

"I never meant...I just got frustrated and wanted to make it happen. It's so hard to wait."

"I know, young friend. We all fight the urge to intervene. It is so hard to understand why they don't just call on God."

"Why would anyone not want to be free?" Flint argued and strode back and forth. "I could blast that demon so easily, if the man would only ask. Why won't he ask? What is he waiting for?"

Galdon nodded as he joined both Meris and Flint, "Yes, I feel the same way. We all do." Galdon gestured to include the large hoard of angels that had gathered in the hope that today would be the day that Carl would make a decision.

"Come on, Carl! Do it!" Flint moved closer to Carl, who remained oblivious to the supernatural beings surrounding him.

"Do it, Carl." The old woman from the front row had spoken softly but the angels, Carl, and the preacher could hear her and they all looked up. She continued to smile at Carl, while he looked in vain around the room to find the voice he had heard so plainly just moments ago.

Pastor John was still trying to comprehend what he had seen only moments before, as the images of the angels burned fresh in his thoughts and his emotions swirled around him. He struggled to keep singing and desperately tried to focus to see them again. The beauty of that small glimpse into the spiritual realm left him craving more. Slowly, his mind began to refocus on Carl and the others in front of him. Most preachers with any experience at all know when to extend or close an invitation to the altar. John's experience as a preacher told him that the moment for Carl to make a decision had passed for now, so he closed the service and rushed through his goodbyes. Quickly, he walked down the hall to Mr. Robert's room and began to pray silently as he walked.

What do I do, Lord? I want to help this man so much. Please let me be able to reach him. Please help me. I need you so much right now. I don't understand it, Lord. Please be with me and use me. Help me understand how to use this gift.

Meris snapped his wings and filled the hall with light, scattering any demons within the area; but he still did not have permission to attack the one with Carl. Meris and Galdon followed the preacher into Mr. Robert's room, where Flint stood with his sword in hand, facing the demon that continued to cling to Carl's shoulder.

"Steady, Flint." Meris ordered. "His days are numbered either way."

The demon growled and snarled. He spat and jumped at Galdon, who in turn punched the demon square on the jaw.

"I thought we couldn't touch him unless he touched us!" Flint said, as he stepped closer, ready to strike.

"We can retaliate any act of aggression."

"Come on, you mangy beast. Get aggressive with me!" Flint beat his chest and dared the demon to make a move.

"Flint, you can't provoke him!" Meris pulled the young angel back. "You have to be patient or I will put you back in training."

"I'm sorry. I can do this. Trust me, please." Flint closed his eyes and sighed. "I can do this, Meris. I have been with him for so long now."

"I am counting on it." Meris turned to watch the interaction of the preacher with the old man. He loved their stories and conversations. He glanced at Galdon, who nodded knowingly that his own heroics had rubbed off too much on the young and impressionable Nardic. He would have to practice more self-control with both Nardic and Flint, who had been watching him too closely.

Mr. Roberts rubbed his crooked hands together and smiled. "Well, Pastor John, that was quite a sermon. I loved it. I will call that a 12 today."

"On a scale of 1 to 10? Thank you!"

"No, I mean 12 people stayed awake. I was one and you and Carl were two and three. I don't count the workers, though."

John laughed. "You should be listening and not counting."

"Well, if I didn't count, then the number would have only been 11."

Even Carl laughed at that.

"So, you didn't like it?"

"No, I didn't say that. I think that I would have liked it more if you had had the passion from last week."

"What do you mean?"

"Now, you know that I love your sermons and what you preached today was fine; but you are more than fine now and I just don't want you to settle for that anymore. Last week was amazing."

"Thank you, I think."

"Oh gosh. Don't get upset or anything. I just mean for you to use whatever you used last week."

They sat in silence for a moment and then John answered, "I don't really know how."

"Well, I am sure that you will figure it out. Your sermon will do for this week, if you can't find that spark again. I am going to pray for you, though. There is something inside you waiting to get out. Some sort of gift."

John's eyes grew wide and all three angels looked at each other. Meris dove forward and held onto John's shoulders to keep him calm. It was not yet time to reveal the whole story to him yet. The word 'gift' reverberated through the room and John felt flush and then an overwhelming calm.

For the next few minutes, the three men danced around other subjects, while John silently continued to pray for an opportunity to witness more to Carl. There is a fine line between salvation and alienation. Some people can cross it easily; but some people will flee, if they are pushed too much. Forming a relationship with Christ usually starts when a Christian takes the time to first form an earthly relationship with a non-believer. Taking time to connect and love another person takes time; but without that bridge, sharing the Gospel can seem like just another option in a world of many choices. John knew this well and had experienced it throughout his time as a preacher. The most effective and real changes always seemed to be related to a one on one friendship between a Christian and a non-Christian. His ministry was built on this principle; and he firmly believed in numbers of genuine followers and not those who felt just the emotional pull during one moment in time. He had also witnessed genuine conversions that laid waste when no one stepped up to help that person develop his or her faith. He and Lindsey had made one of their goals in the ministry to spread the love of Christ and to do so one person at a time. As he sat there that afternoon enjoying time with Carl and Mr. Roberts, he could see the pain behind Carl's facade; and John knew that this would take more time. He also contemplated the words of Mr. Roberts. He had felt it too. This week's message didn't feel as powerful to him either. Somehow his gift was related to his preaching; and he needed to find out how.

"Pastor John, did I ever tell you about the man who lived next door to me when I was growing up?"

"I don't think so."

"Dad, I don't think we need to tell that one."

"I think the preacher would love to hear it. This man was always outside with his old dog. We could never decide who was older, him or the dog; but he took that dog out every day and walked him around his yard on a leash, or I say walked, more like he stood. For some reason, we all thought it was funny. I think what seemed so strange was that the dog never seemed to care if he was outside or not and they both just stood there. They made a sort of living statue in their own yard."

"That is kind of funny."

"I guess you had to see it; but imagine me with a dog as old as me and every time you looked out your window we were there but in a different spot. I never once saw the man or the dog walk much; but they were outside a lot and just seemed to be in a different spot, standing there looking around every time we came home or left to go somewhere."

John smiled. He was starting to get the visual picture of how comical this might be over time. Carl rolled his eyes and stood. "I need to be going."

John stood and shook Carl's hand. "Thank you for coming today. I hope to see soon."

"Um...Well, thank you too." Carl turned to his dad and patted him on the shoulder. "Dad, I will see you soon." Carl began to walk toward the door and he stopped.

Meris looked at Flint, who shrugged.

Carl turned back around and looked at his father and then at Pastor John. "What is your sermon about next week?"

John silently thanked God for Carl's interest and tried not to sound too anxious, as he answered. "Well, I am starting a series on love. It's a three part sermon series that I just developed."

"Love? So, like marriage and relationships?"

"Much more than that. More about the love of God." John hoped that it sounded appealing. He wasn't sure what Carl was struggling with; but he knew it was a dark secret.

"Okay." Carl turned to leave again.

"I hope you can make it. I was really glad you that came back today." John tried not to sound desperate; but he knew that this next series would be perfect for Carl. He had written it with Carl on his mind.

"Thank you." Carl turned back again with a solemn face; but tears were forming in the corners of his eyes. The demon growled and snarled; and Flint stepped forward again. Carl continued, "I am glad that I came."

John's mind was filtering through his training as a counselor to decide what to say next, when Mr. Robert's chimed in, "Carl, I am glad you came too. I love you, son."

The demon screamed in pain as a light from Heaven radiated the room in response to the outpouring of love and Flint used the moment to reflect the light onto the demon, who fell to the floor in response.

Carl responded, "I love you too, Dad."

That moment would forever be one of Pastor John's greatest memories in all of his ministry. Something passed between that father and son that was beyond words. Over the next few weeks, John witnessed the father and son start to repair a relationship that had obviously been destroyed years ago; and he again wondered what the story was behind both these men and why they both never talked about it.

John was about to leave himself, when he asked, "What ever happened to your neighbor, the one with the dog?"

"Oh, well about a month after he moved, we were talking to another neighbor who knew him better and found out he was only about fifty years old. He looked like he was my age!"

"So, like a hundred?"

Mr. Roberts doubled over laughing and pointed his finger at John. "I deserved that! Crazy, though. We found out he was very sick and we never knew. I think that is why he didn't move much. It made us all feel awful."

"What was wrong with him?"

"I am not sure. I think it was his heart. That is why he didn't have much energy to walk around. Anyway, he got better and occasionally, I would see him at the store and he would wave."

John stood to leave and shook hands with his friend. "I will see you next week. Keep praying for me! I need it. I am going to try to figure out how to up my ratings with you."

"You are doing fine, Pastor John; but I will keep praying. Let us both keep praying for Carl too."

"Absolutely."

After that day, Carl started to come more often to see his father and hear the sermons; but he remained closed to the idea of salvation. He wrestled with his emotions until he finally decided he needed help. The demon struggled to keep attached to Carl and continued to whisper thoughts and ideas to him, while Flint worked on planting positive thoughts and physically blocking the demon when he could. Carl continued to stay and began to enjoy talking with the preacher in his father's room, where the conversation was less personal. He was nowhere near ready to talk about his past; and he wrestled with how anyone, especially God, could want him at all after what he had done.

Chapter 12: New Light

 Several more months passed and John settled into a good rhythm with his visits to the nursing home and his regular ministry at the church, which was starting to grow again. Rosie was now 8 1/2 and John could now see either a shimmer or a glow around her all the time for seemingly no reason. The interactions with Carl were slow and labored; but he could sense that the man was starting to enjoy the services more and even singing some of the songs now. John saw the glow around Lindsey again and was starting to see shadows around different people in the church and at the nursing home; but the shadow around Carl bothered him the most. He knew what that had to mean. The swirling shadows around his in-law's home were also back, causing him great concern as well. He prayed regularly with Lindsey and with Darron; but he wasn't sure how much he should tell them. Most of their conversations were about scripture and how to use a gift like his; and so far, they all decided to not talk about it openly until God revealed more about it to them.

On his visits to the nursing home, John began to see the old lady on the front row with her Bible more regularly attending his services and decided to try to make contact and at least learn her name. Every week she would usually be the first to leave; and he could never seem to break away from the other patrons in time to talk to her directly. After the next Thursday service, John gathered his materials and left to walk toward the nursing home office to try to find out who she was and where to meet with her before he went to visit Mr. Roberts. Rounding the corner, he saw Linda, the manager, and decided to ask her about the elderly woman; but before he could call out to Linda, he heard a small voice.

"Are you looking for me?"

John spun around to face the frail old lady sitting in her wheelchair in the doorway of one of the residential rooms. He noted the glow around the old woman and found it both appealing and familiar, yet he felt foolish and somewhat scared too. The lights, the glowing, the angels, the flashes, and now facing this lady all seemed normal and his apprehension was replaced by peace, leaving him longing for more.

"Yes, I was actually. I wanted to talk to you."

"Well, come on in then." She moved back to allow John to enter and she closed the door behind him. "So what do you want to talk about?"

John looked around the room, which was smaller than Mr. Robert's large suite; and it was humbly decorated with only a few items. The bed and dresser looked like they belonged to some distant era, when buying furniture had seemed important and required a great deal of effort and time. Now, these relics were all that remained of a home that had once been fussed over and decorated for years. John scanned the pictures and counted a dozen or more on top of the dresser, most of them of a young woman and man; and only one of a child. The child was small and young and the picture looked like it had been taken years ago. He turned to see the woman facing him, still smiling.

"I guess I wanted to formally meet you, first. I don't even know your name."

"Forgive me, my name is Minnamia Hunt; but please just call me Mia. Don't try to figure out my first name, my mom was just plain crazy to come up with that. Believe me, I gave her fits about it when I was young."

John smiled in response and said, "Okay, then Mia it is."

"Pastor John, I need to talk with you about so many things. I hope you have some time. If not, we can meet another day to continue. I think that you will need some time to listen to what I am going to say."

What is she talking about? John thought and then he spoke, "I've noticed that...I guess I have wanted to talk to you several times; but you seem to leave so quickly--"

"I know. I never hang around after the sermon. I apologize; but it is overwhelming to me each week and I usually need time to just rest."

Before he could ask his first question, she began, "Well, I need to tell you that you sort of need to understand what is going on with everything. I have had the gift for many years now. It takes some time to get used to it."

"Gift?"

"Yes, the ability to see the spiritual world."

John could feel his heart beginning to race; and he sat down in a frail looking chair next to a table. "So you see things too?"

"Oh, Pastor, I have seen so many things."

Questions swirled through his mind and he wasn't sure what to ask first. "Have you had the gift your whole life?"

"No. It started for me when I was in my middle years. I had been sick for many years and nearly died. I stayed in the hospital a lot and when I got better, I had the gift. My husband was so afraid he would lose me--it was an awful time for us both. That's him with me in all the pictures." Mia pointed to one of the many picture frames on her dresser. "That one is my favorite. It was taken the week after we were married." The images were slightly faded; but in the picture, Mia was sitting in a small Queen Anne chair with her proud new husband standing beside her with his hand on her shoulder.

John studied the picture and could easily see Mia's familiar smile and nodded. Mia had been a beautiful woman in her youth. "Is that your child?" he asked, as he pointed to the picture of the toddler.

Mia's face changed quickly; and for the first time, John saw her frown.

"No, that is a very special person. I have always been a law-abiding citizen, Pastor John; but my husband circumvented the law one time and obtained that picture through a favor from a friend. I am not supposed to have that."

John looked at her with a puzzled expression. "Why is it against the law for you to have that child's picture?"

"That child...well let's just say that he was a miracle to me. My sickness that I spoke of was severe kidney disease. Several months of dialysis and medicines helped me stay alive; but I needed a transplant or I would not last much longer. That little boy died and his parents donated his kidneys; and I was the lucky one who received them."

"I didn't know that a child could donate a kidney to an adult."

"Oh, yes. Even the kidneys from an infant can, in most cases, be placed in an adult. Believe me, I became an expert on all of this. Anyway, I am eternally indebted to that beautiful young child and the selfless act of his family."

"I--"

"Yes, I know. You have a donated organ too."

"How do you know that? I don't really talk about it."

"I have been asking some questions."

John tried to manage the thoughts in his head and determine the next question. There was so much that he didn't quite understand. He looked back at the picture of the child.

"He was beautiful, wasn't he? I thought I would never know who my donor was. They are very adamant that the organ donor not be from the same town; and I never could find out his full name. I was allowed to write a letter to the parents a year after I had recovered; but the letter was returned to me along with another letter a few days later. The family must have read the first one and then decided to return it. I never did understand that. Anyway, the second letter confused me and I wanted to know more about this family. My husband knew how much it meant to me and called in a few favors. Within a few months, he was able to get that picture over there. I framed it and kept it all these years. The boy's name was Lou."

John thought about this for a moment; but he still desperately wanted to discuss the glow and the angels, and so much more. His phone buzzed and he looked down. It was a text from Lindsey. Quickly, he responded and then looked back up at Mia.

"Sorry, my wife was worried about me."

"It's fine, you should never keep her waiting. Treasure her, Pastor John. My time with my husband, Madison, was too short. Anyway, I guess you want to talk about the angels."

John looked up, surprised at her bluntness. "Yes, I thought I was going crazy at first. It started with lights and glowing; and I thought I had some type of terminal disease."

Mia laughed. "Well, you do have a terminal disease Pastor John, it's called humanity. You are not getting out of here alive!" They both laughed and then she continued, "Pastor John, the light and the glow, well, they are all from God. The darkness is demonic. Have you seen that too?"

"Yes, I think so. I sometimes see some weird shadows swimming in the air; but mainly, I just see a glow around my wife, my daughter, and sometimes around you. Then, during the service here, I saw a flash and--"

"That was very special!" Mia smiled and patted John's arm. "I hope we both get to witness something like that again. I have never seen so many angels at once."

"That was the first time I have ever seen an actual angel. So you saw them too?"

"Pastor John, I see them all the time. I hear them too, sometimes before I see them."

John's mouth fell open and in any other situation he might have believed this woman was crazy; but he had seen them too. "How often do you see them?"

Mia laughed again. "Pastor John, you have one standing behind you right now. I thought you knew!"

John jumped to his feet and whipped around but saw nothing. His face was pale and his breathing increased. Was he scared or excited or both?

"It's okay. He is with you all the time. In fact, he brings the light on you as you preach. It is beautiful to see. Can you not see the light as you preach?"

John backed up to the chair and slowly sat back down, then immediately jumped up.

Mia laughed. "Don't worry, you won't sit on him."

Gingerly, John sat back down. He stared off into space and tried to put the information into his mind in a way that would fit. There was too much to comprehend and his mind was too full. Of course he believed in angels; but he had never contemplated ever seeing one, at least not until he died. He looked over at Mia; and she was smiling and nodding, as if listening to someone speak. When she noticed he was looking at her, she put her fingers to her lips and looked back at the space beside John. His eyes followed her gaze but saw nothing. The glow was around her again; but he felt an overwhelming peace, despite his incredibly confused and conflicted state. Finally, she looked back at him.

"Pastor, you will learn more soon. For now, we think you have seen and heard enough for one day. Go on home."

"I...uh...okay." John stood and walked to the door. He turned and thanked her and began to walk down the hall toward Mr. Roberts' room.

She said, 'we think you have heard enough.' Was she listening to an angel or is she just crazy? Am I crazy too? I know what I saw today and it was very real. I need to talk to Darron again.

He reached the room and was glad when Mr. Roberts announced that he was tired and cut their visit short. As John drove home in complete silence, his thoughts swirled in a million directions around him. By the time he arrived home, he had convinced himself that Mia was not just an elderly woman at the end of her days. He had seen some of this too, so if Mia was crazy, that would make him crazy too. He leaned forward with his head on the steering wheel and began to pray. His eyes were closed and he prayed fervently for strength and understanding and to be able to keep this gift that he now embraced instead of shunned. That evening, he wrestled with how much to share with Lindsey; but he didn't want her to worry and he decided to wait until he talked with Darron. Maybe the two of them could decipher what it all meant.

The next day, Darron and John met for their weekly Friday meeting in the large conference room to review the weekend ahead. John arrived at the church early noting Darron's car was not there yet, so he decided to head to his office, where he knelt beside his desk and prayed for guidance. He desperately wanted to use this gift the right way, even though he didn't really understand how. Light radiated through the room and John opened his eyes. All around him was a bright light that made him feel safe and loved. The light was brighter than anything he had ever seen, yet it did not blind him. Just as John was about to speak, his phone rang and the light disappeared. John sat staring at the office, which now seemed drab and almost painful to look at. He rubbed his eyes and wanted to cry. Something inside him wanted to be with that light again and he couldn't stand the thought of being without it. Galdon watched the preacher and realized that he had seen too much of the Glory of God and needed help. He placed his hands on his shoulders and looked up to the Father, who filled the room with peace. The phone continued to ring and John suddenly felt better. He fumbled for his phone and answered, "Hello?"

"Hey John!"

"Hey Darron."

"Are you okay? You sound a little weird."

"Yeah. Yeah, I'm fine. Where are you right now?"

"I was just leaving the hospital. Remember I told you I was going by there today instead of tomorrow because of my daughter's soccer game?"

"Oh, yeah right." He had forgotten that Darron was going by this morning to check on several members that had been sick. "So, how is everyone?" John didn't want to go through all the small talk. He wanted to go back to the moment before when he was bathed in the light. A deep yearning began to build in his soul and he had difficulty listening to his friend. Galdon spread his wings slightly and John relaxed again. He wanted to talk with Darron about what he had just seen; but he didn't even know where to start.

"We only have Mrs. Fisher in the hospital right now, but she was enough to keep me busy all morning."

John laughed. Mrs. Fisher loved to talk and had a story about everything. Her stories were not simple and usually rambled on for what seemed like hours before ending abruptly with seemingly no connection to the beginning. John was relieved it was Darron's week for hospital visits. "So, is she doing okay?"

"Yes, she has been battling some type of hip problem. Looks like she may need a hip replacement.

"Sorry to hear that."

"Are we still meeting today?"

John answered, "Yes, I am ready whenever you get here." He took off his glasses and wiped his eyes, as he leaned back in his office chair. It was only morning and he felt exhausted. Why was he so tired? He had prayed late into the night after Lindsey and Rosie were asleep; but he had done that countless times before and had never been this exhausted. The strain of it all was beginning to wear him down and he knew he needed to take some time off soon to relax. As quickly as he thought this through, he began to feel better. Galdon was using his power to minister and help the young pastor. This was another amazing ability the angels had been given from God to help humans. It was used sparingly, as it required a great deal of the angel's strength. Galdon would need several minutes to recover himself; but Meris had now arrived to assist.

"Okay, well I should be there in about fifteen minutes. I will just head to the conference room."

"Sure. See you there." John hung up and looked around the room. His heart was full of emotions that he didn't understand. Part of him was exhilarated and happy; and mixed within these feelings was the yearning he still felt to be with the light again. There was also a strong desire building to tell everyone what he had seen; but there was another part of him that wondered what everyone would think of this gift. He didn't worry about the world as much as he did his own congregation. This was not something you could just openly talk about without sounding like a crazy person. He had to admit that he had always been very skeptical in the past, when he heard people talk about their experiences with angels. Of course, he believed in angels; but there was a comfort in believing something without ever having that belief challenged. He knew that there would be many Christians that would be blessed by what he was seeing; but many others would doubt what they could not see themselves. It occurred to him that this was not too unlike the days when Jesus revealed Himself and the people rejected Him. Many times in his ministry he was asked why God doesn't just do a bunch of miracles or show Himself more today. Of course, he would answer that miracles do still happen and site some story or another; but the truth of it was that John firmly believed that people would reject Jesus just as much or more today as they did back then, even with all the miracles.

As John thought this through, he instinctively picked up a pen and made some notes. Within a few minutes, he had another sermon and knew with all of his heart that he needed to deliver it this week. He now knew that when he had something laid so strongly on his heart, he didn't want to ignore it. He quickly gathered his notes and his Bible and headed to the conference room to wait on Darron. Galdon was resting and recovering his strength, while Meris lifted his hands from Pastor John's shoulders and stepped back. The two angels exchanged a smile, knowing that God's message was flowing well through this man.

The two preacher's schedules had been very full lately even with the decline in the congregation. John had a lot to review with Darron, especially with the change in his sermon; but he really needed to just talk about his gift and how much it was changing.

"Are you sure you're okay? You look like you saw..." Darron's face changed, as he realized what he was about to say.

Before he could speak again, John answered, "I'm seeing more things now."

Darron broke into a smile and leaned back in his chair with his lanky arms behind his head. He was a 6' 2" and most of it came from his long legs, with arms to match. If he had had more ability to dribble and shoot, not many would have been able to get a shot past his wing span on the basketball court. "So, are there more demons at the in-laws' home again?"

John watched his friend, who seemed to be enjoying this a little too much. "Well, yes actually."

Darron could hear the change in his friend's voice and his smile disappeared as he cleared his throat. "So, is that it, or is there more?"

Both men were silent, while John tried to find the right words. "Darron, I'm seeing much more now." John looked down at his notes. Why was this so hard? They should be rejoicing together.

Darron's tone changed and he leaned forward. "Tell me what you are seeing."

For the next thirty minutes, John described what he was seeing and the encounter with Mia. He also described the new sermon he felt led to do this week. Darron listened and asked questions, while he sat and made some notes. When John stopped talking, Darron looked at the paper in front of him. "John, this is an amazing gift. I think that you and Mia have been incredibly blessed with the ability to see some of the spiritual world around us. I don't know why the rest of us can't see it; but I will say that there are a lot of people who would love to see what you see, including me. As for the sermon, I think that if God has led you that direction, you should follow it."

"I really want this gift, Darron; and I feel blessed and humbled that God would allow me to have it. I'm worried, though. I'm not sure what people will think about it or how much I should even tell anyone else."

"I don't think we should shout it out all at once. Why don't we see where God leads you with it?"

More silence followed and Darron could see John fighting his emotions. After several long seconds, John answered, "I do want to follow God's Will with this. I just...well it makes it hard to just keep on going."

Darron was not sure that he had heard his friend correctly. He leaned forward, as if that would help him understand better. "What do you mean?"

"It is more beautiful than anything you can ever imagine. It would almost be easier if I knew it was a medical condition or something or if I had never been allowed to see it at all. Seeing that glimpse of the angels and the light is almost too much to bear. I really wish I could explain it to you in a way that makes sense. The beauty...well, Heaven has got to be more unbelievable than we can ever imagine."

"That's it, then."

"That's what?"

"That must be what the gift is for. You can use what you have seen to preach and explain the majesty of Heaven as well as the spiritual beings that are around us every day."

"Yeah, I definitely believe that that is part of it. There is more, though. I can feel it now. Something is happening and I can actually feel it."

"Like what kind of feeling?"

"Well, just a joy and an overwhelming peace when I am around the light and an incredible gloom and fear around the shadows. It's exactly what you would think it would be like; but it has a really strong pull on me."

"Wow. That is amazing! Do you know how many people would love to experience that?"

"I am not sure. It's not something I ever sought; but anyway, it's here. I need you to keep praying for me."

"Of course."

"I need you to commit to praying for me every day. Please promise me that you will."

"Sure, John. You do the same. We all need it, I am sure."

"I will. Thanks, man."

"No problem."

The two men prayed together for the next few minutes and wrapped up their meeting. The surge of power immediately lifted to Heaven and was distributed to the angels surrounding John. For the next hour, John wrote the next three week's sermon outlines and began searching through scriptures to use. After another thirty minutes, he had a complete sermon series ready to deliver.

Chapter 13: Expanding World

Carl arrived early to see his father the next week. He and Mr. Roberts were the first ones in the activity hall, which surprised John when he arrived. They barely had time to speak before the others began to arrive. The service went well and John was able to remove himself easily from the residents and get to Mr. Roberts's room within just a few minutes. He noticed that Mia had not come this week; and he made a mental note to stop by her room later. Carl had stayed to see John after the service this week, which partially surprised John even though he had been praying for this. He silently thanked God and asked him for words of wisdom to help Carl.

"How are you doing, Carl? Glad you stayed to visit."

Carl nodded and looked at his feet. John turned to Mr. Roberts and shook his hand. "So, what did you think today, Mr. Roberts?"

Mr. Roberts rubbed his pointed chin as he thought and then answered. "I think I will give that one a 6."

John laughed and said, "Explain."

With a twinkle in his eye, Mr Roberts stated, "Well, of the ten people who stayed awake, six of them seemed to at least be looking at you."

Both men laughed and Carl smiled.

"Well, I am glad that six people enjoyed it."

"Oh, I didn't say that they enjoyed it, just that they were looking at you."

John laughed. "Good, good. Maybe I can get seven next week."

"I hope so. On the serious side, I did enjoy some of the scripture you quoted and the examples you gave. I think that your ideas and scripture references were sound."

"Thank you. Is there anything you would change?"

"I guess not. I think you have a winner this week."

"Wonderful! I was truly inspired for this one." John turned to Carl and continued, "What did you think?"

"Um...I don't know, I mean I guess it was fine." In truth, Carl had loved it; but he was not able to admit that just yet.

"No, really. Did you follow it and understand it all? I am trying hard to not get too technical. Lindsey, my wife, is always saying to keep it all simple."

Carl cleared his throat and looked down before he answered. "No, I think I got it."

"Good. Well, enough sermon talk. How was this week, Mr. Roberts?"

"I would say a 4."

"Okay. Tell me why a 4." John smiled and looked over at Carl, who seemed to be waiting for the answer as well.

"Well, I was able to count four people who had visitors, including me."

Carl looked confused and asked, "Four people? How many residents live here?"

Both John and Mr. Roberts answered simultaneously, "One hundred fifty."

"That is terrible! Where are their families?"

"The same place you were not too long ago." Mr. Roberts answered.

"I know." Carl said and hung his head.

Mr. Roberts reached over and patted his son's hand. "It's really okay. I don't blame you. I wouldn't visit here either. Too depressing."

The three men talked and visited for another half hour and finally, John stood to prepare to leave. "I hate to go; but I need to get some work done back at the office. I have a counseling session later today that I want to prepare for."

Carl perked up. "Counseling? I didn't know preachers did counseling."

"Yes, in reality, I do quite a bit of it."

"For what?"

"Really anything. Today, for example, I am working with a new Christian; but I work with people who struggle with just about anything from their marriages to drug problems, etc."

"Why would you work with a new Christian? I thought Jesus was supposed to solve all the problems for someone."

John thought for a moment before he answered. "I am sorry if I ever made it sound that way. It is far from that. Jesus gives us freedom from sin; but we will always have problems. Our problems should draw us closer to God by making us need Him more."

"I don't mean to offend you; but that sounds kind of mean. I thought we had Free Will to choose what we wanted to do. Now you say that He sets up a system where we need Him to fix our problems. Sounds like He has stacked the deck against us."

"Carl--"

John held up his hand to Mr. Roberts. "No, it's okay. I like the questions. Questions are how we all learn." He turned to Carl and responded. "I am going to try to say this in simple terms; but like I said before, my wife says I am too complicated with my words sometimes. You are right; but you are also wrong. Yes, we have the freedom to decide what to do, whom to worship, what to believe, etc. We also have the right to make decisions that affect everything that we do. We don't always have control over what happens to us; but sometimes we make decisions that affect our future. Either way, we have problems throughout life. We are not promised a perfect life, only redemption from our sins-- kind of an absolute absolution."

"I like that: absolute absolution or how about supreme sanctification. I need a T-shirt that says that!" Mr. Roberts was smiling.

"Does that answer your question, Carl?"

"I guess. I think it would just be easier if He showed Himself. I think I would find it easier."

"He did. He came and performed miracles and tried to teach as many people as he could...and they crucified Him."

The room fell silent and then Carl responded. "I never thought about it like that. I really think that if I saw a miracle, I would believe."

"So many people feel like that; but many who saw the miracles over two thousand years ago were the ones who still demanded that He be put to death. Even His own disciples denied who He was."

"Well, even if I didn't need that, why would God want me? I am a terrible man. I don't deserve to go to Heaven."

"None of us do. That is why we are all so thankful. The Bible says in Romans 3:23: 'All have sinned and fall short of the glory of God.' That means that all of us deserve Hell. Jesus paid the price that we are all supposed to pay."

Carl dropped his head and then looked up at Pastor John. "I don't think that He would want me after what I have done."

John leaned forward in his chair and then answered, "Carl, Jesus is perfect. He defeated all sin for all time. The Bible also says in Romans 8:38-39: 'Nothing can separate us from God's love.' That means that God will always love you no matter what."

"I am not a good person. There is no way that I could be accepted. I mean, look at someone like you. How could God want me to be included with you? I have done nothing but cause pain."

Mr. Roberts interjected. "That is not true, Carl. You have brought me a lot of joy in my life."

"Yeah, maybe when I was young. I have been a terrible adult and I know I have only caused you pain since then. How could God love me?"

"Carl, everyone has sinned like I said before. Now, the Bible also teaches in Romans 6:23: 'For the wages of sin is death; but the gift of God is eternal life through Jesus Christ our Lord.' Then the Bible goes on to say in Romans 5:8: 'But God demonstrates His own love toward us, in that while we were still sinners, Christ died for us.' That means that Christ died for us all and he paid the price for us--you and me and your father and everyone while we were still sinners and when we did not deserve it."

"Pastor John, is Romans the only book in the Bible that you know?"

John and Mr. Roberts laughed. "That is called the Roman Road, Carl. It is a series of verses in that one book of the Bible that has become a traditional way to explain the entire concept of salvation to someone."

"Oh. It does make it sound simple. I guess I still don't think God would want me. I don't think you would care, if you knew. I deserve Hell." Carl hung his head again. "I need to get going." Carl stood and hugged his father and shook John's hand. After he was gone, Mr. Roberts and John sat in silence for about a minute and then Mr. Roberts spoke.

"Pastor John, I know you mean well; but I just want to make sure that you understand Carl. He has been through quite a lot."

"I don't really know him like you, of course. I do think that today was genuine. He seemed to understand and really be searching. Maybe he will think about what I said."

"I hope so. He has had a rough life. I guess he will tell you all about it when he is ready. It's not my place to do it. He lost his whole family over his past mistakes and pushed me away so hard that I let him. I resented him when my health declined and I only had my daughter and son-in-law left to help me. They are the ones that stuffed me in here; and I don't have much to say about them at all. Losing my wife and having such a terrible son-in-law controlling my daughter, I decided to let the past be the past with Carl. I forgave him for the way he treated me and let him back into my life."

"I'm sorry to hear about your family problems. When did you lose your wife?"

"It's been many years now and she was sick for such a long time. Unfortunately we don't get a pass on suffering down here. I think that I will have a talk with God about that some day."

"I'll bet you will." John smiled thinking that he would like to be there for that conversation. "I can only imagine what you will say."

"That's it? I thought you would for sure launch into the whole we-learn-to-lean-on-God-through-suffering speech. I thought that pastors had to memorize that or something."

"No, you have suffered enough. You don't need to suffer through that too."

Mr. Roberts laughed and pointed his finger at John. "That's why I like you, son. You get me."

"Oh no! That is scary to think about."

Mr. Roberts laughed again and then his expression grew pensive. "Just be careful. That boy has a haunted past."

Pastor John nodded and stood to leave. "Sounds like you both have."

Mr. Roberts sighed. "There is no way to describe it. When my wife died, it nearly killed me. Thank goodness she didn't have to witness everything with Carl and my daughter. Anyway, be gentle with Carl. He has a lot of baggage."

"You know me well enough to know that I won't push him. He can tell me what he wants and leave out what he wants. I am just interested in helping him move on with his life."

"Yes, I agree. He needs to move on. I do want you to know that he was in prison, though. You should at least know that; and then you can watch your back from there."

The word prison rattled John slightly, but only for a second. Linda, the nursing home manager, had mentioned jail; but John had not really considered the meaning behind those words until now. He had no idea what Carl had done; but he wanted to help this man move forward. Before he left the nursing home, he wanted to visit briefly with Mia again; but he couldn't find her. Her room was locked with a 'Do Not Disturb' sign outside, so he decided to head to the office and get his work done, so that he could head home to his own family.

John drove to his office praying the entire time, as his mind churned through all the events of the day as well as all the strange things he had been seeing. He arrived at the office to find that his counseling session had been cancelled, so he decided to go home. As he drove, a sense of urgency came over him and he really felt the need to talk to someone again. Maybe he should call Darron. Telling Lindsey seemed inevitable and necessary at this point; and he decided that tonight he would find a time to talk with her.

Meris rode on top of John's car and watched, as a large shadow followed closely behind the car. John's prayers gave the angel enough power to create a large bubble of light around the car that prevented the shadow from getting close; but Meris knew that this was more than just an ordinary demon. When they arrived home, Meris called in a few other angels to stand guard throughout the night, while he kept watch over the shadow that hunkered down across the street. Great concern spread across Meris's face when the shadow seemed undaunted by the angel patrol.

The evening routine went smoothly, despite how anxious John was to talk with his wife; and he waited until late in the evening after Lindsey had put Rosie to bed so that they would have plenty of time to discuss everything. He spent the next hour explaining all that he had seen both with the glow that had been growing around Lindsey and the group of angels he had seen during the service at the nursing home. He told her about talking to Darron and meeting the sweet old lady named Mia. Lindsey held his hand and listened intently until he was finished.

"John, I have never heard of anything like that before. I think that your spiritual gift is special and you should never run from it."

"Darron thinks so as well and I really am thankful; but..I guess I'm...scared."

"So, a preacher who is scared that he is experiencing something spiritual. That is more strange than what you have been seeing."

"I want to use it; but I'm not sure what I am supposed to do or who I should tell. What do I do with a gift like that except sound crazy?"

"You don't sound crazy to me. Doesn't the Bible teach us in Ephesians 6:12 'We wrestle not against flesh and blood but against principalities, against powers, against the rulers of the darkness of this world, against spiritual wickedness in high places'?"

"Yes, it does. I know that I am seeing things that are not of this world. I know in my heart that I have seen angels and it was the most beautiful thing in the world; but Lindsey, I feel like I am losing my mind. I never know when something will appear."

"I guess it would scare me a little too, not knowing. You did say that Rosie and I always glow, right? Is there anything else that is always the same?"

"I haven't really considered that. Yes, there is always a light or a glow around you both and Mia. I mean it's always a light but I don't always see it. The dark shadows are always in the same places too."

"What dark shadows?"

John kicked himself mentally. He had not planned to tell Lindsey this yet. He stood and walked around the room and finally sat back down beside her.

"John, you are scaring me. Are you seeing demons too?"

He grabbed her hands and shook his head. "No, just dark areas or shadows."

"So, shadows. I see shadows too."

John shook his head and looked directly at her. "No, like shadows that move when nothing else moves and shadows that seem to be attached to people."

Lindsey kept her eyes on him as she asked, "Like who?"

John's eyes dropped for a moment and then returned to hers. "It doesn't really matter. I guess the important thing is to understand what God wants me to do with this."

"John, tell me who has a shadow attached to them. You are scaring me."

He cleared his throat and pulled his hands away to rub his face. When he looked back at her, she sank back into the couch with tears welling in her eyes. Finally, he spoke in a soft voice and said, "Your mother."

Lindsey's hand instinctively went to her mouth and tears slowly traveled down her cheeks. John pulled her into his arms and they held each other for several minutes.

"Now do you see why I want to know what it all means? I need to understand it and how God wants me to use it."

"Who would even know that? Where would you go to get an answer like that except directly to God?"

"I have been praying, believe me. More than ever. Please pray for me about this. We need help."

"Of course I will. Is there anything else? Anything that I should know?"

John didn't want to hurt her any more; but he couldn't lie either. "I think it would be best if you don't go to your parent's house without me."

"Why?"

John hesitated and then answered. "Because I have seen a large number of dark shadows flying around their home. They aren't always there; but it scares me every time I see it."

"How long have you been seeing this? You should have told me!"

"I am telling you. I thought I saw it a while ago; but I definitely saw it two days ago when I went to pick up Rosie. It's hard to explain, though. The shadows don't seem to be able to get to the home. It's like they are being kept away."

"Kept away by what? Did you see any angels?"

"No, but I don't see everything spiritual. I was talking with Mia and she could see an angel that I couldn't see. She said there is an angel that is always with me."

"A guardian?"

"I guess. I really don't know. I believe we have guardian angels; but I never really thought about it being so real. I guess I just don't understand all that is going on."

"Me either. It is a gift, though. I really believe that."

"If it is a gift, I'm not sure that I want it. How can I use it to help anyone? Everyone will just think that I am crazy."

"You keep saying that; but I don't think you are crazy."

"Please pray for me. I am not sure what to do with all of this."

"I always pray for you. It will be okay. God would never give you something like this if He didn't have a reason."

John nodded and tried to believe her.

"Maybe you should call Darron and talk to him again."

"I guess so." John looked at his watch. It was only 9:30 PM and Darron was a night owl.

"You know Darron is still up and won't mind. You would do the same for him."

John nodded and picked up his phone while Lindsey left him alone to talk. Darron answered on the second ring and they talked for over an hour by phone and then agreed to extend their weekly meeting to talk and pray some more. Darron promised to keep praying for his friend and both pastors decided to do some research and compare notes when they met. The rest of the week was uneventful, as John continued his normal activities at the church and returned to preach at the nursing home. Mia did not attend the service again, which was beginning to concern him. After visiting with Mr. Roberts, John went to her room; but it was still locked with a sign posted outside that the room was being cleaned. He wanted to try to find Linda and ask about Mia; but his phone buzzed with an urgent message from his secretary about a church member needing Pastor John. He sighed and headed back to the church.

Chapter 14: A Preacher's Life

Wednesday

John sat in his office reviewing some notes from the building committee and their recommendations. Fortunately, they had found a repair man for the heating and cooling system who was going to volunteer his time if the church would pay for any supplies. The search for a new building was narrowing down as well. He heard a small tap on his door and looked up as his secretary, Mary, nervously entered.

"Pastor John, I am sorry to bother you, but there is someone here to see you. He came in off the street and asked to talk to you as soon as possible."

"Can you make him an appointment? I am due at the hospital soon for some extra visits."

"I tried, but he was insistent that he see you right now. He said it was urgent."

John stacked his papers and sighed. "Let him in. I will see him; but please tell him I only have a few minutes."

"Sure thing, pastor."

Mary exited and returned, leading in a well dressed man with an air of distinction.

"What can I do for you today?" John waited, while the man looked around the room and then back at the pastor.

The man sat in a chair across from John and answered, "I need to talk with you about your church."

"Well, I am about to leave for some visitations at the hospital. Is there any way that you can come back another day? My secretary can find a time for you in my schedule next week." John felt a strange chill in the air and looked up at his vent and then over at the nearby window to find the source. The window was closed and secure and the vent had not been touched.

The man looked at John for a long minute and smiled. "Of course, I can do that. I apologize for interrupting your busy schedule." The smile lingered on his lips; and John felt the chill again.

The man stood to leave and again locked eyes with the pastor. John felt his knees weaken slightly, sensing something very powerful lurking behind the man's facade; and it was both frightening and alluring at the same time. He was about to answer the man again, when instead, the man offered his hand and said, "My name is...well, you can just call me Mr. B. I will look forward to meeting with you soon."

The name didn't phase John because many people used fake names; but he had never seen someone use such an obvious one. The two men exchanged a handshake and Mr. B left to find Mary to schedule an appointment.

John stood by his desk and gathered the few items he needed to take with him and waited a few extra minutes to make sure Mr. B had plenty of time to make his appointment and leave. He didn't want to seem rude and rush past; but he also wanted to talk with Mary before he left. When he was sure the man was gone, he moved toward the reception area.

"Hey, Mary. Did you get my schedule ready for next week like I asked? I am going straight home after my visits at the hospital today. I want to take a look at it."

"Yes, I have it ready." Mary looked past John with a confused expression.

"Where is Mr. B?"

"He left."

"Oh, Pastor John! I am so sorry that we interrupted you; but Mr. B was very adamant that he meet with you today."

"Well, we met. Did he make an appointment?"

Mary looked puzzled and replied, "What do you mean?"

"He was supposed to come here and make an appointment."

"I never saw him leave. He must have gone out the side door."

John shrugged and grabbed his schedule, then thanked Mary. As he walked to his car, he glanced down at the print out of the next week's appointments. Several were standard meetings with various committees and one was with a disgruntled nursery worker. He was about to stuff it inside his notebook when he saw an entry for his 1:00 PM meeting with a Mr. B printed clearly in the column for next Tuesday. He opened the car door and shoved his papers and notebook over onto the passenger seat and grabbed his phone to call Mary.

"Hey Mary."

"Yes, pastor? What do you need?"

"I was looking through the schedule for next week. You said Mr. B never came by the desk and made an appointment, right?"

"Yes, that is correct."

"Can you pull up the schedule on your computer and tell me who my 1:00 PM appointment is with next Tuesday?"

"Sure. Hang on." John could hear her typing. "Um...it says here that you have a 1:00 PM with..." Mary gasped and then answered, "Mr. B."

"Yes, that is what I have too."

"But, Pastor John, I was here the entire time. I mean, I turned around to grab some files from under the coffee pot; but I would have seen or heard him. How did the appointment get onto my computer?"

"I don't know. Maybe Mr. B can tell us that next Tuesday."

"Okay."

Meris, Galdon, and Nardic all stood outside the church and discussed how to handle this latest development. A large group of demons were assembled now near the pastor's home and the church. Meris spoke first and with authority,

"We now know how important this has become. Do not back down and stand your ground. We need all of our power to help the pastor. He has no idea what is coming."

Galdon glowed slightly and Nardic whipped out his sword. "I will never stop! They will not win this battle!"

Galdon placed his hand on Nardic and spoke gently, "We will win. It is written so; but we have to be patient and go with the Father's plan. His will and His plan are perfect."

Meris nodded in approval at Galdon, who was learning to keep his behavior in check around the young and impressionable Nardic.

John hung up the phone and continued on his way to the hospital, deep in thought and slightly concerned. He did not like this man that had waltzed into his church, demanded a meeting, exited so easily, and somehow managed to get on the church computer without anyone knowing how. He would get to the bottom of it next week. For now, he had enough on his mind to think about. He pulled into the hospital and grabbed his list. Only two visits today and one should be short; but the second visit could be fairly involved.

John greeted everyone at the nurse's station on the cardiac wing and asked where he could find Mrs. Jensen. She had had some chest pain and was brought in for some tests. After visiting with her for about a half hour, he said goodbye and headed to the nurse's station on the surgical floor.

As he approached, Ann Montgomery, an elderly nurse, looked up from her paperwork and stated, "Oh hey, Pastor John."

"Hey Ann. Do you know where I can find Carl Roberts?"

She smiled and answered, "I think Mr. Roberts is in room 306. You can go on down."

John thanked Ann and walked slowly down to the room, while he considered how to approach Carl. He stood outside the door and said a short prayer asking for guidance and wisdom before he entered the room. John had developed a good relationship with Carl over the last several months but had not been able to really connect with him. There was a part of Carl that seemed locked behind a hidden wall that remained unreachable no matter what John said or did. When he received the request to come to the hospital to visit Carl, John was more than surprised.

With the prayer finished, John gently knocked on the door to room 306 and he heard Carl's voice telling him to come in.

"Hey Carl, how are you doing?"

When the preacher walked through the door, a low growl erupted from the corner of the room, as the demon that had tormented Carl for years stepped forward. Meris followed Pastor John into the room and the demon immediately cowered on the floor.

"Oh hey, Pastor John. I guess I'm doing okay."

"So I hear you have been having a little trouble with your gallbladder, is that right?"

"Yeah. It bothers me from time to time; but yesterday it hit me hard and it had to come out. I feel better now."

"Do you need anything? I think my wife would be angry if I didn't let her at least set up some meals for you when you get home."

"Oh... I guess that would be fine. I haven't really thought about that. I'm supposed to go home tomorrow." Carl's mind was reeling. He wasn't sure if he wanted any of those church people getting so close to him; but home-cooked meals were very appealing to a single man. He had long since been divorced since...well...since everything had changed.

The two men sat in silence for a few minutes and John silently prayed.

Please God, if I can help this man in some way, please show me how. Please let his heart open up to me. He is holding something back. Please help him let it go.

Meris used the extra prayer power to shove the squirming demon outside the building, where he was forced to stay for the remainder of the visit.

"Pastor?" John looked up and Carl's eyes were full of tears.

"Yes?"

"Can I tell you something? There is something that is difficult for me to talk about; but I want you to know this about me. I want you to understand why I always thought that God would not want me."

"Carl, God could never stop wanting you. There is nothing you can do or say that could make him not want you."

"You have told me that before; but I am still struggling with something. I know that you say I can be forgiven; but you don't know what I have done. What I've done is worse than you can ever imagine. I am fairly sure that everyone at the church would probably hate me too, if they found out the truth. I know God has to hate me."

"No, Carl. God doesn't hate you. He can't. He *is* love. I don't think anyone at the church would ever hate you either. I know that I couldn't hate you no matter what."

Carl put his hand over his eyes for a moment to gather himself. "I've done something and I am having a hard time believing God can forgive me."

"You know, I think that about myself sometimes. That is what makes salvation so amazing. When you give yourself over to God, it just doesn't matter what you have done. God wipes your slate clean and continues to do so. Jesus was the perfect sacrifice, wiping away all of sin forever for those who will just believe and accept Him."

"But, I didn't just lie or cheat or steal! I have sinned in the worst way possible!"

John looked at the man before him and felt pity. Why wouldn't he just listen to him? "Carl, all sin is equal to God."

"How? How can a murder be the same as telling a lie?"

The words fell like a hammer and John stood still for a moment before he answered. "I don't know."

"What? A preacher without an answer?"

"There are many things that I don't understand or know about God. I do know this: He loves you and wants you to love Him. He has not given up on you."

"Why? Why am I so important? There are so many other people in the world--so many that are innocent and deserving."

"No one is innocent or deserving. We all deserve Hell. He would have sent His son if you were the only human alive."

"You are wrong. There are innocent people." Carl broke down and cried. The pain spilled out with the tears and John simply waited and prayed. The power from his prayer caused a faint glow to begin to grow around the edge of the room. John noticed it immediately and watched it grow with each word from his prayer. As he stopped praying, the glow began to reduce. Within seconds of him ending his prayer for Carl, a thought entered his mind: *When I pray, the glow grows. The power from the prayer is somehow connected to the glow.* He turned his attention to the broken man before him.

"Carl, no one is perfect or innocent, only Jesus. You can make a choice to accept Him and you will be made perfect before God. It's just a choice to give up your pain and allow Him to take it."

"It's so simple that it seems hard. It's almost like it can't be that easy. I guess I struggle with it being so easy to just wipe away my past. It still hurts me so much and I know I have hurt other people too. The pain I have caused doesn't go away. I don't deserve anything."

"No, none of us deserve Heaven. Sin does hurt us. We still have the consequences of our sin to deal with, like your time in prison."

Carl looked up quickly. "You know about that?"

John stopped and cleared his throat. "Well, I know that you were in prison, yes."

"Do you know why?"

"No. I just know that you were there. You need to know that just like you paid for your crimes in prison, Jesus paid for your crimes for all eternity. Your eternal life is secure and forgiven when you accept Him. After you do that, you need to learn how to accept that your earthly life can be just as free. We all struggle with the simplicity of salvation; but make no mistake--it was not simple for God. He had to give up his one and only son and allow him to become sin for us."

Carl put his hands across his lap and seemed to be completely absorbed in watching his fingers. John began wondering if Carl had even heard what he had said, when Carl raised his head slowly and asked, "Do you want to know what I did?"

"You don't have to tell me, unless you want to do so. I am your friend either way."

"I've served some time. I didn't argue when I was sentenced because I felt like I deserved even more. I lost my wife and basically everything I had at that point. When I got out of prison, it was hard to find a job. I have to say that I even stole some things just to get by; but that is not what God can't forgive me for. It's much worse."

John thought about that last statement before he answered.

"Carl, God has seen to it that all of your sins are already forgiven. Even the ones you haven't committed yet. I know it's hard to understand; but you can have a clean slate with

God. He doesn't want you to be perfect when you come to him. He just wants you to come. Sometimes it takes time to understand it fully and forgive yourself."

"I am thankful for God's love and I don't understand any of it. If I tell you what I have done, will you promise to not tell anyone? At least give yourself some time to think about it before I have to face other people who know. All I know is I deserve to be hated; but the thought of disappointing more people is too much to bear right now. I am just starting to feel like I can function again."

"You don't have to tell me what you've done; but I won't judge you and I will never stop being your friend. Whatever is in your past is in your past. You have paid your debt to society and now you can start over with us. As far as God, he never stopped loving you from the moment he created you. He will forgive you the moment you ask Him to."

Carl began to sob; and it took several minutes for him to gain control again. John handed him some tissues and sat back down and waited for his friend. He knew this might take some time; but there was no reason to rush. The angels began to gather again in anticipation that Carl might make a decision. The demon stood outside the hospital window and cursed and hissed.

"I killed someone." The tears flowed freely now and John began to silently pray for his friend. Immediately, the glow returned and John watched it grow with his prayer. When he stopped to speak again, the glow now remained.

"It's okay. Remember, you have paid your price."

"No…it's much worse than that. I…I killed a child."

John's heart almost stopped. He had been shocked by the murder confession; but killing a child was so unthinkable to him, that he had trouble keeping his composure. He could not find anything to say and fought hard not to get upset. His thoughts reeled through a variety of scenarios and hoped that he would be able to keep his promise not to judge his new friend. If Carl was some type of child molester, John was not sure that he could stay true to his promise. As if sensing the preacher's change, Carl's head hung in shame. Meris stepped forward and spread his wings. He had saved some power for this and allowed a calming peace to radiate around the two men. He knew that the demon would be back soon, if this didn't work.

"Pastor John?"

John willed himself to remain calm and simply said a quick prayer for strength. Meris whipped his wings and the glow increased with a sharp beam of light.

"Oh!" John jumped back, startled from the change in the light. Carl looked at John, while he tried to determine what the preacher was looking at and why he had jumped.

"Pastor? Are you okay?"

Meris saw the reaction and smiled. Soon the plan would be fully developed; and he was glad.

"Do you see that?"

"What?"

"The light? It's so bright..."

"Um...I mean I see the light up there." Carl pointed to the overhead light in the room. Pastor John continued to stare at the middle of the room and seemed to be in some type of trance.

"No...it's..." John seemed to realize that Carl could not see the light and how crazy he must look right now. "I just saw...well...I thought I saw something. Um...I know that you need to get some rest. I really want you to tell me the whole story when you are ready."

Carl nodded. Something had changed and he was sure that the preacher now thought he was some kind of monster. The remainder of the visit John steered the conversation to lighter subjects and then said his goodbyes to Carl, promising to come back to see him at his home the next day. John offered to bring Carl home; but Carl declined, claiming that his neighbor was supposed to pick him up to bring him home.

I should have never told him what I did. He hates me now.

John closed the door to Carl's room and slowly began the walk to the elevators. The hospital was relatively quiet; and as he passed the nurses station, he heard Ann ask, "How did it go?"

"I think he's feeling better. He goes home tomorrow, right?"

"Yes, I think he leaves first thing in the morning after the doctors make their rounds."

John handed her his card and asked her to call him when Carl was headed home.

Ann took the card and kept her eyes on the pastor. She had prayed about this and decided that she needed to talk to him. He needed to know.

"Pastor John?"

"Yes?"

"Do you know?"

"Know what?"

Ann dropped her head and then looked back up with tears welling in her eyes. "I have worked at this hospital for over 10 years now. Before that, I lived in Cincinnati. I always work PRN, meaning that I float around to where I am needed. I...well...when you were a small boy and you were sick...I remember your family and I remember all the things that happened."

"Really? I had no idea. That's amazing. How did you figure it out?"

"I saw your parents when your baby was born. It took me some time to sort out my old memory and then about a week ago when you were here visiting some patients, it came to me. I remembered your mom and all the tests...well...it was a tough time for your parents. Thank goodness it all worked out so well, though."

"What a small world, Ann. You should call my mom sometime."

"No, I don't think she would really want to relive that. It was sad and scary. I just thought you might want to know. By the way, you were the cutest little thing!"

John smiled. "I understand the doctors gave me very little hope to live."

Ann's face clouded over. "You really don't know much about it, do you?"

"Well, I mean, I know I was very sick and had to get a transplant. I suppose I would have died without it."

"Pastor, you were dying. As far as the doctor's were concerned, you were not going to make it. Only the persistence of your mom and dad and the timing of the liver...anyway, it was a miracle at the very least."

"I don't really remember much except that I was tired a lot. My older brother would want to play and wrestle and my parents wouldn't let us."

Ann smiled and patted his hand. "You were precious and I was so happy when you got to go home...I prayed...well...let's say that you were at the top of my list for months afterward too."

"I appreciate prayer anytime! Thank you for telling me that. I need to sit down with my parents and talk to them about it. It has always been something that I have meant to do; but to be honest, no one in my family really brings it up."

"I think that is a normal response. Although, it was miraculous, really. It might make a good sermon about suffering and answered prayer."

"That is a great idea. I might look into that. Have a great day!" As he turned to leave, a strange feeling came over him. He looked back at Ann working on some paperwork and he could see a faint glow around her. Shaking his head, he continued on to his car. This gift seemed to be growing even more. He needed to get back to the nursing home to talk to Mia again, when he returned for his weekly visit. She was the only one who seemed to know what was going on. Another thought hit him as well: maybe his parents could be the ones he could reference with his sermon on suffering. His mind also sifted through the strange man Mr. B, Carl's confession, and Ann's words at the hospital. He started to pray and he prayed until he pulled into his driveway and he stopped. All around his home was a shimmery glow.

Chapter 15: Connections

Thursday

    The next day was Thursday, which had become John's favorite day because he was able to visit the nursing home and his good friend Mr. Roberts. Carl, of course, was heading home today to continue recovering from his surgery. Sometime today or tomorrow, John needed to at least call or go see him again. He had built in some extra time to find Mia, knowing he needed some answers from her as well. John had several things on his mind, when he arrived at his office thirty minutes earlier than normal to prepare a few notes he wanted to add to his sermon. As he entered the foyer of the church, he discovered the Martin sisters waiting out in the hall. Kathy immediately jumped to her feet and hurried toward him before he could say a word in greeting.

"Pastor John! We are so glad you are finally here! We have been waiting so long!" She squealed and clapped her hands. Marian shuffled up beside her and smiled.

John pushed up his glasses and tried to think of anything that they could possibly need this early in the morning. A part of him secretly wondered how long they had been waiting.

Did they spend the night? He smiled to himself and thought about the two of them trying to camp out on the bench outside his office. *What could they possibly want?*

"Well, I am really early. I usually don't arrive until 8:00 or later." He pointed to the sign beside his door with the hours clearly posted, which hadn't changed in all the years he had been at the church.

"Oh, well, we just knew you would want to see our next song. We have been rehearsing for several weeks and we are ready for someone to see it!"

Marian squealed in delight and immediately began jumping up and down. "We have the best show for you! I am going to be an angel! I have wings and everything!"

John's mouth dropped open when he saw the props along the wall that the two sisters had made. Kathy proudly picked up and displayed the white gowns and halos that they had put together; and John could not imagine what they had in store. He couldn't help but ask, "What song are you going to do?" Immediately, he regretted his question.

"We thought you would never ask! Meet us in the sanctuary--we will surprise you! Give us ten minutes to get into our costumes. Please know that we won't have time for full make up."

"Oh, um...okay." John turned and closed his eyes. How could he possibly get out of this? He had no one to rescue him this time and he was going to have to force himself to watch the newest production of the Martin sisters. He unlocked his door and turned on the lights.

"Oh gosh!" He half-screamed, as his secretary, Mary, timidly peeked out from behind his desk.

"I'm sorry to scare you, Pastor John," She whispered, "I saw them coming and just instinctively ran in here and locked the door to hide." Mary looked genuinely upset and worried that Pastor John would be disappointed in her. Her small frame looked even smaller behind his large desk and she looked almost like a child waiting for a punishment from her father. John quickly shut the door behind him and burst out laughing.

"I wish I had been able to make it in here with you!"

Mary smiled and a look of relief spread across her face. "I'm sorry, I just had some filing and things to do. Anyway, I ended up sitting here in the dark unable to do anything."

"Well, I am heading into the sanctuary to see the latest performance, if you would like to join me."

Mary shook her head and stepped backward reflexively. "I need to do a few things."

John held up both hands in surrender. "Okay, okay! It's my turn to take it."

"Yes, you still owe me from last time. Hey, did you ever figure out how that man made that appointment yesterday? It worried me all last night."

"No, but I intend to talk to him about it next week when he comes." John's list of things to check on continued to grow.

"Well, you had better hurry to see what the Martin sister's have in store for you! I will be right here hiding."

They both laughed and John left to see what kind of show that Kathy and Marian Martin had planned for this weeks' service. As he neared the sanctuary, he could hear music with a strong drum beat thumping so hard that the sanctuary doors vibrated with each beat. Adding to the dread of entering the room, purple lights leaked through the crack between the doors; and John could not imagine what he might find when he finally went inside.

With his hand on the door, he took a deep breath and prayed for help to endure what was coming; and he quickly slipped in to find a seat. Meris quietly followed and absorbed the prayer surge, then waited in the back of the room as John walked slowly forward. The room was dark except for two purple spotlights shining on the stage, where the two sisters were marching in a circle, wearing long white gowns and silver halos made from aluminum foil. Kathy also held a large stick covered in aluminum foil as well. The music was worse than he had thought and was a mixture of a drum cadence and animal noises. Galdon landed in the room next to Meris and took one look at the stage and smiled, shaking his head. He knew this coming Sunday would be hard for Nardic to keep a straight face. The sight of those costumes was enough; but their disharmonious melodies were becoming something of a legend in the spiritual world as well.

"Pastor John! We are ready! Take a seat!"

John waved and sat down in the middle row, trying to keep a little distance from the speakers up front, where the booming from the horrible tribal music continued to play. He would definitely talk to the music minister to have them keep the volume lower this Sunday. Marian rushed over to start the music from the beginning, then ran to take her place. For the next three minutes, the two women enacted some type of interpretive dance followed by the singing of "When We All Get to Heaven." As the song progressed, Kathy began to march and point her makeshift scepter toward the ceiling, while Marian stood stoically belting out the words in more of a chant than a song. John remained thankful that at least the chant didn't seem as off key as their normal singing; but by the third verse, Marian walked to the edge of the stage and then shouted the final verse with great pageantry. Simultaneously, both sisters then dropped to the ground in some type of dramatic finish perfectly in sync with the last drumbeat from their soundtrack. Meris remained still and Galdon wiped his hand across his face and shook his head again and said, "That may be the worst thing that I ever witnessed."

John heard Galdon and thought it came from his own thoughts, *That may be the worst thing that I have ever witnessed,* his mind echoed the words of the angel. Meris looked at Galdon; but the angels could not read the pastor's mind. Angels have been watching humans for so many years, though, that they recognize subtle changes in behaviors. They moved closer to inspect the preacher's face, since they both thought he had reacted to Galdon's words. If the preacher was now hearing the angels too, it would be a huge step forward in his gift.

John was too stunned to move and thanked God that the horrible show from the Martin sisters was finally over. The power surge from that prayer was sent straight to Heaven for the Father to keep. Both angels stood still, waiting. Silence had never sounded so good, as the horrible singing was now over and John tried to figure out exactly what to say. Finally, the two women stood up from the floor and clapped for themselves, shattering the small relief of silence that both the angels and John had been enjoying.

"Did you like it?" Both sisters moved expectantly toward their pastor in the glow of the purple lights. Pastor John tried to think of anything he could say that wouldn't be a lie; but he didn't want to hurt their feelings with the truth either. He started to clap to pass the seconds, while he searched for something to say. Finally, he cleared his throat and simply said, "Ladies, I can honestly say that I have never seen anything like it!"

Both sisters squealed with delight and jumped up and down. Galdon laughed out loud and even Meris had to cover his face to hide a smile at that response. The sound from the sisters drowned out most of Galdon's laugh; but John looked over his shoulder, thinking he had heard something again. Nothing was there; but he glanced longingly at the door, hoping to make a quick exit soon. Both angels saw his reaction and looked at each other.

Kathy Martin squealed, "We are so glad you liked it! Please stay--we will do it again!"

With the reflexes of a cat, John jumped to his feet and quickly stated, "Oh, I am sorry, but I need to get some paperwork done. Thank you, though!"

He exited as fast as he could move and headed straight to his office in a fast walk that would put most speed walkers to shame; then he quickly shut the door behind him. When he turned around, Mary peeped up from behind the desk again and they both burst out laughing.

"Looks like you need a better hiding place!"

"I guess so!" Mary crept back through to the reception area by the front door trying to keep from alerting the Martin sisters she was there, while Pastor John decided to look over his sermon notes before he headed to the nursing home later that morning. As he was finishing up some research for an upcoming series, his cell phone buzzed in his pocket. He pulled it out and frowned at the unfamiliar number.

"This is Pastor John Miles."

"Well, so formal! Hello Pastor John. This is Mia."

"Hello, Mia! What a surprise. I am so glad that you called. I have missed seeing you."

"Yes, I have been away for a bit. I really want to hear you preach again."

"Great! I was worried about you. I have been thinking about our conversation and wanted to know if we could talk more when I come today."

"Well, I would love that; but I will probably be a little more inclined to listen, the next time we meet."

"Oh. Okay, um...so you are going to be at the service?"

There was a pause, and then Mia sighed and answered, "I know that you probably have a wonderful sermon planned already; but can you please do the one you did a few weeks ago about the Gates of Heaven? I would really love to hear that again sometime."

"Oh. Well, I mean I guess I can do that. I have it still here on my desk where my secretary typed it for me. I will be glad to do that today." He looked at his prepared sermon and sighed. He was not really happy with it yet anyway. He could practice it at home on Saturday.

Mia paused again and John could hear her labored breathing as she answered, "Thank you so much. I will be looking forward to it."

"You are wel--" The phone clicked and Pastor John knew that Mia had hung up. He checked his watch and decided to go ahead and leave, so he grabbed the set of sermon notes that Mia had requested and headed for the door.

John arrived at the nursing home early to try to find Mia and see if they could talk briefly before he was due to deliver his sermon. When he reached her room, it was locked and no one answered, so he strolled down the hall expecting to see the familiar smile of Mia in her wheelchair somewhere in one of the community rooms; but he could not find her anywhere. He walked up to the office to find Linda, the manager.

"Hey Linda. How are you doing today?"

"Hey Pastor John. Are you ready to preach for us?"

"I think so! I was wondering if you knew where Mrs. Minnamia Hunt is? I wanted to talk to her before my service today."

Linda's expression clouded over and John immediately knew that something was wrong. "I'm sorry, Pastor John. I didn't know that you two were that close. How long did you know her?"

"Not long, we were just beginning to get to know each other."

"Well, she has been in the hospital now for several weeks and now..."

"Oh, I was wondering where she has been."

Linda paused and softly answered, "She passed away this morning. I just received the call from the hospital. I am so sorry. She was a precious woman."

John felt his knees buckle slightly and he tried to make sense of what Linda had said. "She's gone? That's not possible!" he barely whispered. Linda grabbed a chair and helped John sit down.

"I am so sorry, Pastor John. I had no idea. She did die peacefully, according to the hospital."

John stared at the floor and then he asked, "You said *this morning*?"

Linda looked up and seemed to be calculating. "I think it was about thirty minutes ago that I got the call."

John looked at his watch and then pulled out his cell phone. He had talked to Mia about forty minutes ago, probably right before she passed away.

"She was a wonderful woman. She was so generous and kind. She even left her dresser and bed to another woman here whose furniture was in bad shape. She was adamant that we give it to this woman if she died."

John stared at the floor and tried to gather his thoughts. He finally looked up at Linda and said, "Did Mia have any family?"

"No, she was all alone. She never had any children; but she did keep a picture of a little child. She told me when she left for the hospital that she wanted me to have it. I have no idea why. Maybe because she knew I would never get rid of it."

John's mind was reeling. "Could I see it?"

"Absolutely. I have it here in my office."

"Can I get a copy of it?"

"Sure. Mine looks like a copy too. I don't know where the original is." Linda walked over to a small drawer in a wooden cabinet and removed the picture frame and carefully slid the picture out into her hand. She quickly copied the picture on her printer and gave it to John, who stared at the picture and tried to understand what was going on. This was the exact picture he had seen in Mia's room when he had visited her there just a few months back. John was filled with sadness; but he thanked Linda and headed to the activity room to deliver the message Mia had requested. He felt an incredible sense of urgency to do exactly as she had requested; but his emotions were completely shredded.

"Pastor John!"

John turned and saw Linda hurrying toward him.

"One more thing, she gave me this envelope before she left and said someone would come for it soon. Do you know anything about it?"

John looked at the outside of the envelope. It was a large manilla envelope and was obviously very old. The outside was addressed to Mia and the addressee was an office with the initials OPTN. John turned it over and looked up at Linda.

"Go ahead, open it. She has no one else."

John lifted the flap and pulled gently. Inside were two other envelopes.

"I am not sure if I should have these. Maybe you should keep these in case anyone comes for them."

"She was here over eight years with not a single visitor; and I really don't think anyone will come now that she is gone. If they do, I will send them to you. There was also one small bag with a pin inside that she left instructions to give it to the same person who came for the envelope." Linda handed John a small plastic bag with a golden pin inside.

John turned the bag over and inspected the pin. It was a simple stick pin with a gold angel. He stared at the pin, he thought he saw a slight glow and again felt an overwhelming sense of confusion and concern.

What is going on?

"Pastor John, are you okay?"

"I'm not sure. I'm also not sure that I am the one who should take these. I think you should keep them for now, in case someone comes and specifically asks for them." John stared at the angel and tried to remember what Mia had said. He had asked if they could talk today and she had answered 'I may be more inclined to listen today.' John thought back through the rest of their conversation and finally stood and thanked Linda, as he headed to the room to try to deliver his sermon. As he drew near the door, he felt an incredible urge to pray. John veered over to a small hallway and knelt down and prayed,

Dear God,
I am not sure what is going on. Please help me. I don't know what to pray for or what to say. Give me strength to preach and then help me find the answers. I'm ready for answers now. I want to do your Will and use what you have given me. Show me how.
In Jesus' name,
Amen

The strength of the prayer lifted Pastor John and carried him through the rest of the day. Meris was able to give John enough strength to deliver the sermon and relax enough to spend some time with Mr. Roberts. The conversation with Linda was still fresh on his mind; but John really wanted to talk to Mr. Roberts about Carl too.

"Well, Pastor John! I'm glad you made it down here after all!" John looked at his elderly friend with confusion and Mr. Roberts laughed, while motioning for him to take a seat. "I just mean that your sermon was at a new level."

John still did not understand; but he wanted to know what was so funny to help lighten his mood. "What is this new level?"

"Oh, I think I will call this one a level A sermon."

"Okay, you got me. What exactly does that mean?"

"You were right up there with the angels today! I mean A for angels!"

The room might have been spinning; but John wasn't sure. He was really glad that he was already sitting down. He opened his mouth; but no sound came out and he just stared at his friend. Galdon and Meris both looked at each other and then at the two men. Neither angel knew what Mr. Roberts was talking about. As far as they knew, this elderly man had never connected with the spiritual world.

"You look surprised! Don't you want to preach as high as the angels? I thought that would get you pumped up to get such a high rating!"

John moved his lips, but no sound emerged.

"A speechless preacher! Now that might be a miracle on top of a great sermon!" Mr. Roberts laughed so hard that tears formed around the edges of his eyes. "Come on, you have to say something!"

"I...well...angels..."

"That's what I said. I think that your sermon was that good. I felt like we were all floating as high as the angels today. That was really something. I usually don't get that excited; but it was the best sermon that I have ever heard. I was teasing you when I said, 'I'm glad you made it down here.' I was talking about coming down from the clouds!"

The words started to sink in and John started to understand. Mr. Roberts hadn't seen any angels. He was just rating the sermon in one of his unusual ways and was trying to give him a compliment. Slowly, John began to relax and a smile spread across his face. "Angels, huh?" Meris and Galdon both smiled as well.

"Yes, angels. I think that you preached us all the way up to the feet of the angels today."

Now it was John's turn to laugh. He laughed so hard that when he stopped, Mr. Roberts had begun to look confused. "It's okay. I have just...just been under a lot of pressure. I'm glad to get an A rating from you." He had to remove his glasses and wipe his eyes.

The two men spent a few minutes on small talk and then fell silent. John silently prayed and both Galdon and Meris slowly opened their wings in response.

"So, I went and spent some time with Carl yesterday."

"Yeah, he told me." Before John could respond, Mr. Roberts continued. "We have begun to talk every day by phone, now. He called me after you left yesterday. I really want to thank you for all that you have done for him."

"I want to do more; but I can't. I wish he would let go and trust Jesus."

Mr. Roberts sighed and looked at his hands. When he lifted his head to speak, he was crying. "Me too. More than anything in the world."

"Would you like to pray with me about it?"

Mr. Roberts nodded and the two men bowed their heads. John was about to start praying, when Mr. Roberts began,

"Dear God,
I thank you for this man before me. He has done more for me than he will ever know. We come together today to pray for my son, Carl. Only you know all that is in his heart and

what keeps him from making that final step. Please let him release whatever demon holds him back and just trust in you. We ask these things together because you have taught us in the book of Corinthians that your Grace is sufficient and your power is made perfect in weakness. We are weak, Lord, and we ask for your Grace and your help.
In Jesus' name, Amen."

"That was beautiful, Mr. Roberts. I could not have said it better myself." John noticed the scripture in the prayer and smiled.

"Thank you. Carl is so close to believing."

"What about the demon comment?" John wanted to know what his friend thought about that, especially with all that he had been experiencing.

"Son, if there is one thing I know, it is that angels and demons are real."

For the next hour, the two men talked in great detail and John poured out all that he was experiencing with Mr. Roberts. When he finished, Mr. Roberts simply said, "Then it is true."

"Yes, it is all true."

"Oh, I believe that; but I mean it is all true. The world we see is just a small part of what is going on around us. Son, you are a blessed man. Use it to reach people."

"That is what I want to do, but how? It makes me sound a little crazy."

"Have you ever told Carl?"

"No, I mean very few people know."

"Why? What are you afraid of?"

"I guess losing everything, including my ministry. I might get shoved out of my church. People would think I am making it all up."

Mr. Roberts shook his head and looked at John. "No, try telling Carl first. He has something to tell you too. By the way, how in the world can you lose a ministry by telling everyone about God and his spiritual world? If you lose anything, then it wasn't worth having. Any church that wouldn't listen to you and try to embrace this is not where you should be anyway. Of course, that is just an old man's opinion."

John was stunned. Of course he shouldn't be scared. How stupid he had been. After a few more minutes together, John headed back to his office. He felt he needed some rest and time with Lindsey and Rosie tonight; but he had to finish the day first. Meris surrounded his car with his wings, as Pastor John headed back to the office to complete his last appointment of the day. Back at the nursing home, Linda placed the bag with the pin along with the envelope inside the safe in her office and wondered if anyone would ever claim them.

John walked into the church and greeted Mary, then hurried into his office to tidy up his last paperwork of the day. Too many things were happening and he knew he needed talk to Lindsey right now more than ever. Her calm and easy manner would help him decipher what to do next. He walked the short hallway to his office deep in thought, while Meris moved alongside him and Galdon stayed outside the building. His mind was too full to work, so he left a message for Darron to call him when he could and then headed home. The prayer surge from Mr. Robert's prayer was absorbed and saved for the right moment, which was not far away.

Chapter 16: Family Time

Thursday Evening

John was surprised when he arrived home to find Rosie enjoying a book with Lindsey's mother, Ellie. Something was happening between them that everyone had noticed and no one could have predicted. Although Ellie had struggled with her past, Rosie had somehow been able to help thaw her frozen heart. At first, she didn't show much of a difference in her behavior; but over the last few years, Rosie and her Mimi Ellie had begun to form a very special bond. None of Lindsey's sisters seemed to mind, as everyone was so glad to see Mimi Ellie starting to enjoy life again.

There was something strange that now drew Ellie to her young granddaughter; and she frequently came and kept Rosie, while Lindsey fulfilled a variety of tasks for the church. Today, though, Ellie had simply come to visit for a few hours, while Lindsey worked in the home on some preparations for the upcoming church clothing sale. While Lindsey busied herself with some paperwork, Ellie played with her granddaughter in the adjoining room. When John walked in, he decided not to disturb them and simply greeted them, then turned to join Lindsey in the kitchen. John had so much he wanted to discuss with his wife; but he was not ready to do so in front of anyone else, so he waited.

"Can I do anything to help start dinner?"

"I have most of it ready to go. The lasagna is in the oven and the bread is buttered and ready to heat up right before we eat. If you want to finish putting the salad together, though, that would be great."

"Sure. So do you want to use all this?" John was standing at the refrigerator door holding up several containers of vegetables.

"Yeah, any of that you want to use. I thought I would combine it all."

"Got it. I will make you a wonderful salad!"

"Just stay away from the stove, Smokey."

"If you remember, that was *you* who left those muffins in too long!" He smiled and walked over to get a quick kiss.

From the other room, they could hear Rosie speak, "Mimi Ellie?" Rosie was curled up in her grandmother's arms, coloring in a new book her Mimi had given her. Lindsey held her fingers to her lips, indicating she wanted to hear what Rosie was saying. She and John continued working quietly as they listened.

"Yes, Rosie." Mimi Ellie stroked the soft brown hair of her young granddaughter, while a deep and secret pain stirred inside.

"What was my Aunt Rose Louise like?" Rosie looked up and then back at her book, as she exchanged the blue crayon for a red one. Lindsey and John both stopped working and looked at each other.

Mimi Ellie's expression clouded over, as she tried to keep her composure. Lindsey dropped her pen and bit her lip, hoping her mom could keep her composure. She knew her mom rarely made it through a conversation about Rose Louise without crying. She looked at John and he shrugged and they both moved closer to the door to listen.

Please, God, don't let her lose it. Lindsey silently prayed.

At the edge of the room, Galdon stood waiting for this added strength. He had been able to get closer to Ellie at times, as she continued to soften her anger toward God; but the demon of Pride still had more control. The added prayer finally gave him enough power to strike the demon, causing him to writhe in pain and back away slightly. He turned to lash out at Galdon; but he missed completely, falling to the floor, and Galdon placed his foot on the demon's chest, holding him there.

"Well, Rosie, she was beautiful and sweet, like you." Mimi Ellie fought to keep the tears in check and was surprised at how strong she felt inside, instead of weak and raw like she usually did when she tried to talk about her daughter that had died so many years ago.

"Did she like to draw like me?" Rosie continued to color in her book as she talked.

This time Lindsey felt the need to say something. "Rosie, I need you come here, please."

"No, Lindsey, it's okay." Mimi Ellie called out as she held up a hand. She hugged her little granddaughter closer and was able to maintain her composure as she asked, "Now what did you ask? Oh yeah. Well, Rose Louise was a very small child when she left us."

Mimi Ellie wiped a small tear away and sniffed. Galdon strained to keep his foot on the demon's chest, as the power from the prayer began to fade. The demon felt the slight change and jumped up to lash out at Galdon. He struck the angel in the leg and Galdon dropped to one knee; but he continued to block the demon from getting to Ellie, while he looked over at Lindsey hoping for her to pray again. When she did not, he was forced to move and allow the creature to crawl to the back of the couch to whisper in Ellie's ear.

Rosie continued to color and then looked over at her grandmother. "Where did Rose Louise go?"

"Rosie!" Lindsey couldn't take it anymore, so she hurried into the family room. "I'm sorry, mom. She just doesn't know." John moved into the room alongside Lindsey.

Ellie held up her hand again. "It's okay, really." Ellie sighed and closed her eyes briefly, then continued, "Rose Louise went to be with Jesus. She was very little, only about two years old." Ellie started to feel a terrible sadness and tried to keep from crying. The feelings of guilt washed over her like a rogue wave, sending her emotions tumbling in a swirling dark fog around her, as the demon kept whispering into her ear.

"I wish I could meet her." Rosie watched her grandmother's face and dropped her crayon. She reached over and grabbed her grandmother's hand.

Ellie squeezed her hand back and answered, "I wish you could too. She would have liked you." Ellie put her arm around Rosie and began to stroke her hair and her thoughts floated back to a day that seemed like yesterday. As her memories drifted back in time, she closed her eyes and tried to control the pain that still tugged at her heart every day. She could feel the wound of bitterness toward God begin to throb; and she didn't want to fight it but something held it back. Rosie squeezed her grandmother's hand and snuggled closer, causing Ellie's emotions to swirl in confusion. John wrapped his arm around Lindsey and they both said a silent prayer for strength for Ellie.

Galdon drug his body over toward Ellie and pushed himself into standing. His leg throbbed; but he gathered every ounce of power that he could to place his sword on the demon's head, making him scream in pain and stop whispering into Ellie's ear. The added prayer gave him enough power to hold his position for a long time or knock the demon off for only a few minutes. He chose the long battle and the two beings locked arms and began a powerful struggle. Galdon felt confident that he could keep the demon occupied for a long enough time to help give Ellie a break. He knew the prayers would provide a certain level of protection; but he also knew that he was not completely out of harms way. They continued to wrestle; but suddenly, the demon realized he had been tricked into focusing on the fight instead of Ellie; and he let go. Both watched Ellie and each other closely; but the demon was outmatched and he knew it.

Thirty-five years ago, Mimi Ellie had been a young woman with a heart full of love and hope. Ellie remembered the details of her last day with Rose Louise with unbelievable clarity. She sat stroking her granddaughter's hair with tears running down her cheeks. She didn't want little Rosie to see her like this.

I was sitting just like this with my baby the last time I held her. I still miss her so much.

Lindsey came over and handed her mom a tissue to wipe her eyes. Rosie looked up and noticed her grandmother crying.

"Mimi, why are you crying?"

"Rosie, let's go get ready for dinner." Lindsey reached for Rosie's hand.

"No, Lindsey, this is good for me." Ellie wiped her eyes and hugged Rosie. "Rosie, I am crying because I miss her."

"At least she is with Jesus. I am sure he is taking good care of her." John moved over to a chair and sat on the edge. Rosie surprised him with her response.

Lindsey smiled and wiped her own eyes. Ellie laughed and said, "Yes, I am positive that he is doing that."

"Mimi, at least she never has to get one of these." Rosie lifted up her knee and showed Mimi where she had a large scrape from falling off of her bike the day before.

"You are right, Rosie. I know she will never hurt again."

"I wish I didn't ever have to hurt again." Rosie kept coloring and Ellie looked up at Lindsey.

"You know, I never thought about it before; but that is really wonderful." Ellie felt a small sense of relief; but the pain was still there. She still had several layers to work through and had no idea how much Rosie would help her do that.

"Rosie, you need to go wash up for dinner." Lindsey helped her daughter clean up the crayons. John stepped in to help too and then took Rosie to wash her hands and allow his wife to have a moment alone with her mother.

"What are we having, dad?"

"Your favorite: lasagna!"

"Yes! I want a big piece!"

"Not as big as mine!" John chased her through the house, leaving the two women alone.

Lindsey sighed and grabbed her mom's hand. "Mom, I am really sorry. Rosie didn't know."

"Nonsense. No need to be sorry. I need to get going too. Your father is probably mad that I didn't bring him over!"

"Why don't you go get him and join us for dinner?"

"Oh, no. We are going on a hot date tonight!"

"Really! Where are you going?"

"We are going to see the new movie about the end of the world...oh gosh...I can't remember the name."

"Time Out?"

"Yes, that's it."

"Wow, I would never guess you guys would see that one."

"You know how your dad loves the movies."

Lindsey gave her mom a hug goodbye and said, "Yes, I do. Please give dad a hug and feel free to come by tomorrow. Love you!"

"You too. I'll call you tomorrow."

Lindsey watched her mom walk to her car and silently prayed for her again. This time she added a Bible verse in her prayer. John had been working on a new sermon series and they talked about the importance of praying scripture. The prayer combined with the scripture gave Galdon enough power to keep the demon's mouth sealed shut until the next day. After a quick call to her dad to warn him about what had happened, Lindsey returned to the kitchen to find Rosie sitting at the table ready to eat.

"Is Mimi eating with us?"

Lindsey grabbed three plates and loaded them with a piece of lasagna and some bread, while John filled bowls with salad. "No, she had to get home to be with Gran Gran."

Rosie watched as her mom sat the steaming plates on the table and her rumbling tummy screamed for her to dive in; but she waited patiently through her dad's prayer. Within a few seconds, the only sound was silverware scraping the plates, as they enjoyed the meal before them.

Lindsey put her fork down and watched her daughter finish eating. She had John's eyes and hair color but was otherwise a very close copy of herself. She had seen the pictures of her sister who had died; and Rosie favored her as well. She braced herself and said a simple prayer for wisdom, as she broached the topic she needed to discuss with her daughter. The subject of her dead sister had long been something that was repressed in her family, as her mom was still not able to talk about it no matter how long it had been. She had learned the details in pieces through the years; but had never had the nerve to ask her mom directly. It had been her own grandmother who had given her the most details with Millie and Sarah filling in the rest as they remembered it.

"Rosie?"

"Yeah?"

"Ma'am" John corrected her.

"Yes, ma'am." Rosie said and smiled at her father, who winked in return.

"I need to talk to you about something."

"I know."

Lindsey sat back in her chair, slightly stunned, as she tried to figure out what her daughter meant. "What do you mean?"

"You want to talk to me about Mimi. I can tell Mimi is very sad."

"Well, she is sad about one thing, but overall is a very happy person. She loves you very much."

"I know. You are wrong, though. She is sad all the time."

"Why would you say that, honey? You know she--"

Rosie dropped her fork and looked at her mom. "I don't mean to be mean, mom, but she always has that dark cloud around her. It's kind of gloomy. I guess I would be sad too."

John almost choked on his bite of bread.

"What? What are you talking about?" John said as he thought about the dark shadow he had told Lindsey he sometimes saw around Ellie. *Rosie must have heard us talking about it.*

"Okay, you know how we all have this light around us?" John looked at Lindsey, who sat staring at her daughter. John was now sure Rosie had heard them talking. How else would she even know this?

Rosie saw the puzzled look on her parent's faces and let out a huge sigh. "Come on, mom. You know like the light around your face and dad's and mine. Mimi's is dark. There is a light underneath, though, not like people who don't love Jesus."

Lindsey nodded only because she could see that Rosie needed her to. She had no idea what her daughter was saying. It scared her, though, because it was so similar to what had happened to John. She wanted to ask more; but what would she even ask? She and John exchanged a look and both decided to wait until they could discuss it together before they talked more with Rosie.

"May I be excused?"

"Um, yeah. Just put your dishes in the dishwasher."

"Sure." Rosie grabbed her plate and cup and put them in the dishwasher and then turned to face her parents. "Don't worry. We are all protected and safe." Both John and Lindsey were too stunned to speak and watched Rosie skip out of the kitchen and go upstairs.

Lindsey opened her mouth to speak but John spoke first, "She had to have heard us talking about this."

"Maybe so. Either way, it scares me."

John reached over and grabbed her hand. He knew he needed to talk to her about all that had happened with Mia but decided to wait until later. "Let's talk to her after her bath."

"Okay, I'll go up first and you come up a few minutes later."

Lindsey and John both stood and cleared the dishes and finished putting the food away, giving Rosie enough time to take a bath and get ready for bed. When Lindsey went upstairs, she found Rosie was sitting up in her bed writing in her notebook. Rosie quickly placed her notebook under her bed and settled into position and both of them looked up when John came through the door.

"Dad, will you let me do the praying tonight?" John looked up in surprise and Lindsey just shrugged.

"She's better than me!" Lindsey said and kissed her daughter on the forehead, while helping her settle back into the bed.

"Fine by me. I'd love for you to pray." John knelt beside his wife and they held hands, as Lindsey reached up and grabbed Rosie's hand as well.

"Dear God, I want to thank you for everything as usual. I mean, you know all the regular stuff I say; but I need to talk to you about something else."

John snuck a peek at Lindsey, who shrugged again and motioned for him to be quiet. He stole a glance at his little girl, who had her eyes squinted tight and her little hands pressed together in front of her face.

"...and you know all about how we need this and that. I need you to look in a little extra on Mimi Ellie. Of course, I want you to take care of Gran Gran and Papa and Mamaw as well. It's just that Mimi is sad. She misses Rose Louise, you know, my Aunt Rose Louise. She should be up there; and I hope you are loving on her and taking good care of her. No one seems to want to talk a bunch about her down here, so I'm just asking you to maybe tell her hello for me and give her a hug from Mimi. I'm sure my mom and Aunt Millie and Aunt Sarah would want her to know that they love her too. Anyway, can you do that tonight? Maybe tomorrow you could do it too. I think Mimi would want you to do that. Anyway, I thank you that I get to have her name. I think that is kind of cool. I love you. Amen."

Lindsey and John exchanged puzzled glances as Rosie popped up and gave her parents each a kiss on the cheek. They kissed her goodnight and went downstairs to the family room, careful not to talk until they were out of range for Rosie to hear them.

"What was that about?" John asked.

"I'm not sure. She usually just prays for everyone and for us to get a dog."

John smiled. "That will take a miracle."

Lindsey waved him off. "You are funny." She punched him gently and then continued, "What is Rosie seeing, John? Do you think she really sees these clouds and lights?"

"No, I think she heard us talking--"

"John, she was sound asleep when we were talking. She is also all the way across the house. We would have seen or heard her coming. I really think she sees something, like you. She must have your spiritual gift."

"How does she have the gift too?"

"I don't know. Have you talked to Darron lately?"

"No, but I left him a message. We have been playing phone tag this afternoon; but I will see him tomorrow at our weekly meeting."

"What about your research? I have done some myself; but I just keep finding stuff we already know."

"Same here. I am looking forward to hearing if Darron found anything new. For now, we need to keep an eye on Rosie."

"I agree."

"Lindsey, I feel like we should commit to praying and using scripture in our prayers. I think we should start praying like this for your mom."

A few seconds passed and John was not sure if Lindsey had registered what he had said. Finally, she answered, "I would like that. I don't know why it's been so hard for me to do that before; but you are right. We need to lift her up to God, especially now. Something spiritual is going on and we need to fight."

"I think you are right about that. I have been studying everything I can find and Darron emailed me some of his research too. Crazy that we work in the same building and usually talk by phone or email! Anyway, the only two offensive weapons that we can find in the Bible are prayer and scripture."

"Ephesians 6:10-18."

"Why did you say that?"

"Well, it says that we wrestle--"

"--not against flesh and blood, but against the rulers, against the authorities, against the powers of this dark world and against the spiritual forces of evil in the heavenly realms." Before John finished saying the verse, Lindsey joined in to finish it. They both looked at each other and smiled. "That is the exact chapter that Darron and I have been studying. We have been looking at that particular verse as well as the rest about the Armor of God."

"The sword of the Spirit, which is the Word of God."

"Exactly. Have you been spying on us?" John smiled, knowing she had not.

"You are funny! I do have my own Bible, you know!" Lindsey punched John in the arm again and he pulled her close for a hug. "Seriously, though, I have been digging too."

"What do you think about our conclusion about the only two weapons?"

"Scripture and prayer? I think you are right."

"We do too. Darron and I have combed all of our sources and they all say the same thing."

"Well, there are specific pieces of armor mentioned in the Ephesians: the gospel of peace fitted around our feet, the helmet of salvation, the belt of truth, the breastplate of righteousness, the shield of faith, and the sword of the Spirit, which is the Word of God."

"Right, and all are defensive except for the word of God, which is an offensive piece."

"I like to think of it as attributes: truth, righteousness, preparation of the Gospel of peace, faith, salvation, and the Word of God and Prayer."

"Yes! That is what Darron and I keep coming back to. I really think this is what God is saying to me. He wants me to preach this."

"Of course he does. It's in His Word."

"No, I mean I think he wants me to concentrate my ministry on this for now at least. I also think that when I see the light and the darkness, it signifies an angel or a demon that a person is dealing with or maybe that someone is saved or not. This is the part I am not sure about yet."

"I don't know either; but I do think that God wants us to pray more. I am guilty myself for not doing it enough and I am the wife of a preacher."

"We all fall short, Lindsey. God doesn't expect perfection--He is the only perfect one."

Lindsey nodded and grabbed John's hand. "Why do you think we all struggle with something so powerful as prayer?"

"I don't think people understand the power it has. Every time I see the light grow or the angels, it seems that prayer or praise is involved. Do you think our prayer gives them power?"

"I guess it's possible. I mean, God gave it to us as a weapon. Maybe the power is expressed at least partially through the angels."

"Let's commit to praying and using scripture with the prayers when we can."

"I am going to do that. I am going to pray with specific scriptures for my mom."

"One thing is for sure. Praying could never be wrong. I really feel convicted to be on my knees more than ever right now. Maybe that is what this gift is doing--reviving my prayer life."

"Mine too.

Chapter 17: Additions

Friday

Lindsey was up early the next morning and made a pan of muffins and cut up some fresh fruit for her two favorite people. She was starving and couldn't wait for them to get up and join her. She decided to bring John breakfast in bed; but before she could get it all on a tray, she felt violently ill and had to run to the bathroom and vomit. John lumbered down the stairs just as she was cleaning up her face with a wet washcloth.

"Are you okay, honey?"

"Yeah, I think those muffins made me sick or something."

John looked at his wife and then started to smile.

"What? You are laughing at me for being sick?" Lindsey was mad. Why in the world was he smiling?

"No, I would never laugh at that. I was just wondering if maybe you woke up starving and then got sick after you ate."

"Yes, but...do you think?"

"Muffins, you know...they are a good indicator for you."

"Okay, Smokey." Lindsey smiled as she walked over to a calendar that they kept on the wall and started to count. John walked up and hugged her from behind. "Well, I guess we have been so busy that I didn't think about it. I mean, this isn't exactly proof or anything. I am pretty late, though."

"Late for what?" Rosie yawned and walked into the kitchen. "Muffins! Yes!" She grabbed two and picked out the strawberries, then sat down at the table. John and Lindsey looked at each other and Lindsey shook her head. She wasn't ready to talk about any of this yet, especially when they weren't even sure themselves.

"Um, we were just trying to figure out something." Lindsey again gave John a threatening look as he walked behind Rosie, mimicking a pregnant woman by pulling out his shirt and waddling. Rosie never looked up from her breakfast and was unaware of her father teasing her mom.

"Figure out what?" Rosie said through a mouthful of muffin.

"Don't talk with your mouth full. It's not lady-like."

"Yeah, and you need to be a lady!" John said and made a face at his daughter, as he handed her a glass of milk. She responded by opening her mouth full of muffin and making a face right back at him.

"Gross! You two deserve each other." Lindsey half scolded and half smiled as she sat down with a glass of sweet tea. John looked at her and her glass and winked. He knew that sweet tea was the only thing Lindsey could drink for weeks in the morning when she was pregnant with Rosie. She always drank the decaffeinated version, so it was safe--and of course, never any lemons.

Rosie finished one muffin and then sat back, picking at the second one. John looked at Lindsey and she nodded.

"Say, Rosie. So did you and Mimi have fun yesterday?"

"Yeah, but I made her cry." Rosie kept picking at the muffin and John looked back at Lindsey, who tried to act nonchalant.

"Maybe we should not talk with her about things that make her sad."

"Well, I didn't *mean* to make her cry. She just, well, you know always feels sad. It's that dark cloud thing."

"Oh, yeah, the cloud. Well, um, is this cloud kind of like a picture in a book?" John looked up at Lindsey and shrugged as if he were saying, 'I really don't know what to ask.'

Rosie rolled her eyes. "No, silly. It's the opposite of our light. Mimi has the light too. She is kind of mixed up."

"Oh. Mixed up like sad."

"No. Well, I guess she just doesn't let the light shine. Kind of like the songs in church."

John looked up at Lindsey again. "So, she is in a dark mood."

"Well, she needs to get that cloud out of there. It's annoying. I love Mimi, though. Anyway, I wanted to know about Aunt Rose Louise. I really want to know what happened to her."

"She died when she was two." Lindsey answered before John could.

"I know; but how and why is it so hard to talk about?"

"Well, she was so little and Mimi and Gran Gran loved her very much. She died in a car accident."

"Yeah, I know all of that. I just thought there was more."

"Well, Mimi has a hard time with it still. I think maybe we shouldn't make her talk about it."

"Okay, but I think she *needs* to talk about it. Haven't you already tried *not* talking about it? That hasn't worked."

John almost laughed out loud at his daughter's logic. It was true. Lindsey's mom had not improved by *not* talking about it. Maybe talking about it would help. "Well, for now, can we all agree to not bring it up unless she does?"

"Yeah, I guess." Rosie sat there for a moment and then asked, "Can I ask Gran Gran about it?"

Again, both parents looked at each other and Lindsey shrugged. Her dad had never had any problem dealing with it as far as she knew. He had been so occupied keeping her mom stable that he had probably learned to recover in his own way.

"Let's just see how it goes for now."

Rosie had no idea if that was a yes or a no. She looked over at Nardic, her guardian angel, who had been with her before she was even born. He smiled and she smiled back. Both parents were too occupied to notice.

John sat back in his chair and looked at Lindsey again. She was glowing more than usual. He silently prayed for some guidance on how to talk to Rosie. Nardic absorbed the prayer and glowed. Meris landed in the room and nodded, indicating that he would help the pastor.

"Rosie, do you see the light a lot?"

Rosie rolled her eyes. "Of course, Dad, you know, like on people who love Jesus. It's just their angel with them."

Both Lindsey and John stopped moving and this time, Lindsey spoke, "Honey, what do you mean?"

"Well, you and daddy and me and everyone who has Jesus gets one. They keep us safe."

"So, you see the light around everyone who loves Jesus?"

Rosie sighed and then nodded. "Yes, can I be excused now?"

John looked at Lindsey and then she shrugged again. "Yes, but put your dishes in the dishwasher please."

Rosie left the table and quickly put her dishes away. Lindsey grabbed John's hand and they both sat in silence for a few seconds until they were sure Rosie was out of earshot. "John, what is going on? How can she see that?"

"I don't know; but maybe it's just her imagination."

"Is it yours too? She is sounding like you now."

John sat and rubbed his hands through his hair, while he again said a silent prayer for help. *What does Rosie see? Could she be seeing the things I am seeing too? How could that be and why is it happening?* So many questions were swirling through his mind. "I don't know. I wish I knew what to do."

"Should we take her to someone?"

"Who? Most people would bring her to someone like me; and I am stumped. I think we should pray about it."

"Okay. I am just worried about her."

"She will be fine. For now, I need to get going. When I meet with Darron this morning, I am going to bring this up too. Maybe he can talk to her and make some sense out of it all with us."

"I like that idea."

"For now, you need to take care of yourself." John winked and patted Lindsey on the tummy, while he grabbed his Bible and notes and then kissed Lindsey on the forehead. "I have a couple of appointments this morning and then I'm counseling a few people after lunch. I should be home early tonight. Do you need me to pick up anything?" He looked at his wife and pointed to her belly and smiled.

Lindsey shook her head and answered, "Now, what makes you think I can wait until you get home? I will be making a quick trip to the store very soon."

"What store?" Rosie came back into the room carrying her backpack and caught the strange interactions from her parents.

"Oh...I just need a few things. I need to get you to school."

"I need a new pencil case, mine broke yesterday."

"What color do you want?"

"I guess pink. Hey mom, are you okay?"

Lindsey looked at Rosie and then at John. "Yes, of course. Why do you ask?"

"I heard you throwing up. I just thought maybe you were sick."

"Oh, well I was feeling kind of bad; but now I feel better."

"Hey Nosy Rosie, go brush your teeth and grab your jacket."

Rosie made at face at her father and they both laughed. "I already brushed."

"That was fast. Did you really brush your teeth or just run the toothbrush through the water again?"

Rosie's mouth dropped open. "How did you know?"

"I see everything!" John pretended to chase her and Rosie ran back upstairs squealing and brushed her teeth for real this time.

When John arrived at his office, he gathered his notes and headed to the conference room, where Darron was already waiting for their weekly meeting.

"Hey John. Sorry I never got back to you. Did you get my texts?"

"Oh, yes. I knew we would see each other today."

John and Darron reviewed the new sermon series and some of the upcoming schedule changes. Both men wanted to get through the regular work so that they could discuss their research. After an hour, all church business was completed and Darron pushed back from the table and looked at John. "So, tell me what is new."

Another hour later and both men were taking notes and discussing what they had found, while searching scriptures and reference materials. John made a list of things that they had either uncovered or suspected to be true. As their conversation waned, John looked down at the list and whistled. "This is quite a list."

"Read it back to me."

"Okay. Here we go:

1.) When we pray, the angels seem to have more power.

2.) The glow is connected to angels and the darkness to demons

3.) Scripture and prayer are the only offensive weapons that we have to fight against demons and together they seem more effective. Scripture is one of the parts to the Armor of God (Ephesians)

4.) Angels and demons are around us all the time (Ephesians)

5.) John, Mia, and maybe Rosie all seem to be able to see the spiritual world in varying degrees

6.) The Glory of God is greater than anything we can even describe or understand

"That is enough to preach about for the next ten years. Just the Armor of God alone is a great place to start."

"Darron. I think I should start by explaining the spiritual world and then a series on angels and demons. I think we should do the book of Ephesians and include the Armor of God as a lead into that."

"Yes, that would be great. I will be glad to do part of it as well. Let's look at the calendar and--"

"I have already done it." John handed Darron a rough draft of the schedule and how they would approach the different series. "Before we get too deep in this, though, I want to tell the congregation some of what I have been seeing."

"Why start there? Let's lead into it and then slowly let them know."

"I thought that at first; but I really think I need to start with explaining about spiritual gifts and let them know what I have experienced."

"Okay, John, I agree with that; but let's prepare them by teaching them first."

John was silent for a few seconds and then he nodded. "Okay. I am just struggling with keeping all of this inside. I need to let it out soon."

"You will. What if we start with the Armor of God and that moves up the schedule a little?"

John smiled and answered, "I think that is a great compromise. Let's pray."

The two men prayed for the next few minutes, while the angels around the church spread their wings and glowed.

Chapter 18: Beginning Signs

Saturday

The next morning, John was finishing brushing his teeth when Lindsey walked in. It was a lazy Saturday morning with nothing on the agenda, which was rare. He rinsed his mouth and turned to hug his wife.

"When do we tell our parents?"

"I may see them today, I'm not sure. I am not good at keeping a secret, you know." Lindsey turned sideways in the mirror. "I already feel fat."

"Oh no! Not that already!" He grabbed her again and hugged her close. "You are perfect to me."

"John, do you think Rosie's okay?"

"You mean the 'cloud' thing?"

"Well, yeah! I mean how many eight-year-olds see clouds around people?"

"I would say quite a few. Isn't that one of the big ages for imaginary friends?"

"No, I think that would be much younger. I'm not sure. Anyway, I just want her to be okay."

"She's fine! She is one of the smartest little girls I've ever known. I am still convinced that she heard us talking about all the things I have seen or something. I talked to Darron at our meeting yesterday. We came up with a plan on how to proceed with the sermons surrounding my gift."

"That's great. Did you guys talk about all the new stuff you are seeing?"

"Yeah. We made a list. Kind of a way of putting together all the facts around this or at least what we think we know."

"I'd like to see that list."

"I've got it in my Bible downstairs. I'll show you later. How are you feeling?"

"A little sick. I just need some sweet tea."

"So you think you will tell your parents today?" John pointed to her belly.

"Even though it's killing me, maybe we should wait until I see the doctor, okay?"

"I can do that, I'm just not sure you can!"

"Well, I can try. I probably need to tell my mom first, though."

"Tell Mimi? What are you gonna tell her?"

John smiled, "Well Miss Nosy Rosie, you are up early!" John reached over and patted Rosie on her head, feeling a tinge of sadness at how big she was now.

Rosie yawned and answered, "I couldn't sleep with all the talking."

John and Lindsey exchanged a puzzled look. They had only been up for a few minutes and had been talking in somewhat hushed tones to keep from disturbing Rosie. "I'm sorry, sweetie. We thought we were being quiet."

"What's for breakfast?" Rosie said as she yawned again.

"Definitely not muffins." John said and laughed.

"Why not?"

John tried to backtrack his thoughts and realized Rosie would not understand the joke about the muffins. She didn't even know about her mom expecting a baby and certainly wouldn't know about the history of the burnt muffins when her mom was expecting her. Rosie looked intently at her father and then started to laugh. Now, John and Lindsey were both completely puzzled.

"What is so funny?" Lindsey asked.

"Oh, you know, how dad burned the muffins and you get sick when you are having a baby."

"How did you know that, honey?" Lindsey was now crouched in front of her daughter and John quickly did the same.

Rosie looked up at both of her parents and matched their confused expressions, while she answered, "Nardic told me all about it."

Lindsey's mouth dropped open and John answered, "Who is Nardic?"

"He's my guardian angel, dad. He told me all about it."

Lindsey looked up at John and then back at Rosie. "So is Nardic with you all the time, then?"

"Kind of. I mean I see him most of the time; but sometimes I don't. He says he is with me when I need him."

"So is he here right now?" John grabbed Lindsey's hand when he saw it starting to shake.

"Yeah. He is over there." Rosie pointed to an empty space beside the door to the room. Both Lindsey and John looked over to the empty space and then back at their daughter.

John squeezed his wife's hand as if to say, it's okay and then he let go to hold Rosie by the shoulders. "What else does Nardic say to you?" A tear rolled down Lindsey's face, as she felt fear creep into her heart.

"He just says God loves us and that he is here to help protect us for God."

"Well, that is true. God does love us."

"I know. He also told me about my baby sister."

Lindsey reached out for Rosie's hand as John released her shoulders. "Honey, what do you mean 'baby sister.'"

"Mom, the baby in your belly. Nardic said God told him it was a girl. I'm hungry, can I go get some cereal?"

"Of course, sweetie. Go ahead." John watched Rosie go down the steps and then sat down next to Lindsey, whose tears now flowed freely.

"Oh John, how could she have known? It has to be true!"

John hugged his wife and thought through what his daughter had said. He felt sure he was now starting to understand what was happening and no longer felt any fear.

He sat and prayed for his wife and daughter and then answered his wife. "It is. It is another gift from God."

"How is this a gift? It scares me that my little girl is seeing angels. How is that helping us or anyone else?"

"I am not completely sure; but I just know in my heart that it is from God. Lindsey, all that has been happening to me for years now is starting to make sense. I see lights, Rosie calls it a cloud. It really is like a haze or glow. If I were her age, I might call it a cloud too. I also see shadows sometimes. She said she saw a dark cloud around your mother. I think we are being shown a glimpse of the spiritual world to help us understand more about it; and I believe God wants me to preach about it. Maybe this is all so that we can help bring about some type of revival for God's people."

Lindsey had stopped crying as she listened to her husband. Along the walls of the room, a hoard of angels had gathered and all began to glow and surround the room with peace. The power was immediately felt by John and now Lindsey. She looked at her husband and then sank into his arms. She prayed silently for strength and immediately felt the renewal. "John, you are right. I don't know how I know; but I know with all of my heart that you are right."

"Prayer and scripture."

"What?"

"That is the message I am supposed to teach. The power of prayer and scripture."

"Then that is what you should do. For now, I am going to commit to praying for all of this. I am not sure how to help my little girl--"

"Love her."

"Of course--"

John held Lindsey's hands and looked directly into her eyes. "I mean just love her and let it be. This is a gift and we need to embrace it. I didn't want it at first and then I lost it when I tried to ignore it. Now its back and I long for more of it."

Lindsey nodded. They sat in silence a few more minutes and then Lindsey finally spoke again. "I do need to call my mom about the new baby, though."

"So we are not going to wait to tell everyone?" John's eyes sparkled. He knew Lindsey would not be able to wait and she smiled in response.

"I guess not. I'll call her now."

"Go ahead if you want. I was going to look through some notes I was writing for this week's sermon."

Lindsey finished praying alone after John left the room. She walked over to her phone and dialed her parent's home. Ellie answered on the third ring and she and Lindsey had a simple lighthearted conversation for about a minute. As the conversation lagged, Lindsey softly said, "Mom, I have something to tell you. Can you put dad on the phone too?"

"You're pregnant!"

For the second time this morning, someone knew she was pregnant before she could tell them. First Rosie, and now her mom. Lindsey sank down to sit on the bed. "How did you know?"

"A mom just knows."

A strange relief swept through Lindsey. For some reason, she was afraid her mom was going to say an angel had told her. "Wow, you are good."

"How far along are you?"

The relief continued to calm Lindsey, as she realized why she had been so scared. Her fear was rooted in a very real idea: she was afraid that somehow everyone else seemed to be seeing spiritual beings and she was not. She was comforted by the knowledge that her mom was not seeing them too. "Um...It's early. I haven't even been to the doctor yet. I just couldn't stand to wait to tell you. We really aren't telling anyone else yet."

"Have you told Rosie?"

"Hey beautiful, so you are expecting another baby?"

"Oh, hi dad. Yes, we are. We just found out. As for Rosie, well...she sort of guessed it like you, mom."

"She is a smart girl." Ellie smiled as she thought about how much she was enjoying Rosie. Her joy had inspired her to connect more with her other grandchildren as well. The effects of this were exhilarating and the demon was having difficulty staying in the same room with her anymore.

Mark answered, "She sure is. She takes after me!"

They all laughed and Lindsey marveled at how much more relaxed her parents seemed. Was it her imagination or was her mom actually happy and excited? Could it be the power of the prayers she had been praying over scripture as John had suggested? Lindsey was in deep thought about this when she heard her father say, "How is Rosie taking it?"

"She is very excited. We--well she knows and seems happy."

Lindsey and her mother talked for several minutes longer about the baby. Finally, there was a lag and Lindsey felt it was time to ask.

"Hey mom, I'm sorry about Rosie bothering you."

"I told you. No big deal. It's okay. I need to talk about it. After all it's been over 30 years. I think I need to go on. I have been holding that in for way too long."

"Well, I'm just sorry if she caused you pain. She didn't mean anything by it."

"It's fine." Ellie finished her conversation with her daughter and hung up the phone. She walked over to her kitchen window and looked out at the rain clouds forming in the distance. No tears came this time, just a sadness that was deep and hollow in her heart. "Okay God. I'm trying. Help me. I don't want to do this anymore. I've carried this burden long enough."

Galdon's wings glowed as he spread them around Ellie; and the dark shadow pulled back even farther; but the demon did not give up so easily. He threw as many thoughts at Ellie as he could; but they were starting to bounce off. He screeched and cursed and writhed in anger; but Galdon simply smiled. Nothing could touch the power of God at work. Ellie was unaware of the spiritual battle going on around her. Although her soul already belonged to God, she did not realize how much the demons had gripped her and increased her bitterness and pain through the years, stealing joy and power in her own life. Throughout the next few days, she felt a lightness and a joy that she had not felt in years. Mark noticed it too. His prayers for his wife had not gone unnoticed in Heaven. Neither of them fully understood the debt they owed to their young granddaughter.

"Mark, I want to talk about it."

Mark looked up at his wife as she sat down next to him on the couch, "Talk about what?"

"I have never asked much about it. I want to talk about the accident."

Mark studied his wife's face and tried to discern what she meant. He had watched her struggle for over thirty years to work through the pain. His own heartache had been difficult enough to bear; but Ellie had simply closed off her heart and gone into some type of robotic mode through the years. He knew she still loved him and the kids and she put up a great show; but Mark also knew that she was deeply depressed and didn't know how to help her. Through the years, he had decided just to love her and had given up on trying to talk about it. Every time anyone wanted to talk about the accident, Ellie would become inconsolable. The subject had become a great taboo in the family, so Mark was incredibly shocked when over thirty years later Ellie wanted to talk about it. He carefully weighed his words, not knowing how much Ellie would be able to handle. "What do you want to talk about exactly?"

"Everything. Tell me everything."

Mark looked at Ellie. "Let's start with you telling me what you remember first."

Chapter 19: Questions

Sunday

So much was happening; but Rosie was still just a little girl who loved to spend time with her family. Sunday afternoon, Lindsey's parents came over for a cookout and Rosie and her Gran Gran sat on the porch swing waiting for dinner.

"Gran Gran? Can I ask you something?"

"Of course Nosy Rosie! You can ask me anything. I may not have the answer, though."

"Can you tell me about my Aunt Rose Louise?"

Mark's eyes narrowed slightly and he dropped his head and looked away. Ellie had warned him that Rosie was very curious about her namesake right now. "Well, Rosie, she was very beautiful like you. We loved her very much."

"Yeah, I know all that and I know she died in a car accident. I just want to know more about what she liked to play with and about the hospital."

"She pretty much liked what most two-year-olds do. She liked playing outside. I think that was her favorite." Rosie laughed and nestled into her grandfather's arms.

They both sat in silence for a few minutes; and then Rosie pulled away and looked up at his face. "What was it like when she died? Were there lights?"

"Well, it was horrible. We were very sad. Your grandmother was still not well from the car accident; and there were so many decisions to be made. Mark's voice trailed off for a moment and then he gathered himself and continued, "Anyway, it was not much fun for any of us."

"Did Rose Louise cry when she was in the hospital?"

"No, she was always sleeping in the hospital."

"Sleeping?" Rosie crinkled up her nose to try to figure that out. "If she was just sleeping, then why did she die?"

"Well, she was very sick and they couldn't wake her up. We had to...I had to let her go."

"That's so sad. I hope I don't die when I sleep."

"No honey. She was in what we call a coma. That's a type of sleep when your body is very sick and can't wake up. She was that way from the car accident. Why don't we talk about something else?"

"I guess I don't want to talk about anything else. I want to know if Rose Louise had light around her when she died."

"I'm not really sure. It was light in the room; and I was there holding her hand."

"No, like was she alone with light all around her all the time."

"I am not sure I understand. It was a very sad time for me and it wasn't something I ever thought I would have to do. I'm just really glad that she was able to help others."

Rosie perked up at this news. She had never heard that before. "What do you mean she was able to help others?"

Mark cleared his throat and sat up. "I mean sometimes when people die...we find a way to make it better for someone else." He was trying desperately to keep the information simple and not scare his young granddaughter. He had not thought about this in years; and it had just slipped out.

"Oh you mean like you donated Aunt Rose Louise's organs?"

Mark's mouth dropped open and he looked at his granddaughter. "How do you know about that?"

"Oh you know, because of daddy. You know he has a liver that used to belong to someone."

Mark thought about that for a moment and tried to remember if he knew that. He knew that Ellie had said Mark was sick when he was young; but no one had ever really explained it.

"I don't think that I knew that about your dad."

"Who did you donate Rose Louise's organs too?"

"Um...well...Rosie, your grandmother couldn't handle knowing something like that. We have had so much healing to do. She is still so fragile. Please just talk to me about it, okay? I will answer questions for you."

"Sure Gran Gran. I think you should tell her, though."

"Tell her what?"

"You know, that you donated Rose Louise's organs."

Mark sat in silence and tried to determine what to say. He had not really admitted anything to Rosie; but he didn't want to lie to her either.

"Hey you two, dinner is ready." John stood holding the door open and Rosie bounded inside. Mark stopped and grabbed John's elbow.

"I'm afraid I might have opened a can of worms with Rosie. She was very curious about our daughter that died years ago and asked a bunch of questions today. I tried to keep it simple; but she was very concerned about it all."

John stopped and looked at his father-in-law. "Oh no, I'm sorry. What did she say now?"

"She was just talking about her Aunt Rose Louise and wanted to know all about her time in the hospital. Do you know what she means about seeing 'light' around people? She really wanted to know if Rose Louise had a light around her."

John froze and looked at Mark. His mind sifted through a variety of responses and he finally settled with, "I'll sit down with her tonight and try to sort it out." John didn't want to scare his father-in-law with any other details.

"She also knew about organ donations. I don't know if you guys know this, but I donated little Rose Louise's organs when she died. I never even told Ellie. She was in a medically induced coma for several weeks, leaving me to make the decision on what to do. It was so horrible losing our baby and Ellie took it the worst of all, so I thought it was best not to tell her any more than necessary."

"No, I didn't know that. That is an amazing gift you gave someone. I...well...I have someone's liver, actually."

Mark answered so quick that John wasn't sure he had heard him. "Rosie was pretty adamant about wanting to know about light. I really didn't know what to say. She is so darn smart."

John was silent as he considered this. Then he asked, "What *did* you tell her?"

"Well, I really didn't know what to say. I just told her there were lights on in the room and I held little Rose Louise's hand when she died."

This time both men were silent for a moment. Finally, Mark said, "I don't think I realized that you were an organ recipient. What exactly happened to you when you were young?"

John was still considering what his daughter meant about the light then answered. "Well, I was a very sick toddler. I had a tumor in my liver and had to have a complete liver transplant. I was gravely ill for several months, until I got strong enough to overcome all the surgery, etc. Since that time, I've been fine.

"You know, I knew you had been sick and that you were better; but it never occurred to me that you had received an organ. I guess that makes me feel better about Rose Louise."

"I don't talk about it much; but I wouldn't be here without it."

"You know, there is something else."

John looked at his father-in-law expectantly.

"Our Rose Louise was only two when we lost her, so she couldn't talk a whole lot; but she said one word very well."

"What was it?"

"Light."

John and Mark joined the others in the back yard for the cookout. For the rest of the evening, John watched his family interacting and laughing; but he could not stop thinking about everything that was happening.

What does Rosie see? What does she mean 'dark cloud' and 'lights'? Is she really seeing angels?

As scary as this had all been for him, how in the world was an eight year old little girl supposed to handle it? It scared John and he knew that he needed to talk to his daughter. His mind filed through all the events of the last few weeks, as he finished helping Lindsey clean up after everyone left.

Lindsey never mentioned that Rose Louise's organs were donated. How would Rosie know that? What an amazing story, though. It is because of people like that that I am still alive today.

That night he lay in bed next to Lindsey, while they talked. "You know, your dad was telling me about how they donated your sister Rose Louise's organs. I'm very thankful that they did such a thing. That is the only reason I'm still here is because someone did that."

Lindsey looked at him puzzled. "What do you mean?"

"Well, I of course have a liver transplant and your dad said they donated Rose Louise's organs when she died. I wouldn't be here without my liver and I am thankful for people who donate. Your dad had to make that decision, while your mom was still in a coma."

Lindsey had never heard that before. She was confused why her dad had never told her before; but there really was no need to do so. Rose Louise was gone and she was born after all of this anyway. "Does my mother know about it?"

"I'm not sure. Wait. No, your dad said she doesn't know."

"What will that do to her if she finds out?"

"I don't know. We need to talk to Rosie and make sure she stops talking about it--especially to her Mimi. We also need to find out how Rosie knows about the donation."

Lindsey sat up and looked at John. "Did my dad tell her that?"

"No. She asked him about it. He said she already knew."

"How?"

"I don't know but we need to talk to her about all of this and soon."

Lindsey nodded. Her little girl was seeing things that were not normal; and now she knew things that she wasn't supposed to know--things Lindsey herself didn't even know. They had to keep this from her mom. Her mom had struggled for so long that anything more might send her into some kind of mental breakdown. Lindsey felt a strong urge to pray for her mom and said a silent prayer for strength. Galdon closed his eyes and thanked the Father that Lindsey had prayed for her mother again. Now, he hoped she would also use the scriptures. The combination of these weapons were extremely powerful in the spiritual world.

John laid in bed that night unable to sleep and stared at the ceiling. He silently prayed for wisdom and guidance and within seconds the room began to fill with a soft glow. Tears filled his eyes as he absorbed the beauty of the light and he rolled over and pulled Lindsey close. There was no more fear and only an indescribable love and peace that washed over him and gently soothed him to sleep. His dreams were filled with the glory and magnificence of heaven as he understood it to be from all of his research through the years. He woke around midnight with a sudden realization that his young daughter could see and talk to an angel. Did that mean she could see the demons too? His fatherly instinct kept him awake for several hours, as he tried to determine how to keep her safe. At least his visions of the spiritual world could be utilized somehow in his ministry; but how would they help an eight year old little girl? He wrestled long into the early morning hours with how to help little Rosie, while Meris shook his head and willed him to just pray.

Chapter 20: More Information

Monday

Normally, he took Monday's off; but there were an uncomfortable number of unresolved events that Pastor John needed to investigate. First, his gift was expanding and growing. Now his daughter was seeing things too; and that scared him more. How did she know so much without being told? She claimed to talk to an angel named Nardic; but how could that be? He and Lindsey were going to have to sit down with her and find out more about this. Then there was the letter and the angel pin--was he supposed to take that? He wanted to talk to his parents about his childhood sickness; but that seemed low on the list of priorities for now. Lindsey's parents were a mess spiritually; but they had been that way for years. Was it his job to reach them? While the church had ministries that tried to reach out to support mission work around the world, he had a ripe mission field right in his own family.

Pastor John sat in his office with the door locked and stared at the Bible in front of him. *God, I just want to get it right. Where do I begin? What is going on?*

His mind churned through a thousand scenarios of where to begin; then he contemplated ignoring it all and trying to do his job, which seemed more difficult now, as he struggled with the issues in front of him. Before he could make a decision, he heard a soft knock on his door. Mary was taking today off, so he had no warning as to who this might be. The inner struggle to stay hidden inside was overtaken by his desire to help people, so he opened the door.

"Hi, pastor."

"Hello, Ann. What a surprise. How can I help you?" John was happy to see the familiar smile of Ann, the nurse from the hospital.

"I just got off work and was on my way home and wanted to talk with you." John instinctively looked at his watch and Ann laughed. "I worked third shift last night. I jump around a lot. It keeps me young--that and a bottle of hair color." Ann touched her light brown hair, which was neatly clipped back on each side of her face.

Now it was John's turn to laugh and he waited for the elderly nurse to continue talking; but when there was only silence, he felt compelled to speak. "Why don't you come in and have a seat?"

Ann timidly followed the pastor inside and sat in a large cozy chair, while she fumbled with her purse. "I am not sure how to say this without sounding crazy."

"I think that no matter what, I would not be one to call you crazy." Galdon chuckled and looked at Meris. Both angels knew how much John had been questioning his own sanity lately.

"Thank you, Pastor John." Ann sighed and finally said, "I have something that I need to give you." She opened her purse and pulled out a picture and handed it to him.

The photograph was old and poor quality compared with today's digital varieties. At first glance, John could see much younger Ann standing beside a young boy and his parents. There were balloons and other hospital staff in the background; but the banner above their heads said, 'Congratulations!' He looked up at Ann and she motioned for him to look closer. This time he could see it clearly: the people in the picture were his parents and the young boy was him.

"How did you..."

"Pastor, do you remember I told you that I used to work at Cincinnati Children's Hospital and I was one of your main nurses when you were undergoing chemotherapy and the transplant?"

"Yes, I remember."

John sensed she wanted to say something else.

Ann looked up quickly. "I think that you need to know some things."

John braced himself. He didn't know how much more he could take. "What kinds of things?"

He could sense she was uncomfortable; and when she finally spoke again, it was almost a whisper. "Pastor, you do believe in prayer, right?"

John laughed slightly and answered, "Of course! It is one of the cornerstones of Christian belief."

Ann's face clouded over slightly, as she seemed to be searching for the right words to say. "Pastor, you were the sweetest child. It affected me so much that I almost quit nursing altogether. I don't know if you know how close you were to dying...it was horrible. When I prayed for you, it was like I really felt God's presence."

"I really owe you for both the nursing care and your prayers."

Ann shook her head quickly and responded, "No, the praise goes only to God. He provided all the strength. I just thank Him that I was a vessel."

"That is correct and well said." John wasn't quite convinced that this was why Ann was here. Surely, she didn't come just to reaffirm that she had prayed for him. He waited patiently for her to continue.

"Pastor, when they gave you that transplant, I saw you both before and after. There was a remarkable difference in you. You were...brighter. I think that I was the only one who could see it; at least no one else said so.

John's head sprung up and he looked at Ann. "What do you mean?"

"You were not supposed to live. The doctor's told us that you would not make it through the night so many times. I have never prayed so much in my life."

"I thank you for the prayers. I wish I remembered more about it."

Again, Ann fumbled with her purse and seemed hesitant. John watched her struggle with something and wasn't sure how to help her. His experience with counseling had taught him to be patient and let the person open up on their own terms; but he was screaming inside for her to tell him what she knew. Finally, she licked her lips and looked up with tears in her eyes.

"Pastor, you were given more than life, you were given...something else."

"Absolutely, there is not a day that goes by--"

"I'm sorry to interrupt; but you don't understand. You were changed."

"Changed?"

Ann leaned forward slightly and looked him straight in the eye. "Have you seen anything unusual?"

John was taken aback and his mouth fell open reflexively. "What--"

"Have you seen anything that you can't explain?"

An incredible feeling of warmth overcame John; and he relaxed and felt as if he could tell Ann anything. His tongue felt heavy; but he found the words and his voice cracked slightly as he answered, "I have seen..." He was careful not to reveal too much. His hands trembled slightly as he continued, "...a sort of glow or light."

Ann nodded and her eyes danced. "Yes, that is it. Does it seem bright but never hurt your eyes?"

Again, John was shocked. "Yes, that is exactly it."

"I don't know how to tell you this except to say that I saw it too; but not only with you."

"What do you mean?"

"When you came out of your surgery, I could see a strange light around you. I didn't tell anyone directly; and I kept thinking that something was wrong with me."

John felt his pulse quicken. "Do you still see it? Am I glowing right now?"

"I don't see it now; but I did when you were with your baby daughter."

"What do you think it is? I thought I was losing my mind. I want to think it is spiritual, I mean...I just know it is." John was still having trouble fully believing all that was happening. Meris watched the pastor with sadness, hoping he would soon stop doubting it all.

Ann nodded. "I did the same. It is not of this world, pastor. You were given a physical gift of the transplant along with a spiritual gift too."

They both stared at the floor and allowed the words to filter through their minds. Of course, John had already come to this conclusion himself with the help of his wife and Darron; but this time, someone completely unexpected was telling *him* about it. Would the religious world accept this or would he be forced to leave his own church? This was the second person to tell him what was going on with him. Why was it so hard to just believe and trust in the gift? Isn't this what he preached all the time?

"Did you ever tell anyone?"

"No, not directly. I knew that everyone would think that I was insane."

"How did you know to come to me?"

"There is so much more to tell you."

"What do you mean?"

"I need to tell you the whole story. It is too hard to give it to you in pieces."

It was so long ago...but I remember it so well...

"The nurses station was really quiet and calm, as the days activities settled into the evening shift. I had only been working at the hospital for about six weeks and loved my job; but this day had been different. Most days, I left work feeling good about what I had been able to do for the kids. There were wide varieties and types of injuries and illness that I saw everyday; but most of the kids were going to heal quickly and it was wonderful to be able to help them.

The day you arrived, though, was terribly different. You were so little and so sick. The doctors finished the major testing and had diagnosed you with a hepatoblastoma; and I knew it was a very aggressive type of liver tumor. Your prognosis was very bad and you needed a liver transplant very soon or you would die. They weren't even sure if it would help. Anyway, I had been in the room when the doctor delivered the news; and watching your family was one of the hardest things that I have ever done. There was nothing I could do to help...but pray.

That evening, I remember just sitting and staring at the charts in front of me, trying to finish up my paperwork so I could head home. I couldn't stop crying. The other nurses were off doing different things and I was really glad, because I had only been working there for a few weeks and didn't really know them well. There was this little room in the back behind the charts where we kept some extra supplies and I slipped back there to pray. Something happened when I fell to my knees that night. I could feel God's presence, almost like a blanket around me. It was really amazing."

Ann hesitated, while she collected her emotions. John sat in silence thinking about how hard it must have been on his parents. He could not imagine what it would be like if Rosie were that sick. As he thought about his parent's grief and struggles, he silently thanked God for them and for this nurse, who had obviously given so much of herself to help him and his family.

"I don't know how to thank you for your prayers."

Ann waved her hand in front of her face and wiped her eyes. "There is no need to thank me. I really should thank you and your family. Something about that experience changed me forever. I don't know how much you know about organ donation; but there was a very slim chance that you would get a donor in time. Most people never think much about organ donation. Anyway, I cried out to God that night and I begged Him to help you. When I got up to leave, I felt I needed to see you one more time. I'll be honest, I wasn't sure how many days or even hours you had left. I really thought...well...I just needed to see you again.

"When I reached the door to your room, I tapped lightly; but there was no answer, so I slowly opened the door. The room was dark and I could see a form curled up on the chair beside your bed; and I knew it was your mom. She never left your side. I stood watching you in your little crib--you were resting so peacefully even though that horrible tumor was ravaging your little body. There just wasn't anything more the doctor's or I could do. I think that was what frustrated me so much and I couldn't imagine how frustrated your parents must have been. I was about to leave when your mom woke up. She sat straight up in her chair and scared me so bad that I froze in place. Anyway, that night...it was the first time that your mom and I really talked. We sat there together for almost the whole night. We prayed together and cried together and honestly just both cried out to God. It was one of the most raw moments of my life.

The next two days I found a way to see your mom and we continued to talk and pray. She had lost her way with God and needed help to reconnect. She began to talk to your dad and within a week, we were all meeting in the hospital room to pray together. When your parents rededicated their lives to God, an organ match came through within the next hour. It was a miracle and we all knew it. Even the doctors were surprised at how quickly the match was made. You came through the surgery so easily--another miracle. It was right after this that I saw your glow. Eventually, when you finished your last chemotherapy treatment, I attended your goodbye party, which is where the picture originated. You had the glow from the moment you got the liver until the day you left the hospital."

When Ann finished telling John the story, he leaned back in his chair thinking it through. The story should have shocked him or in some way sent him into a whirlwind of emotions; but instead, he felt at peace. "Did you ever get scared?"

"I did; but then again I didn't. I was scared to tell anyone else; but the light made me feel good; and I really wanted to be around it and you."

"What happened, then? Why didn't you keep in touch?"

"I don't really know. It was just strange to do so. We weren't relatives and I didn't really know what to do."

"Have you ever seen light like that again, besides with Rosie?"

"Yes, one time. That is why I am here. I think there is some weird connection."

"What do you mean?"

"A few weeks ago, I was working an extra shift and they moved me to help in the ER because they were short staffed. I was more or less helping the nurses that worked there regularly and didn't have my own patients. The nurses were all busy when one of the call lights came on, so I went to the room to see if I could help the patient. I opened the door to the room and found an old woman sitting up on the side of the bed. She asked me to get her a drink of water, so I hurried away and returned to find her laying down again. She took a sip of the water and thanked me; and as she handed the water back, I saw the glow around her. She smiled the most beautiful smile and she grabbed my hand and squeezed. When she let go, she simply said the weirdest thing. She said; "You should tell him to take my letters."

John sat up straighter. "Did you say, 'letters?'"

"Yes, letters; but it gets even stranger than that. I left the room and went to grab her chart to get her meds--sorry, medicines--ready. When I came back to the room, she had a room full of light. I could hear voices singing...but when I looked inside, it was only her smiling and looking at nothing. Anyway, I didn't tell anyone. I will never forget it as long as I live. The voices...they were so beautiful."

John's mind was swirling. "Do you happen to remember her name or what she looked like?"

"I am not sure...I only saw her that one night. I think that they admitted her, though."

John let out a small sigh. He had hoped that this would all be connected somehow. "That's okay."

"I think I can remember at least part of her name--it was unusual. I believe she went by Mia; but I can't remember the last name."

John's head snapped up and he said, "Did you say, Mia?"

"Yes, hang on, it was Minnamia Hunt! I can't believe I remember it!"

"That's it!" Ann looked confused at his outburst. "I'm sorry, I didn't mean to scare you. I know...knew Mia too."

"Really! That's amazing. When did you meet her?"

There was no way that he could say what he needed to say without his emotions taking over. He looked away and tried to think. Somehow, he knew Ann would understand.

"Pastor John. Are you okay?"

"Yes, I think so. I met Mia at a nursing home that I visit each week. I didn't know her well; but she...well...had a spiritual gift too."

"You said she *had* a gift. Is she..."

"Yes, she is gone."

"I'm so sorry." Ann said and she and John both allowed a brief pause before she continued, "Do you know what she was talking about with the letters?"

"Yes, I believe that I do. It's a long story; but basically, she had some old letters that she left when she died."

"Did you take them?"

"No, I looked at them; but I wasn't sure whether I should be the one to take them or not."

"Then that is it."

"What?"

"Why I had to come here today. I have had an overwhelming feeling to come and visit you to tell you that story. I have not been able to sleep well the last two nights. I knew I had to come today; but I didn't know why until now. You are supposed to take those letters. I don't know why; but maybe you will find out someday."

Silence draped the room when so many words needed to be said, so many questions needed to be asked. Finally, John was able to speak. "This is amazing."

"It really is."

John thanked Ann for coming and closed the door as she left. He needed more time to think and pray. For the next hour, he prayed fervently for guidance and help and then picked up his keys and headed home.

Meris, Galdon, and Nardic all moved swiftly to keep Pastor John and his family safe, as they began to finally put their story together. The next few days would be critical.

Chapter 21: Digging Deeper

Monday (Noon)

There was no other place to go except to see his wife. They had shared everything and he needed her now. They took Rosie to his parent's home and went for a long lunch. John reviewed everything from start to finish with Lindsey, holding nothing back this time; and they both sat in silence when he was through. Finally, Lindsey broke the silence.

"Why don't we go get them now?"

"What, the letters?"

"Absolutely. I think you are supposed to get them. They might have some of the answers."

"Why, though? They are just letters between Mia and the family that donated the organ to her."

"John, I am going to leave you here and get them myself, if you don't take me."

John smiled and then realized she was dead serious. "Okay, then. Let's go."

They arrived at the nursing home and John introduced his wife to Linda. There was the usual small talk and finally, John asked to see the letters.

"I was hoping you would return for them. I can't think of anyone else who would even want them."

"I would at least like to open them."

"Well, if you open them, you keep them. I don't want them back. I know where to find you, if I do need them." Linda smiled then she turned to Lindsey. "You know, I wanted him to have them before. No one has ever come around asking about any of Mia's things." Linda handed the large manilla envelope to John.

"That is so sad. Thank you, Linda. We can bring them back anytime. Please let me know if anyone else comes."

"They won't; but I will. Have a great day! By the way, Mr. Roberts is at his son's house today."

"Oh, thank you. We were going there next."

"I figured. Take care, now."

Pastor John and Lindsey walked out to his car and they both sat looking at the letters in John's hands. "Should we read them here?" asked John.

"Why not?"

He opened the first envelope and pulled out the folded letter inside. The paper crinkled as John unfolded the page; and he moved slowly to keep from tearing it. As he unfolded the letter, a picture fell out. John picked it up and they both looked at the picture of Lou that Mia had kept on her dresser.

Lindsey gasped, "Oh my gosh!"

"What? Do you know Lou?"

"Lou?"

"The boy in the picture. Mia kept this framed picture on her dresser."

"I don't know Lou; but my mom has that same picture! That's Rose Louise!" She turned the picture over to see the word Lou in the middle. She noticed something else, a faint R in front of the name Lou. "I think this is supposed to be an R for Rose and Lou is abbreviated for Louise."

John looked over Lindsey's shoulder and smiled. "All that time Mia thought it was a boy named Lou. I guess her eyesight was not so good. It is hard to see."

"Wow. That means...Rose Louise was the donor for her kidneys! That's amazing! I didn't know that she was a donor at all until a few days ago and now this. Read the letter."

John held the letter in his hands and slowly began to read the words, as Lindsey continued to stare at the picture of her dead sister.

Dear Someone,

I really don't know where to begin. I don't know how to thank you for your gift. I began my journey when I was forty years old and I was very sick. I was told I needed a kidney transplant or I would soon die and was put on dialysis and had to endure this treatment three times a week for four hours at a time. Needless to say, it changed my life dramatically. Even with the treatment, I was very weak.

Normally, someone my age would be able to endure it much better than someone older; but it nearly killed me. Anyway, I was put on the donor list quickly; but I knew it was a waiting game. We prayed vehemently, as did our friends and family; and within a year, we received news that a pair of kidneys was available for me. We rejoiced, of course, and I immediately underwent the long and difficult surgery followed by an even longer recovery, which was complicated by some infection and pneumonia. Through it all, I stayed strong through the help of many people in my life.

Days and months went by; and I often wondered who had given me this wonderful gift. I tried to talk to different people at the OPTN; but there are strict guidelines on that information and I was only allowed to write to say thank you. I can't thank you enough, though, because you have given something beyond what mere words can express in gratitude. You have given me my life back and I have no way to make it up to you. I want you to know that every day I promise to live life to the fullest and keep your loved one with me every step that I take.

There is no more that I can say. I am forever indebted to you and your family. Your sacrifice and gift have allowed another family to thrive. Thanking you is too small of a thing. You are my hero.

Sincerely,

M

"What is the OPTN?"

"That is the Organ Procurement and Transplantation Network. They are responsible for connecting and counseling families."

"Wait, there is more! Look at the back!" Lindsey pointed to the back side, where another small letter had been scribbled.

Here is the rest of my story. My husband obtained this picture and now I know that Lou was the one who gave me life. I am sixty years old now and I know it will not be long before the Lord calls me home. Since the day that I woke up from my transplant surgery, I discovered that I had been given another gift: I see spiritual things. Most of the time, I see light or darkness around people; but I have also seen angels. I want whoever is reading this to know. They are real and they are all around us all the time. I have no idea why I can do this; but as much as it scared me at first, it now brings me great comfort. I can in no way repay the gift that was bestowed upon me and I am forever grateful.

Sincerely,

Minnemia Hunt

Lindsey spoke first, but in a whisper. "She...could see angels. Like you, John."

John was silent; but his thoughts moved quickly through the obvious conclusions. "She had Rose Louise's kidneys..." A thought entered John's mind and he knew he needed to check on several things. He needed to talk to his in-laws; but there was so much else to work through as well and he didn't want to alarm anyone yet. Lindsey just stared straight ahead, as if in a trance.

"What does the other letter say?"

In all the emotions surrounding the first letter, John had forgotten about the second one. "Oh, it is addressed to Mia."

Dear M,

Thank you for your letter. My family can't endure more of this memory; but we are all glad for you.

M

"That's it?" Lindsey peered over at the letter.

"Looks like it was handwritten."

"That looks like my dad's handwriting. The M could be for Mark."

"That would make sense. He never told your mom about it all and maybe he just snatched this up and sent it back so she would never know."

"I am sure that he did. That is probably what he would still do. He was always trying to protect her."

"Makes sense. This would have only been a year after the accident. Your mom would have had you by now. I am sure that it was just too much for him."

"Do you think I should tell my mom? Maybe this would give her some closure or something."

"I don't know. Maybe you should talk to your dad. Obviously, he read it and returned it and didn't want her to know. I am not sure that he would want to open up old wounds."

"Those wounds stay open."

They both reflected on the information; and finally, John spoke, "I think you should ask your dad about it before you bring any of this up to your mom."

"You are right. I would like to know if he is definitely the one who got that letter and returned it."

John sat quietly looking at his hands. "I wish Mia was still here. She was an amazing woman. I had no idea she had passed until the other day."

"She sounds like it. I would have liked meeting her too."

John straightened up slightly and cleared his throat. "So much is happening. Darron and I have put together several sermons about it and we are excited to start teaching and preaching about it; but I am really afraid of what other people are going to think. I know I shouldn't care; but we are going to take some type of kick back from this for sure. I'm worried about you and Rosie too."

Lindsey held his hand and squeezed it gently, "Don't worry, that is what the devil and his demons would want you to do." After a short pause, she continued, "Why do you think that you see the glow and not me? Why does Rosie seem to see light too? It makes me feel like I am not close enough to God or something."

John instinctively placed his other hand on top of Lindsey's hand. "I don't think that at all. I really don't know what I think. If angels are all around us all the time, then why in the world would God only let us see glimpses of them? Why not more? I don't have all the answers; but I now know God wants me to preach about it. What I don't know is how everyone will react. The more I pray about it, the more I just don't really care what they will think. My biggest concern is for you and Rosie."

Lindsey watched her husband wrestling with the logic and then it came to her, as if someone had whispered it into her ear. In truth, Galdon had.

"John, it's not about us. It's about God and his work."

"Of course, Lindsey--"

"No, you don't get it. I am talking about a genuine and wholehearted belief in God and the work that he does. I think God wants you to use this gift for Him to convince people that they need Him. Maybe even start a revival of some kind."

"What do you think that I do every single day? That is my life's work. I have dedicated myself to teaching people about God."

"Yes, but you said yourself you don't have all the answers. Maybe the revival starts with you and with me. We need to pray and study the Bible. He is trying to tell you and the rest of us something."

"That just sounds too easy. I mean, why doesn't he just tell us what he wants to say. What is the point of making me, Mia, and now Rosie look crazy?"

"You sound like a non believer who won't commit. You keep saying, 'look crazy.' That is not how you look at all to me. I think it is incredible; and like I said before, I'm a little jealous that I can't see it too. When you talk about it, I don't think about your sanity at all. It just grabs my attention and I immediately want to learn more."

"It now has that affect on me too. At first I tried to run from it, kind of like Jonah; but now I really almost crave it. I just...I guess everything has been so comfortable and I'm not so sure it will stay that way."

"Comfortable. Hmm...I don't think we were called to be comfortable. What should we do?" Lindsey rubbed her eyes and leaned back in the car seat.

"I'm starting this Sunday. The series begins this week and I need more prayer support. I think we need to talk to our parents too. We need to tell mine about the new baby anyway."

"Oh! Sorry, I already did! Your mom called this morning and I forgot that you hadn't told her. I was sick...anyway they know."

"Well, that takes care of that! Now we just need to tell them that Rosie and I see angels and demons. I'm sure they will be proud to have a son that sounds nuts, I mean, uncomfortable!"

"At least I'm not the crazy one. I don't see anything!" Lindsey smiled and John reciprocated.

"When we talk to your parents, we need to somehow talk with your dad alone about the letter too."

"So we are going to tell them about what you are seeing before you preach about some of it."

"I think so. I really want their prayer support too. I also want to explain it before they hear it from the pulpit."

"Okay. Let's see if I can get my dad alone tonight when we pick up Rosie and then maybe we can mention the sermon to them both."

"Boy, you don't waste any time!"

"Might as well do it now." Lindsey called them but they insisted on bringing Rosie home instead and promised to have her there within the hour. John drove home and the two of them held hands and prayed for thirty minutes, while they waited for Rosie to be brought back home. By the end of their prayers, a gathering of angels had surrounded their home. Their strength was building and there was nothing the demons could do but watch.

Chapter 22: Secrets Revealed

Monday night

When Mark and Ellie arrived with Rosie, she was sound asleep. John carried her inside and put her to bed and Lindsey asked her parents to come inside. Before they could settle into their chairs, John came back down to announce Rosie was awake and wanted her Mimi. Ellie smiled and jumped up to go see her granddaughter, while the other three sat down in the den. When Ellie left the room, Lindsey could take it no more and she decided to ask her dad about the letter.

"So, dad. How is mom doing?"

"She and I have talked about Rosie's questions. I think everything is okay. Your mom has had to adjust; but I really think that this has helped her in many ways."

"Oh. I am glad to hear that. I guess there is a lot to discuss." Lindsey looked at John and he nodded.

Lindsey's dad looked at her with a puzzled expression.

"Dad, John told me that you donated Rose Louise's organs."

Mark smiled a sweet but sad smile. "Yes, I had to make a decision and needed to act quickly. I signed the forms and tried to never look back."

"I know you never told mom back then; but does she know now?"

Mark's face darkened slightly. "She didn't know about it then--she was still in a coma. I had to decide it all alone. It was one of the worst times in my life. I just never thought it would help her to tell her. She could barely handle losing your sister much less anything else. Besides, we had you so soon after; and then our lives were just so busy. I never really thought it was that important."

"I understand. We stay so busy now that I don't know what we will do when we have this new baby."

"You will figure it out. It has a way of working its way out on its own. If you have one child or fifty, you will forever and always be busy."

"Dad, did you guys ever get a letter from anyone who received organs from Rose Louise?"

Mark nodded and a strange look crossed his face. "Yes, we got three letters."

"Do you remember who were they from?"

"Well, everything is kept confidential; but about a year after the donations, the people who received an organ had the chance to write to us. About a year and a half after we lost Rose Louise, I found an envelope in the mail on a Saturday that was sent from the organization that helped connect our families. The envelope had one letter inside. I hid it from your mom, because I wasn't sure exactly how she would react. About three weeks later, I got another envelope with two more letters inside. All the letters were signed with initials only by design, so that we would have no connection to the families."

"Do you still have all three of them?"

"Well, I still have two of them. I used to get them out occasionally to read them."

"Why only two?"

"I returned the first one with a letter from me. I didn't know how to handle it all and was afraid your mom might find it. Once I returned it, I thought it was all; but apparently, one person can provide up to eight different organs to donate. When the other two letters came, I just didn't want to part with them."

"Dad, could I see the letters? John and I would both like to read them, if that is okay."

Mark stood and walked over to a small desk in the corner of the room. He pulled on the top drawer until it completely came out. Reaching underneath, he pulled a manilla envelope loose that was taped there and replaced the drawer. He turned the envelope over in his hands as if handling a fragile flower and slowly walked over to Lindsey with a painful expression on his face.

"That's the desk you gave us. I remember you asked me to never get rid of it without talking to you first. Is that why?"

"Yes, I put them under there to keep them far away from your mom. These letters are all I have left of Rose Louise; but I want you to have them."

"No, dad. I don't want to keep them, just read them."

"Either way, take them and keep them here."

Lindsey hugged her father and took the envelope from him. She could see how the envelope had been handled a great deal and thought of how her dad must have read them many times.

"I have never told anyone about these. They just sort of became my own personal shrine to her. I didn't worship Rose Louise; but I needed a way to grieve too. Your mom and I were never able to heal together."

"I understand. Thank you for sharing them with us. I will keep them safe."

With a raspy voice that bubbles to the surface when someone is trying desperately to maintain their control, Mark answered his daughter. "No, thank you."

"Why...why didn't you tell me?" Everyone turned to see Ellie, ashen faced and trembling in the doorway.

"Oh honey!" Mark stood and grabbed Ellie before she slumped to the ground. John helped him carry her to the couch, where they all talked for over an hour. Ellie was surprisingly calm but not sad. She wasn't crying at all, which everyone noticed. The more she learned about the organ donations, the happier she seemed to be.

"Mark, do you know what this means?"

Mark looked hopelessly from John and Lindsey to his wife. "No, honey, I don't know what you mean."

"Rose Louise is still alive! I mean, I know she isn't but part of her is or at least was. Our little princess was able to help these people live." Several angels were now in the room, including Galdon, Nardic, and Meris. All of them spread their wings from the strong prayers of a little girl, who sat in the hallway listening to the adults in the other room. Nardic had already told her most of this story and she was glad that everyone else now knew it too. She prayed and thanked God for Rose Louise.

When Mark and Ellie left, Lindsey hugged John. "I don't know what to call that except a miracle."

"You mean your mom's reaction to all of this?"

"Yes. No one could have guessed that this would help her heal."

"I don't think it was just this. I really think that it has been a combination of the prayers, the timing, and Rosie."

"Look, they left the letters."

"I'm sure they will want them back. Let's read through them again."

"I'm game. I am not at all tired."

John smiled and said. "Me either."

The first letter was written by a family of a man that had received Rose Louise's heart. The extreme gratitude and love expressed to Lindsey's parents from the family was overwhelming. The second letter was from a family that had received Rose Louise's liver. This letter was sweet and direct and extremely well written as well. John and Lindsey each read both letters several times and both agreed that the families that had received the organs sounded incredibly overwhelmed.

Lindsey pushed the letters toward the center of the table and looked up at John with wet eyes. "That is one of the most beautiful displays of love that I have ever seen. To know that one family's heartache could heal so many others is incredible. I'm glad my mom got to see this and see how God took something so awful and made it beautiful through the act of my dad signing those papers."

"I understand why your father was reluctant to show them to her. She was so fragile and sad."

"I guess so. Anyway, I am glad that he shared them with us all now."

"Me too."

"That makes three."

"Three what?"

"Three families that Rose Louise was able to help through her death. She saved three people."

"You mean including Mia."

"Yes, including Mia."

"What do we do now?" Lindsey stood and walked over to the window overlooking the dark backyard. Her eyes strained to see the swing set in the moonlight and then without warning, she began to focus on the reflection in the window instead of what was outside. Behind her she saw something white and glowing standing beside her husband. The glowing object was surrounding her husband with what looked like large wings.

Lindsey gasped and turned around but the light was gone. She turned back to the window and could not see it there either.

"What's wrong?"

"I saw...well...I saw something."

"What?" John could see the concern in Lindsey's eyes; and he stood and walked over to his wife. He held her hands and watched the fear slowly subside. "What is it?"

"I think I saw an angel. At least I saw a light and some wings."

"Where? In back yard?"

"No, in the reflection...it was hugging you."

"Hugging me?"

"Well, surrounding you with it's wings. It was...beautiful."

John looked into Lindsey's eyes and could sense the calm that was building. It had been the same for him. First an overwhelming fear followed by an even more overwhelming calm. Without a doubt in his mind, he knew that Lindsey had been given a glimpse into the spiritual world.

"Now you see. It has been difficult to explain."

"John...I..."

"I know."

Chapter 23: Angels and Demons

Tuesday

So much was changing and both John and Lindsey could feel it. They spent as much time together as they could to pray and talk; and then they started to dig for more information. The families that had received the heart and the liver were going to be difficult to find. The records for these transplants were sealed and meant to stay that way to protect the families. John called a lawyer from the church to get his opinion; and after some extensive checking, he confirmed that this information was strictly guarded and would not be possible to obtain.

John's suspicions about something were growing and he called his mom. They talked for over an hour and he was convinced he was right; and when he told Lindsey his thoughts, she immediately agreed too. The time frame was almost perfect; and there was only one way to prove it. He and Lindsey went straight to his parent's home, bringing Rosie along to play. One look at the letter in John's hand and his mom started to cry. He told his parents all about Ann's visit and all that had been happening with the lights and glowing, while Lindsey played with Rosie in the other room. When he was through talking, they all sat and worked through the details. It was obvious that he had been right: the liver he had received that had saved his life had come from Rose Louise. His parents agreed to pray for them all; and John, Lindsey, and Rosie headed home. After they put Rosie to bed, John and Lindsey sat in their family room reviewing what they knew.

"John, this is the most amazing story that I have ever heard. I can't believe that you have part of my sister living in you--that you would not even be here without it."

John's emotions had been tested so much lately and he was simply stunned. "I know. I can never thank your family enough for what they did. I wish we could find the other family, though. I think that the story is not quite finished."

"Even if we knew who had Rose Louise's heart and could find the family, the odds are that the recipient is probably no longer living. That was over 35 years ago." Lindsey was staring at her laptop, as she scanned through several articles about transplants.

"I guess that is true. I would still love to meet that family." John didn't finish what he wanted to say; but Lindsey understood. She also wanted to know if this family had seen angels. So far, Mia and John had both been blessed by spiritual awareness of some kind. For some reason, Rosie was also blessed with this gift.

Lindsey sat up and closed her laptop. "John. Do you think that Rose Louise had some deep spiritual gift that maybe she transferred to you and Mia and possibly this other person? I mean, what if she had a strong spiritual gift and when you and Mia received a part of her you both also received this gift? Is that too weird?"

"I don't think it is weird at all. It would explain a lot. Your dad said Rose Louise used to say the word light a lot. I am not sure what we are supposed to believe about the transfer of a spiritual gift. All I know is that it is definitely what seems to have happened. I can't understand why Rosie seems to have it too, though."

"Maybe because she has a part of Rose Louise through both me and you. I am a blood relative and you have a part of her."

"Maybe. This is just all so strange."

"I loved seeing the angel around you. It was overwhelming but beautiful."

"I know. I have been running from this since I first started suspecting it was spiritual. I am a man who has dedicated himself to spreading the gospel and all I wanted to do was explain it away. It has made me really rethink what I believe and whether or not I should still be a preacher or not."

Lindsey grabbed his hand. "If there is one thing that I feel sure about it is that you are an amazing preacher. I can't imagine that God would want you to stop doing that."

"What if he is calling me to do something else?"

"I can't answer that one for you; but I can help you pray about it."

John looked at his watch. It was 12:30 and he needed to head to the office for the appointment with the strange man, Mr. B. He stood and kissed Lindsey and drove the short trip over with both Meris and Galdon staying close, as both knew how dangerous this might become. John strolled in and noticed Mary was not at her desk. As they drew near the door, Meris gave a shout, bringing Galdon instantly to his side. Both could sense the danger lurking within and knew that Pastor John needed help. There was a foul stench and a cold chill in the air, which could only mean one thing.

John walked into his office, oblivious to the danger within. He placed his sermon notes on his desk and sat down. Within seconds, the door opened and Mr. B stood before him in the opening. John jumped to his feet; but Mr. B held up his hands, causing John to fall back into his chair.

"I am here for our time together, Pastor John."

"Who are you?"

"Really? You haven't figured it out yet? Mr. B?" He laughed in a low sadistic tone and then continued, "I thought you were smarter than that."

"What is your real name?"

"Well, I guess you would know me as Bune."

John shifted in his seat and tried to remember if he was familiar with the name or not. Since the name wasn't familiar, he asked the obvious next question. "What do you want?" For reasons he didn't understand, John was not afraid; but he was very alert. The peace and protection from the two powerful angels enveloped him. Bune paced back and forth slowly as he eyed the two large angels standing in front of the desk protecting the pastor.

"So smart, Pastor John, yet still you don't get it."

John watched the strange man before him as the man walked back and forth but never closer to his desk. He tried to remember anything in his past that might help him right now, when he noticed that the man had a dark outline around him. "You are...not a Christian."

Bune laughed. "Far from it! Very good. Now you are getting it."

Meris and Galdon moved beside John, ready to do whatever was required. The Father had told them to stand down for now.

"Are you a demon?"

"What do you think?"

"What do you want from me?"

"Well, nothing really that important to you. I just want you to get the help that you need."

"What are you talking about?"

"I can see how stressed you are. It's all these lights and glowing...it's really just a matter of getting you some help." Bune's voice had a high-pitched quality that seemed to echo as he spoke.

John's mouth dropped open. "How do you know about that?"

"You would be surprised what a few busybodies in a church can find out and spread around."

"Clara Burton?"

Bune laughed again. "Yes, I am very fond of her!"

"Well, I'm fine, and I am not alone. Others see it too."

"Yes, yes. So what? What about those who don't see it? What will that make them think?"

John was silent for a few seconds and then answered, "Well, I guess they will listen."

"What makes you think that? Didn't you doubt it all at first too; and you are a preacher?"

John felt anger rising up inside at Bune; and he really didn't understand why. "What do you want anyway? Did you just come here to challenge what I see or don't see?"

"What do I want? Wow, that is a loaded question!"

"How did you get an appointment with me last week? My secretary--"

"Does that even matter at this point? Come on, Pastor John. We all know that the real problem here is what to do with this little gift of yours."

"What--?" John was speechless for the moment, unable to think of what he wanted to ask.

Bune smiled and John felt sick to his stomach. Galdon removed his sword and pointed it at the demon, who held up his hands in surrender. "Look, I am just concerned about how the rest of the world is going to deal with all of this...stuff." Bune smiled. "I guess I am here to help you."

"Help me? How?"

"Well, I see how much your church has grown and I am sure you don't want that to change."

"So?"

"I want to make a deal with you."

"A deal. You can't be serious. What kind of deal?"

Galdon inched forward and Meris pulled him back. Nardic now landed in the room and the demon looked over at him briefly before he continued.

"Well, I don't think that you realize what your little venture into the spiritual world will potentially cost you. I just think that you need to ignore it all. Eventually, you will stop seeing it and things will stay the same. Remember back when it started, you pushed it out of your mind and it kind of stopped?"

"How do you know about that?"

A new smile crept across Bune's face; and John felt a cold chill in the room. "John, can I call you John?"

"I prefer Pastor John."

"Okay, whatever! Pastor John, let's get back to the important issue here. The more you nose around in this spiritual stuff, the crazier you are going to look. I feel sure that you don't want to see your little life here disrupted. Leave it alone. Ignore it and you get to have your church, your life, you know, exactly what any good pastor would want."

"Ignore it? I don't even know when it is going to happen."

"Well, then stop talking about it to people!" Bune shook violently and the room seemed to grow slightly darker. John looked around and thought he saw a flash of light. The moment the light flashed, Bune took a step back and his arms instinctively went up. Silence draped the room and slowly Bune lowered his arms and continued. "I think that you want a good solid church with steady growth and a happy, healthy home, right?"

John had seen the flash and he noted that there was a glow around the outer edge of the room now. A thought came to him, as Meris whispered it into his ear. He was not alone. After a pause, he answered, "Of course, that is what any preacher would want." He felt no fear; and he began to understand what was happening to him. His gift was to see the spiritual world; but it was more than that. He could see when the power of God or of Satan was at work. The light and glow was obviously from God and the darkness was demonic or from Satan. He had known this in his heart; but so much of what Bune was saying was true. He really did want the status quo, no wrinkles, just a quiet life serving God. Now that it was being suggested, he realized that this was not God's plan for his life anymore now that he had this gift. The clarity of this realization made John bold and sure, as he faced Bune, who was obviously not on God's side.

Bune continued talking, "Let's just say that you keep talking and digging into all this light and glowing and angels stuff. What exactly will that get you? Probably a trip to a mental hospital and maybe you lose...everything." Bune opened his arms to indicate John would lose his church.

"Are you threatening me? Is this a Job moment or something?" John's mind quickly flashed through the story of Job in the Bible.

A look of mock concern swept over Bune's face as his shrill voice continued, "No, no, no. I just think you are making a big mistake."

John laughed. "I don't think so. I will not do what you ask."

"Your future is yours to choose. I would say that a little more digging and you will soon find yourself much worse off than your friend Carl." Bune's face broke into a wicked smile.

"I think it's time for you to leave." John almost shouted, being slightly rattled at the sound of his friend's name coming out of this man's mouth.

"Have it your way. Just remember that I warned you. Your precious Lindsey and your little Rosie are just a part of what you will lose." Bune eyed the preacher closely to see his response to the mentioning of his family.

This was more than John could take and he moved around the desk. The room began to glow more, as all three angels surrounded Bune. "Leave my family out of it!" John shouted.

Immediately, Meris yelled, "Enough! You can't touch them, they are covered by the blood!"

John fell to the ground looking in all directions, as he heard the words of the angel reverberating around him. Suddenly, he could see all three large beings in the room surrounding Bune. John caught his glasses as they slid down his nose and he slowly scooted back toward his desk, watching the scene before him.

Bune was visibly shaken at Meris coming toward him; but he tried to keep his composure as he continued to back away slowly. He looked over at the pastor and then at each angel and their position around him, then he answered, "Oh my, you brought up blood so quickly! I am not threatening anyone. I was merely suggesting how the world will react to all this. You know as well as I do that everyone will call him crazy!"

"You have nothing more to say here. Leave!" Meris moved forward again and Bune cowered slightly.

"Okay, okay!" He looked at John and said, "I must go now. I will be watching you and your family. Remember, Pastor John, if you want things to be the same as they were--"

"Now!" Meris thrust his sword forward and Bune was immediately shoved out to the edge of town. John looked around the room; everyone was gone except for him.

John's mind was racing, as the words hung in the air like a thick fog. Fear ripped through his soul and he began to shake. Meris slowly opened his wings and John immediately felt the peace and calm. He fell on his knees and began to pray out loud.

"Oh Lord! What is happening to me? Please help me and my family! Things were easier before the lights and the angels started showing up everywhere. I am not sure what you want from me. Please help me! Please!"

Meris and Galdon remained in the room, while Nardic went back to John's home. The two angels absorbed the power and Meris motioned for Galdon to join Nardic, while he talked to the Father about what to do next.

John stayed face down a few more seconds and slowly stood up and walked around the room trying to gather his thoughts. How could he protect his family? Who was Bune anyway? Should he call the police? What would he even say?

He decided to call Darron.

"This is Darron Mitchell."

"Hey Darron. It's John."

"Hey John, what's up?"

Over the next ten minutes, John talked without stopping, explaining all that had happened. Darron said little and simply listened. When he was through telling the story, Darron sat in silence a few more seconds before responding.

"What do you think I should do?"

"I am not sure; but I can tell you from what I have learned that I think you are stirring things up in the spiritual world for some reason."

"Why would it matter if I tell people what I see or not? I have purposefully kept it a secret through all these years precisely because I don't want to seem crazy."

Darron sighed and answered, "I know. I think I even advised that at one time. Listen, John, you are not going to like this; but you need to figure out how far you are willing to go with this."

"What do you mean?"

"Are you willing to risk it all for this?"

"You sound like that crazy man or demon or whatever he was." John removed his glasses and wiped his eyes.

"I know; but in a sense, he was right. Not all people will not embrace this."

"I know what I see. I know what my daughter and Mia said they see...Oh my gosh!"

"What?"

"I'm not sure, but I need you to do something for me."

John talked with Darron for several more minutes and gave him some specific instructions. Both men had a list of items to look for before they planned to meet in a few days to compare notes. John leaned back in his chair with a sense of relief at this latest realization. He was not sure how it all fit; but if his instincts were right, then everything would finally make sense. Even though this latest event today had drained him emotionally, he had a renewed energy, as he replayed it all through his mind to fit the pieces together. Suddenly, he sat up straight as an overwhelming urge began to overtake John's thoughts. Bune had threatened his family in some form and he needed to check on them. He grabbed his phone and called Lindsey.

"Hey! Are you..." John paused. He didn't want to scare his wife. "Um, I mean what are you doing?"

"Hey sweetie. I am just finishing up some grocery shopping. Nothing exciting. I did get you some more of that awesome--hang on, honey."

John gripped the phone and listened to Lindsey pull away from the phone to talk to a familiar voice in the background.

"Oh...yes..."

John listened and tried to hear what the other person was saying. The voice grew stronger and John bolted up straight in his chair. His hands began to shake and he could barely grip the phone, as he strained to hear the conversation. He could hear Lindsey laugh and then the last words came through clear from Bune:

"I must go; but I hope to see you again."

"Thank you! Have a great day! Hey again. Sorry. This nice gentleman needed some help and then he recognized me as being from the church; and you know--"

John finally found his voice, "Lindsey! Stop talking. I need you to get Rosie and just go home. I will be there soon to explain."

"You are scaring me. What's wrong?"

"It's just...I just need you to go home and then I want to spend some time with you all tonight." John put his fist on his forehead and tried to calm himself to sound less panicked. "I love you."

"I love you too. I will be home soon."

He sat in his office and tried to gather his thoughts and figure out what to do. A quick search on the internet revealed that Bune was the name of a powerful demon. He flipped through several pages, printing out several and taking notes as well; and then pushed away from his desk with his head in his hands. Prayer seemed so futile and so weak right now. He felt like he needed to do something more. He bowed his head and simply said, "Help me, God."

A strong light burst into the room and John sat upright again. Inside the light, John could see a large form that moved through the light and stepped into the room, reducing the light to a glow around the edge of a large man. The man smiled and John felt an incredible calm filter through his soul, while his mind continued to try to analyze what was happening.

"Pastor John Miles. I am honored to meet you."

"Who are you?" The calm and peace continued to radiate through the room, eliminating all fear and doubt in his heart.

"I am Meris, an angel from our Heavenly Father and sent to watch over you."

John felt such an incredible love and peace that he wanted to remain with this angel and never leave. Even though the angel was in the form of a man, John's eyes filled with tears at the beauty of this being before him. "What--"

"I will answer your questions. First, though, do not take this gift of yours lightly. It is very special and we have waited years for it to develop."

"I don't understand what it means."

"Trust in God. He will lead you through."

"I do trust Him. I don't know what I am supposed to do."

"Pastor John, use the weapons that God has given you: prayer and the scripture. They are very powerful alone and exponentially so, when used together. For now, you and your family are safe."

Before John could ask any of the hundreds of questions he still had, Meris disappeared and the room fell silent. He should have been scared but he wasn't. He was more troubled with what to do. One spiritual visit would have been enough; but two was too much.

Oh God. Please help me. I want to do your Will. I love you. Please protect my family. Amen

Then he thought about what Meris had said to him: '...use the weapons that God has given you: prayer and scripture. They are very powerful alone and exponentially so, when used together.' He bowed his head again.

Father, you said you would never leave or forsake us. Please protect me and my family and my home; and help us serve you. For me and my house, we will serve the Lord.

When John finished praying, light burst forth and surrounded the room once more. He opened his eyes and fell to the ground in tears. As he lay face down on the floor, he felt a warmth envelop him and a peace washed over his body, filling him with love and hope. Slowly, he lifted his head and looked around the room. It was still glowing and in his heart he knew that everything was going to be okay. He picked up his phone to call home but it began to buzz before he could do so.

"Hello, this is Pastor John."

"Hey Pastor, this is Carl."

"Hey Carl, what can I do for you?"

"I need to see you, if you are available."

"Okay, I can probably meet with you this week--"

"No, I mean right now."

John removed his glasses and pinched his nose. He knew he couldn't turn Carl away. Somehow, he felt assured that everything would be okay and he simply sighed and answered, "Sure, Carl. I'm at my office or we could meet--"

"I'll be there in a few minutes." There was a pause and then Carl added, "Thank you."

When Carl hung up, John called home. Lindsey answered after the second ring.

"Hey honey."

"Hey stranger. I was just wondering when you were coming home."

"Lindsey, you know the man Carl that I have told you about--he's the son of Mr. Roberts from the nursing home?"

"Yes, of course."

"Well, he wants to meet me at my office. He sounded really upset. I am going to meet with him and then I'd love to meet you and Rosie for dinner."

"You just made my day. I was staring at this crazy chicken in the freezer and trying to decide how I was going to turn that into something. Where were you thinking?"

"You girls surprise me. Plan on about 6:30 or so. I'll call you to confirm...and honey...please don't talk to any strangers."

"Okay. You are scaring me a little."

"No, just be careful. I will call you around 6:20 to see where you guys want to meet."

"Wow! Carl must really must be upset. You are blocking out over two hours."

"Just want to give myself plenty of time and I don't want to have my two girls waiting!"

"We will even dress up for you a little." Lindsey smiled and John laughed. He knew that that meant that Rosie would be wearing one of her many dresses that had suddenly become her choice of clothing.

Meris surrounded John with his wings and allowed the Father to calm Pastor John's heart from all the events of the last several minutes. John waited in his office, praying and gathering his thoughts; and within ten minutes, he heard a soft knock on his door. Carl was red-faced and had obviously been crying. John greeted him and quickly escorted him into his office to keep anyone from seeing him and reduce any embarrassment he was feeling.

"Thank you for meeting me. I didn't know where else to turn."

"What is going on, Carl?" John had already confirmed that his father, Mr. Roberts was not the problem. When John first heard the sound of Carl's voice on the phone, he had immediately suspected that something horrible had happened to his dear friend from the nursing home; and he had been relieved when Carl assured him Mr. Roberts was fine.

"It's my grandson. He is very sick."

"Oh. I don't think that I knew you had any grandkids. What's wrong with him?"

"I have one son. When I went to prison, my wife left me and she made sure that I never saw my son. I really didn't try to fight her because I didn't want my boy to know he had a bum dad. Anyway, I never really was much of a father to him."

"It's never too late, Carl."

"I'm trying. I am trying to make up for it through my grandson. He's 7 and...anyway, he was just diagnosed with leukemia." Carl broke down and openly wept.

John moved his chair closer and handed Carl some tissues. "Where does he live?"

Carl wiped his eyes and looked up at John. "He lives here in Louisville; but they are sending him up to Cincinnati to the Children's Hospital for treatment. They said he needs a bone marrow transplant."

"What can we do for your son and his family? I would be glad to set up meals--"

"Don't you see? It's my fault! God is punishing me!"

John let Carl cry and waited until he relaxed again. "Carl, God--"

"Yeah I know, He loves me so much! Don't you understand? I killed a child and now he is going to take my grandson to punish me."

John tried to ignore what Carl had said about his past; but it still bothered him. "What about the treatments? Don't you think that those will help?" John was trying to stay calm; but the image of Carl killing a child continued to swirl through his mind.

"The bone marrow might work; but they said it's hard to find a match."

"I would bet that they find one soon. The good thing about bone marrow transplants is that you don't have to wait for them."

"What do you mean?" Carl perked up slightly.

"Well, with most transplants, someone has to die first; but for bone marrow, they have a large registry where people have had their marrow typed and entered. For instance, I registered mine because I knew how important it was for someone to receive a transplant. I also signed my driver's license to be an organ donor."

"I didn't know that. I thought they would have to wait on someone to die. That is amazing that they have a data bank. So did you donate your marrow and they freeze it or something?"

"No. I just had it checked and registered so that if someone needed my type, I would donate to them."

"What made you do that? I didn't even know that was possible."

"I guess you may not know; but I wouldn't be here if it were not for someone donating their liver to me. I was very sick when I was young. In fact, you won't believe this but we just recently found out that my wife's sister was where I got my liver from--she died as a small child."

"Did your families know each other?"

"No. It was just by chance that Lindsey and I met and married. There is no connection made after a donation. They keep the information secret so that the families don't have to deal with any of the pain or possible problems that could result."

Carl sat in silence for a few seconds, absorbing all of this information. "So how do you guys know about your wife's sister being your donor?"

"It's a long story. Basically, it's a small world; but enough about me. What can we do to help you and your family?"

Carl shook his head. "I don't know. I am not exactly welcome around them. My son has allowed me to interact with my grandson some; but I am not sure if they want me around now."

"Carl, I don't mean to pry; but if you ever want to tell me what happened, I will listen and try to help you. I want you to know that if you never tell me, that is okay too."

Carl sat wringing his hands and then he stood to pace back and forth. "Pastor John, I think I need to tell you. I need you to understand why God can't forgive me. I just don't know if I can right now."

"Carl, do you believe in God?"

Carl looked at John with a puzzled expression. "Of course I do."

"Do you believe that he created the world and all that is in it?"

"Yes, of course."

"Do you believe that God has the power to do what He wants to our world, that He is in charge?"

Carl cleared his throat and rubbed his hands together. "Yes, I do."

"Then you need to know and believe that He has the power to forgive you no matter what. I don't need you to tell me what you have done. You have already been punished through the court system; and as far as I am concerned, you are a free man and God wants to give you a clean slate too. It is yours for the asking."

Several angels arrived in the room along with Galdon and Meris. All within the room, both spiritual and human, fell silent, as Carl wrestled with his decision. The demon began whispering in desperation, fearing he was losing his favorite charge. Meris used some of his reserved power and placed his blade on the demon's lips to seal them closed.

"Pastor, I really want to. I really want to do it." Tears streamed down his face and he wept for a few seconds, while John waited patiently. Meris knew that the demon's lips would only stay sealed for a few more minutes and waited nervously for Carl to make a decision.

"Then do it, Carl. All you have to do is ask."

"Will you help me? I don't know what to say."

"Of course."

John led Carl through the simple prayer of salvation, having him profess Jesus as the Son of God and asking to have Jesus come into his heart as his Savior. The words poured out and fell around them sending a light beam radiating out into the room. Slowly the light continued to grow but also began to separate into all the colors of the rainbow. The deep hues emanated for several miles in all directions, visible only in the spiritual realm. Outside the building, hundreds of angels gathered and spread their wings in unison, praising God and singing while basking in the spectacle of color. For several minutes the colors continued to get brighter until every demon within range screamed and howled; and many of them fled to get out of reach of the light. The demon that had been with Carl ran in shame and hid, hoping to avoid being punished for losing the battle for Carl's soul.

The angels continued singing for over an hour, basking in the colors and enjoying the power surge from Heaven. John and Carl continued to talk after their prayer long into the late afternoon. Finally, both men rose and John agreed to check on Carl's family at the hospital.

"Wait. Pastor John, I need to tell you everything."

John froze and looked at Carl. He knew that this moment might come; and he felt ready for it. "Of course, Carl. Please have a seat." Both men sat down and Carl rocked back and forth for a few seconds and then began his story.

"I had a family--I had a wife and a son. There were problems in our marriage; but for the most part, we were doing okay. Anyway, I liked to drink a little after work each day; but I had developed a little problem with overdoing it and so I promised my wife not to do it anymore except at home. I really meant to do that and I had bought some whiskey to keep at home. That day was different, though. A few buddies talked me into meeting them for a few beers. I really didn't want to; but I went anyway. I didn't even stay that long." Carl started to cry but quickly wiped his eyes and took a deep breath.

"The sun was setting. I remember it was really pretty and I also remember that the light was green. I swear it was green!" He had to stand up and walk this time. Carl paced back and forth as John listened intently. Something in John's mind clicked; and he sat up taller.

"I was in a hurry. I really didn't want my wife to be mad. She had threatened to leave me if I was late and drinking again. The light...it was green and then all of a sudden it was yellow, then red. It was so fast and I couldn't stop...there was no way to stop." Carl wept openly and sat back down in the chair.

"Carl, it's okay. It was just an accident." John knew where this was going and he also knew that if he was right, this was going to be more than incredible. Carl continued to cry and John spoke gently, "Carl, was it a van?" *The timing would be right. Oh Lord, could this be?*

Carl stopped crying and looked up. "Yes! How do you know? Did my dad tell you?"

"No. I need you to tell me the date when this happened." John's heart was racing and he could hardly breathe.

"I will never forget that day. It was May 10, 1974."

The date rang through the room like a bell and John smiled. "Carl, one last question. Was it a child that died in the crash?"

"Yes, I killed a little girl. She was only two years old!"

Before John could ask anything further, Carl continued, "I spent fifteen years in prison for drunk driving and involuntary manslaughter. I lost my wife and son; and my dad and I didn't speak for years.

John leaned back in his chair and then laughed out loud. Carl looked up, appalled at the pastor's behavior. "Why are you laughing?"

John's eyes danced and Carl watched him with confusion. "Carl, I think that your mistake led us here today."

"Please, I don't--"

"Wait! Hear me out. I need to do some checking; but it sounds like you saved more lives than you took that day."

Carl was completely confused; but over the next thirty minutes the two men worked through the details until both were convinced that Carl had been the one driving the truck that had slammed into the van, killing Rose Louise; but he had opened the door for three other people to live.

"Don't you see, Carl? In a way, you saved yourself. If I had not lived; we would not have been here today, working together to help you find Jesus."

"Do you think God wanted me to kill Rose Louise?"

"Absolutely not! I think: '...all things work together for good to them that love God, to them who are the called according to his purpose.' Romans 8:28. Carl, God took your mistake and turned it into something beautiful. That is how God works!"

"Romans again!"

Carl laughed for the first time in years, because the past no longer felt like a burden. The release of his pain and the knowledge that his mistake had been used for good along with his salvation, left Carl speechless and humbled. He fell to his knees and praised God. All throughout the town, the glow from the Glory of God filled every corner and crevice, scattering the demons in every direction.

Sitting in his car, John tried several times to reach his wife to tell her the good news about Carl and find out where to meet them. Lindsey was never one to keep her phone nearby and usually only looked at it a couple of times a day, so John tried the home phone; but it was busy. John decided to go home and Lindsey met him at the door with a strange expression on her face.

"Hey, I was trying to reach you. You need to keep your phone with you. You will never guess what happened! Carl accepted Jesus!"

Lindsey broke into a smile and hugged John. "That is amazing!"

"It was so awesome."

Lindsey walked back into the kitchen and sat down. Rosie came bounding in and grabbed her dad. "Are you going to do it, dad?"

John looked up at Lindsey and then back to Rosie.

"Are you going to give your bones away?"

"What--"

"Rosie, can you go get your papers from school? Dad wants to see your pictures."

"Sure! Stay there, dad!"

Rosie ran off and John looked at Lindsey. "You had a phone call today. You are a match for a bone marrow transplant."

John's mouth dropped open and he sat down. "Are you serious?"

Rosie came running back into the room and placed a stack of pictures in front of John for him to admire. "I added one! This one is you, dad."

John and Lindsey looked down at the paper and then at each other. John jumped to his feet and ran to get his phone. Within a few minutes, Darron was on his way to their house. No demon could come within a block of any of them as Meris, Galdon, and Nardic, along with a large group of angels, surrounded the home with light. When Darron arrived, he prayed with Lindsey and John and they all worked throughout the evening to piece all the information together.

Meris, Galdon, and Nardic all stayed close to the pastor and his family for the next several days. An overwhelming urge overtook John and he began to write a sermon on the power of prayer and scripture that would become the cornerstone of his ministry for the rest of his life. Over the next few weeks, Pastor John preached about the Armor of God and began a journey through scripture about the spiritual world around us. As he revealed his experiences, some of his members did leave; but in their place, many others came. The church grew so rapidly, that they were forced to open up rooms with big screen TV's to broadcast the sermon. People were flocking to see the pastor that talked about angels but also to hear the messages of love and hope. There was still more to tell and he needed to give his members the full story of what his family had experienced through the spiritual and physical gifts of a small child named Rose Louise. Ellie was touched and moved beyond words, as she began to understand God's incredible ability to use her young daughter to help so many people. Within a short time, Ellie and Mark began to attend church every week as well.

Friday morning of the week that John planned to tell the entire story of Rose Louise, he received a phone call from a young woman in a nearby town. She told John the story of her father who had received a heart transplant and how he had claimed to see angels afterward. After comparing stories, they both concluded that this man had received Rose Louise's heart. Not only that; but before the transplant, this man had been very ill for several years and was so sick that he was limited to walking only in his home and a few steps in his yard every day, which he did with his old friend, a dog named Red. Within a few hours, John confirmed that this man had been Mr. Robert's neighbor. Not only that, but the man had moved and attended a church in Florence, Kentucky for several years before his death. He was the man that John had seen as a child in his hometown church, the first time he had seen anyone glow.

Chapter 24: Putting It All Together

Sunday at the church

"My heart is full this morning. The last few weeks have been somewhat unusual for our family. So much has occurred that I only know to address you all with the facts and share what we have just now learned ourselves."

Not one sound could be heard except the preacher's voice. Something had happened and no one wanted to miss a single word. Listening to her son, Terry sat at her husband's side and glanced over at the church busy body, Clara Burton, who was poised to memorize each and every morsel of information. Clara needed a new crusade, since there had been very little to do lately.

"All of you know my daughter, Rosie."

Several people nodded and Clara congratulated herself for already noting Rosie was not sitting with her mom today. There was a small ripple of response; and Pastor John looked down to try to catch his breath before he continued. He knew he had a lot yet to tell them and he wanted to get it right.

"You are all familiar with something that I say every week. I always start my sermon by telling you that I am here because of a gift, yet few of you know the double meaning behind those words." Pastor John paused and looked at his notes, more to gain control of his emotions than to see the words written before him.

"Most of you have probably assumed that I have been alluding to the gift of salvation, which is partially correct; but it is not the full meaning. There has been another gift, one that I was aware of but never had the curiosity or the courage to know more about." Pastor John looked over at his wife, Lindsey, and then at his parents, who never missed a service and then at Lindsey's parents, who had only started to come over the last few weeks. He wiped the corner of his eyes and tried again to regain his composure.

"I think it's important for you all to know that what I am about to tell you all is a story that is still difficult for even me to understand." He looked back at Rosie, sitting on the seat behind him. She and her mother looked so much alike, almost like sisters. The meaning behind that thought hit him hard; and then he broke down slightly and had to take a moment to gather himself so that he could continue.

Several women began to cry, as they watched their beloved pastor struggle to tell them something that was incredibly painful. Lindsey mouthed 'I love you' and wiped the tears from her eyes as well. Besides their parents and

Darron, she and Rosie were the only ones that knew all the details of what Pastor John was about to say; and she began to silently pray for strength for everyone involved. Galdon and Nardic began to glow from the added prayer and both instinctively spread their wings in response. Galdon moved into place behind the preacher and placed a hand on him to give him added strength.

In response, Pastor John stood up straight and gained some control over his emotions as he continued, "I spent some time yesterday reviewing all of this with my family and well...I'm not sure how to say this, so I think it's important for me to start at the beginning. Bear with me as I try to put this all together for you to understand."

John began the tale that would define his ministry for years to come and possibly forever. The whole congregation sat motionless, as their pastor told them the events that had brought a revival not only in his own life and the life of both his and Lindsey's parents, but also in the life of his dear friend Carl. His hope was that by telling what had happened, there would be a similar response in his congregation. The story itself, although incredible enough on its own, was only the beginning of what God had revealed to him; and John knew that he had found his purpose. Outside, a large group of angels stood watch over the area to allow the pastor time to talk and tell what had happened. They spread their wings and dared any of the demons to draw near, for their power was now fully charged.

"First let me tell you about my wife. Lindsey is from a family that experienced a terrible tragedy. When her mom was expecting Lindsey, she was on her way to pick up her oldest daughter and had her two younger girls in the van with her. She was in a terrible car wreck, which left her mom in a coma for about two months and killed her 2 year old sister, Rose Louise. Lindsey's dad, Mark, had to make some decisions quickly and he allowed Rose Louise's organs to be donated. At the same time, I was a young toddler and I was very sick. I was diagnosed with terminal cancer of the liver and had been put in the hospital for chemotherapy to wait for a liver transplant. As you have probably guessed, I received Rose Louise's liver. Without that gift, I would not be here today. There are no words that can express my gratitude for that incredible gift. If that were the end of the story, it would be incredible enough; but there is more. During the last few years, I have met another one of the recipients of Rose Louise's organs. There was an elderly woman at the nursing home that happened to be the recipient of Rose Louise's kidneys. Unfortunately, she has now passed away." John paused and waited for the information to sink in before he continued.

"One other piece to the puzzle came into place just a few days ago. I met a woman whose father received little Rose Louise's heart. Now, there is another man with whom I have become close friends with over the last several months. He has shared with me that he had a troubled past. He fought for years with the notion that he was guilty of killing someone and even went to prison for this crime. Recently, he accepted Jesus and then shared with me that his crime was killing a child. This obviously disturbed me greatly until I learned the entire story of what happened.

You see, he killed a child but not intentionally. He ran a red light and plowed into a van--the van carrying young Rose Louise. This man has been haunted by his past for years and even lost his own family through divorce and his prison term. Now that he knows his terrible mistake saved my life and two others, he has been feeling better; but this is still not the end of the story." John paused to let this information sink in before he continued. "This man, Carl, has a grandson who is now sick with leukemia. I just found out that I am a match to save this young man's life through a bone marrow transplant. Through a series of incredible events, Carl is in effect saving his own grandchild's life through a terrible tragedy that haunted him for years. Do I believe that the accident was good? No of course not. I can only say that God has taken something horrible and created something beautiful. This is just what he does. Through this entire experience, a picture of the significance of prayer and scripture has been revealed to me. God has revealed to me that prayer and scripture are the only two weapons that the Bible mentions as offensive weapons. That means that with these two weapons, we can fight the dark forces that try to influence us in this world. If we combine these two, we have even more power to help us."

John paused again and continued his sermon. Lindsey smiled at him and prayed as well. When John finished, she and Rosie joined him at the pulpit. After a few more words in prayer, he took a seat, while she and Rosie tried to answer questions about their past and the amazing story of sacrifice and love that allowed one family to give a gift to another to allow life to continue and the full ramifications of that event. At the end, they shared more about the story of Carl's grandson and the donor match from John's bone marrow that saved the young boy's life. The boy's name was Jonathan.

Chapter 25: New Days

Galdon and Meris stood outside Pastor John's home and watched the angels that surrounded the property.

"What an amazing few weeks. The outpouring of support and love has been beautiful to watch."

Meris nodded and Galdon spread his wings slightly. The scars along the back of his wings blocked much of his glow now. Nardic landed softly and reported that Rosie was asleep and well. He, too, looked at his friend and mentor's wings, noting the decreased light. Nardic stepped back from the other two and silently opened his own wings to see how much light he had lost from his scar. There was a distinct area on his wing where the glow was missing from his battle with the demon. He still had plenty of glow left; but he knew that Galdon's days were numbered as a warrior. Suddenly, a large light opened from Heaven and all the angels around the home instinctively stepped aside to watch. Thousands of other angels suddenly appeared and in the middle of the light was an even stronger light with a man dressed completely in white. His eyes glowed and on his hands had light emanating from the palms. He spoke in musical tones that echoed softly, yet with authority, to all the angels that had gathered.

Meris half whispered, "Jesus!" Then he knelt to the ground, followed by all the angels that had gathered.

Jesus stood in the window from Heaven and said, "For bravery and sacrifice, I have been given authority to heal you both this one time." He reached forward and light struck both Nardic and Galdon, lifting them up and then gently setting them back down. All the angels began singing and praising Jesus and both Galdon and Nardic slowly stood and opened their wings. Both were fully healed with the full Glory of God reflected over the entire surface of their wings.

Inside the home, Rosie watched from her window and smiled. She knew that her father was teaching about the angels in church and that there were many new people flocking to hear what he had to say. In her heart, though, she also knew that no words could ever describe how beautiful it all was; and she treasured it in her heart. Rosie climbed back into her bed and curled up on her side. Nardic appeared and she rolled over to see him.

"That was so beautiful! I saw Jesus heal you!"

"Yes, He is everything. Please don't ever stop loving Him."

"Never! Show me your wings!"

Rosie watched, as Nardic smiled and opened his wings to test them again. The room filled with light and Nardic relaxed and slowly let the light fade, as he tucked his wings in again.

Rosie clapped and then said, "Nardic, did you know Rose Louise?"

Nardic shook his head. "I do now; but I did not know her here on earth, because she was with another angel. She was well cared for and loved, just like you, though."

"It's really something, isn't it?"

Nardic was not sure exactly what she was referring to. "What is something?"

"How God gave Rose for Jonathan. Now she has saved five lives. The first three through the organ donations and the fourth through Jonathan. She also saved Carl, through Jesus."

"Yes, that is right. The Father can make something good out of anything."

"I can't wait to go to Heaven and meet everyone. I really want to meet Rose."

"Someday you will meet everyone there and Rose will be waiting for you."

"I can't wait!"

"For now, sleep. You need to concentrate on getting ready for your baby sister."

"Good night, Nardic. Tell Rose hello for me."

"I will."

Epilogue

Two weeks later, Pastor John was sitting in his office reading when there was a knock at the door. Before he could answer, the door opened softly and Ellie, his mother-in-law, timidly peaked around the corner.

"John, I'm so sorry to bother you. I just...well I just wanted to talk to you for a minute."

"Of course, anytime. Please come in and have a seat." John stood and helped guide her to a chair across from his.

Ellie nervously sat on the edge of her seat and fumbled with her purse, fighting back the tears. John immediately prayed silently for her to be at peace and the effects were almost immediate. Meris and Galdon surrounded Ellie with their wings and John smiled at the slight shimmer around her chair. He sat up slightly when he suddenly noticed that his mother-in-law no longer had the dark shadow around or near her.

"John, I'm kind of embarrassed; but I feel like I need to talk to someone and I know we are family but anyway…I'm here."

"Of course, you can talk to me. What is said in this room stays in this room, unless you give me permission to do otherwise."

"This may seem strange; but I don't want it to stay here. I feel like God is leading me to talk about everything that I have been through. I don't know how to explain it; but God has healed me. It has taken over 35 years; but I am now healed from my pain and it's because of you." Ellie paused and seemed to gather strength as she continued, "I think I am supposed to testify about it. That is the only way I know how to explain it. I know that I am being led to tell others about my suffering and pain and how God healed me."

John sat up a little straighter. The words of his friend, Mr. Roberts, replayed in his mind about John needing someone to give their story to compliment and undergird his sermon on suffering. John silently thanked God and prayed for wisdom and the right words.

"You're not going to believe this, but I prepared a sermon a long time ago and have been waiting for someone to give a testimony just like yours in order to complete the message. Someone once told me that God would lead a person to me when the time was right. Would you feel comfortable speaking in a church service?"

Ellie's mouth dropped open and her face turned slightly white; but Galdon and Meris continued to wash her with peace and love and suddenlty she smiled. "Yes, I think I can. I can do that."

The following Sunday, Pastor John took his seat behind the podium after introducing Ellie. As she unwrapped the story of her pain and anguish followed by the years of resentment, several people began to cry. The heartache followed by the Grace and the joy in her life was overwhelming. Copies of this service were delivered to over 300 people the following week.

Meris and Galdon landed on a hill at the edge of town where it all began so long ago.

"What are my orders, sir?"

Meris stood and watched the town for a few seconds and then turned to face his friend. "Your orders are as always to do the Will of our Lord. For now, continue to stay with this family. When another battle comes, we need to be ready. For now, stay alert and remember in 1 Peter 5:8 that our enemy the devil prowls around like a roaring lion looking for someone to devour. Be vigilant, my friend."

"Yes sir. I am and we will win, as always."

Meris turned to face his friend and answered, "Yes, it is written so."